Elementary

BIG BOOK of Bible Story Coloring Activities

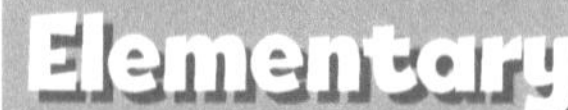

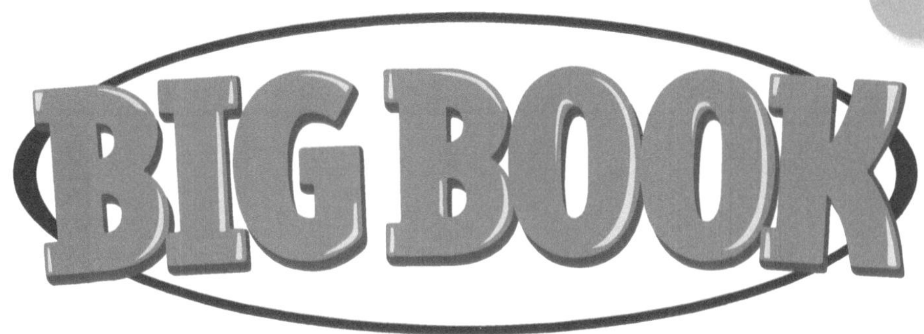

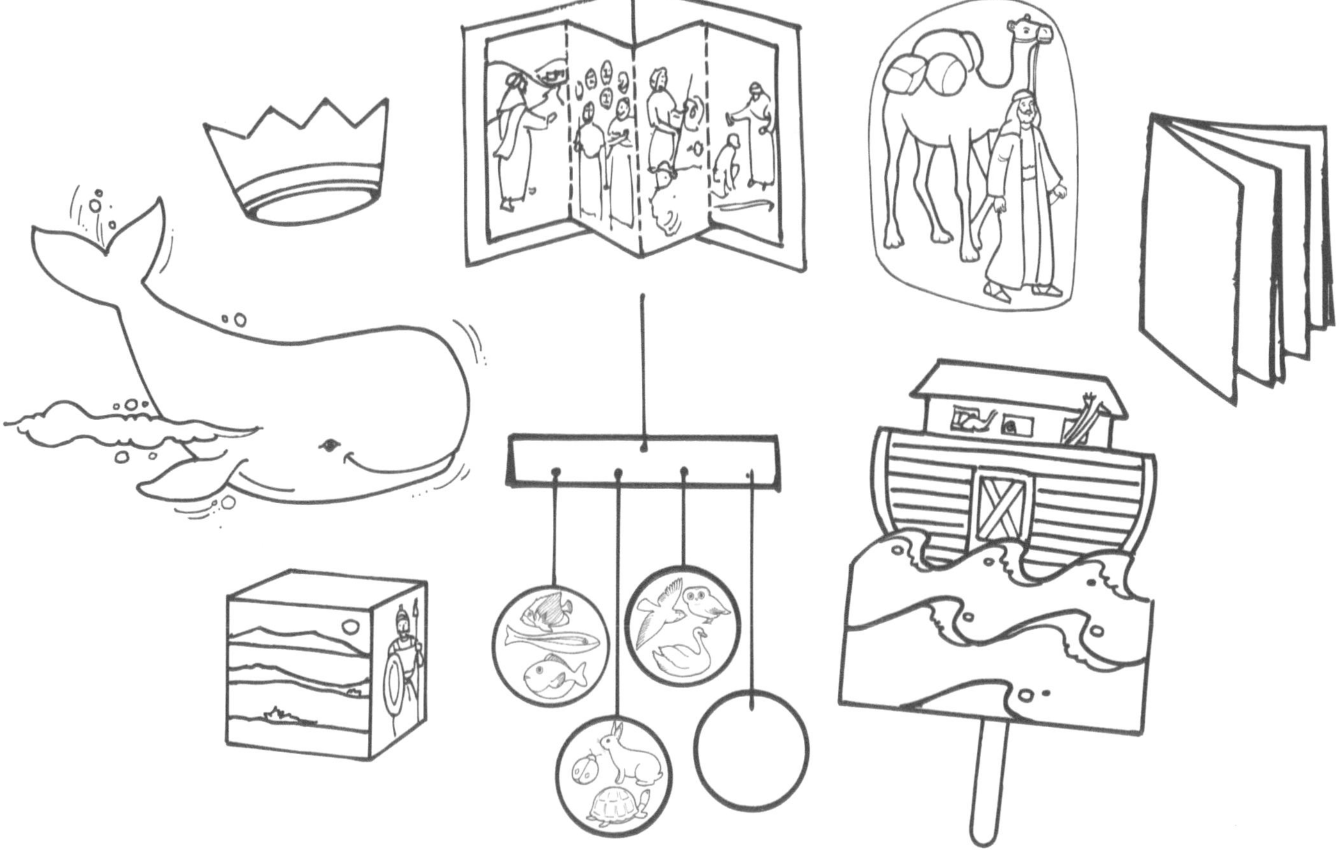

DAVID C COOK
transforming lives together

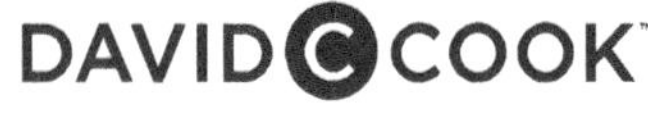

BIG BOOK OF BIBLE STORY COLORING ACTIVITIES FOR ELEMENTARY KIDS
Published by David C Cook
4050 Lee Vance Drive
Colorado Springs, CO 80918 U.S.A.

Integrity Music Limited, a Division of David C Cook
Brighton, East Sussex BN1 2RE, England

ISBN 978-0-8307-7230-8

Content included in this book was originally published in *Bible Stories to Color & Tell Ages 6–8*
by Standard Publishing in 2005 © Standard Publishing, ISBN 0-8307-4272-7.

Cover Design: James Hershberger
Illustrator: Len Ebert

Printed in the United States of America

7 8 9 10 11 12 13 14 15 16

101424

Contents

New Testament

Introduction

Big Book of Bible Story Coloring Activities for Elementary Kids includes Bible story pictures and related activities kids can do that correlate to the most popular Bible lessons for elementary children.

Coloring Pictures

Coloring pictures provide a quick and easy way to introduce a Bible story. These coloring pages can help young children develop fine-motor skills as they color, and will allow them to experiment with working toward a finished piece. While a simple coloring picture is fun for many children, consider making it part of a more active learning experience. Try one of these creative ideas for using coloring pictures as teaching tools to encourage more active learning for kids:

- **Touch-and-Feel Pictures**—Provide rice, beans, cotton, buttons, fabric, felt, or popcorn for kids to glue to their coloring pages.
- **Thematic Bulletin Boards**—Add specific coloring pictures based on a teaching theme to a bulletin board with an appropriate title.
- **Bible Lesson Visuals**—Enlarge a coloring picture that illustrates a story you are teaching. Use the picture to introduce or review a story.
- **Personal Coloring Books**—Copy about ten different coloring pages based on a theme you are teaching. Help children create their own coloring books using staples, yarn, or folders to keep the pages together.
- **Puzzles**—Mount a coloring picture on poster board and cut the page into puzzle pieces. Kids can work the puzzle as they review the Bible story.
- **Mosaic Pictures**—Have children glue small pieces of torn tissue paper or construction paper onto a coloring picture, rather than simply coloring the page.
- **Mail It Home**—Children love to get mail! Welcome a visitor or stay in touch with an absentee by mailing a coloring picture to a child's home address, along with a personal note to the child.

Activity Pages

The activities in this book were specifically designed so kids can complete them with little or no assistance. The activities teach kids to retell the Bible stories in their own words, using pictures and word clues that help them remember the order of important events. When kids retell Bible stories in their own words, they remember them long after they leave the classroom.

Special Activity Instructions

For some activities you will be directed to this page for assembly directions.

Smush Book Instructions

(pp. 40, 95, 170, 212)

Make a copy of the activity for each child. Provide crayons and scissors. Color and cut out the smush book around the outside edge. Fold the pages to make a book, as illustrated. The numbers on each page of the book will help you determine the order of each fold.

Red Sea Pamphlet Instructions (p. 44)

Make a copy of the activity for each child. Provide crayons and scissors. Color and cut out the pamphlet around the outside edges (do not cut along the dotted lines). Color the back of the pamphlet blue to look like water. Lay the pamphlet in front of you with the picture facing up. Fold the right panel in on the dotted line so that it covers the center panel. Fold the left panel in on the dotted line so that it covers both the right and center panels. Open the left panel and then the right panel as you retell the story of God's people crossing the Red Sea.

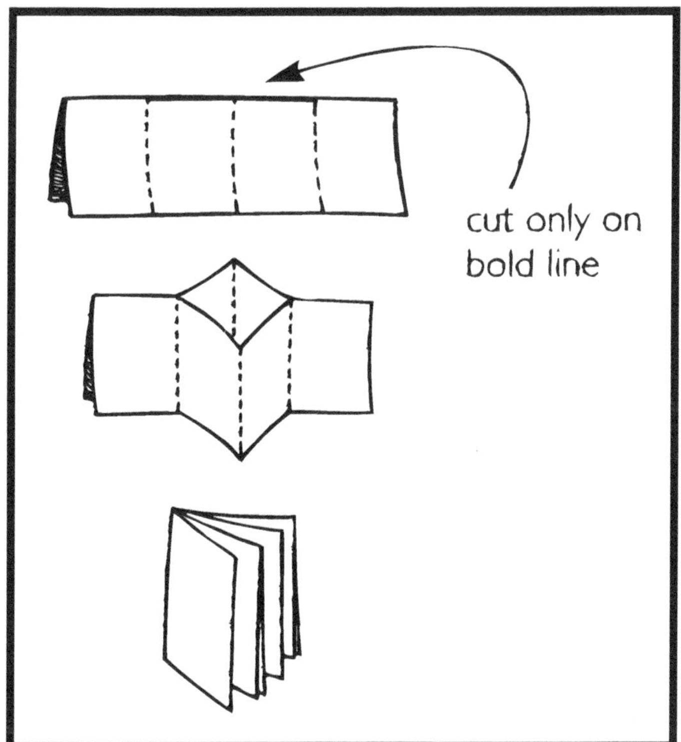

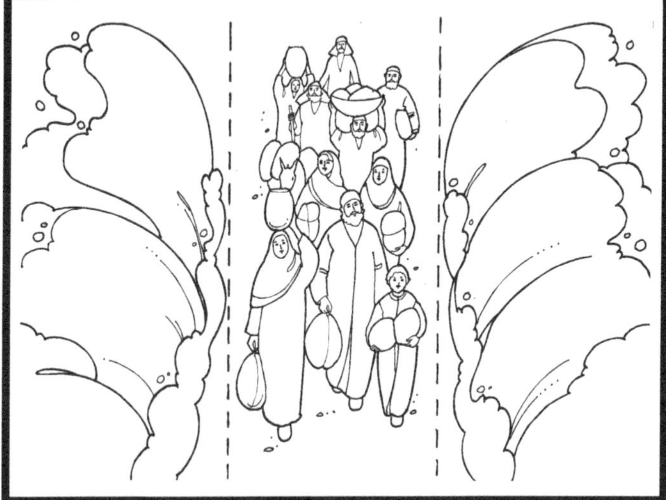

Leading a Child to Christ

One of the greatest privileges of serving in children's ministry is to help guide children to become members of God's family. Pray and ask God to prepare the kids you know to understand and receive the good news about Jesus. Ask God to give you the sensitivity and wisdom to communicate effectively and to be aware as opportunities occur.

When talking with children about salvation, use words and phrases they understand; never assume kids understand a concept just because they can repeat certain words. Avoid symbolic terms that will confuse literal-minded thinkers. As you watch and pray, you will see kids developing relationships with God.

Here are some questions you can ask and things you can discuss with a child who is interested in accepting Jesus as their Lord and Savior. Encourage the child to look up and read the Bible verses along with you.

Read John 3:16. **Why did God send Jesus to earth?** (God loved us so much that He wants us to have eternal life with Him.)

First John 3:1 says that God wants us to be His children. But sin, doing wrong, separates us from God. Read Romans 6:23. **What do you think should happen to us when we sin?** (die) **But what is God's gift to us?** (eternal life in Jesus)

Jesus willingly died on the cross to take the punishment for our sins. Read 1 Corinthians 15:3. **But Jesus didn't stay in the tomb. After three days, He came back to life! Jesus died so that we can live forever in heaven with Him.**

Are you sorry for the wrong things that you've done? If you are, what should you do? Read 1 John 1:9. **Our sins are wiped away when we're truly sorry for what we've done and when we turn to God.**

Read Ephesians 2:8. **How are we saved?** (by God's grace, through faith) **Christian faith is a life-long adventure here on earth. With Jesus as Lord of our lives, we build a life of submitting to God, following Jesus, and keeping in step with the Spirit.**

At this point, continue to talk with the child about accepting Jesus as Lord and Savior. Include what your church teaches about how this happens. If you have any questions about salvation, talk with your pastor or children's ministry leader.

God wants every person to accept the free gift of eternal life that He's offering. What do you need to do about this?

Old Testament Bible Story Coloring Activities

God Makes the World

Genesis 1: God Makes the World

Creation Puzzle

Supplies

- copy of the Creation Puzzle (preferably on white card stock) for each child (continued on p. 12)
- crayons or markers
- scissors

Directions

Color and cut out each puzzle piece and assemble the puzzle according to the numbers on each piece. Color piece 1 a light color and piece 2 a dark color to show that God made light and darkness. The completed puzzle will form a circle. Use the puzzle to tell about what God made on days one through four of creation (each row equals one day).

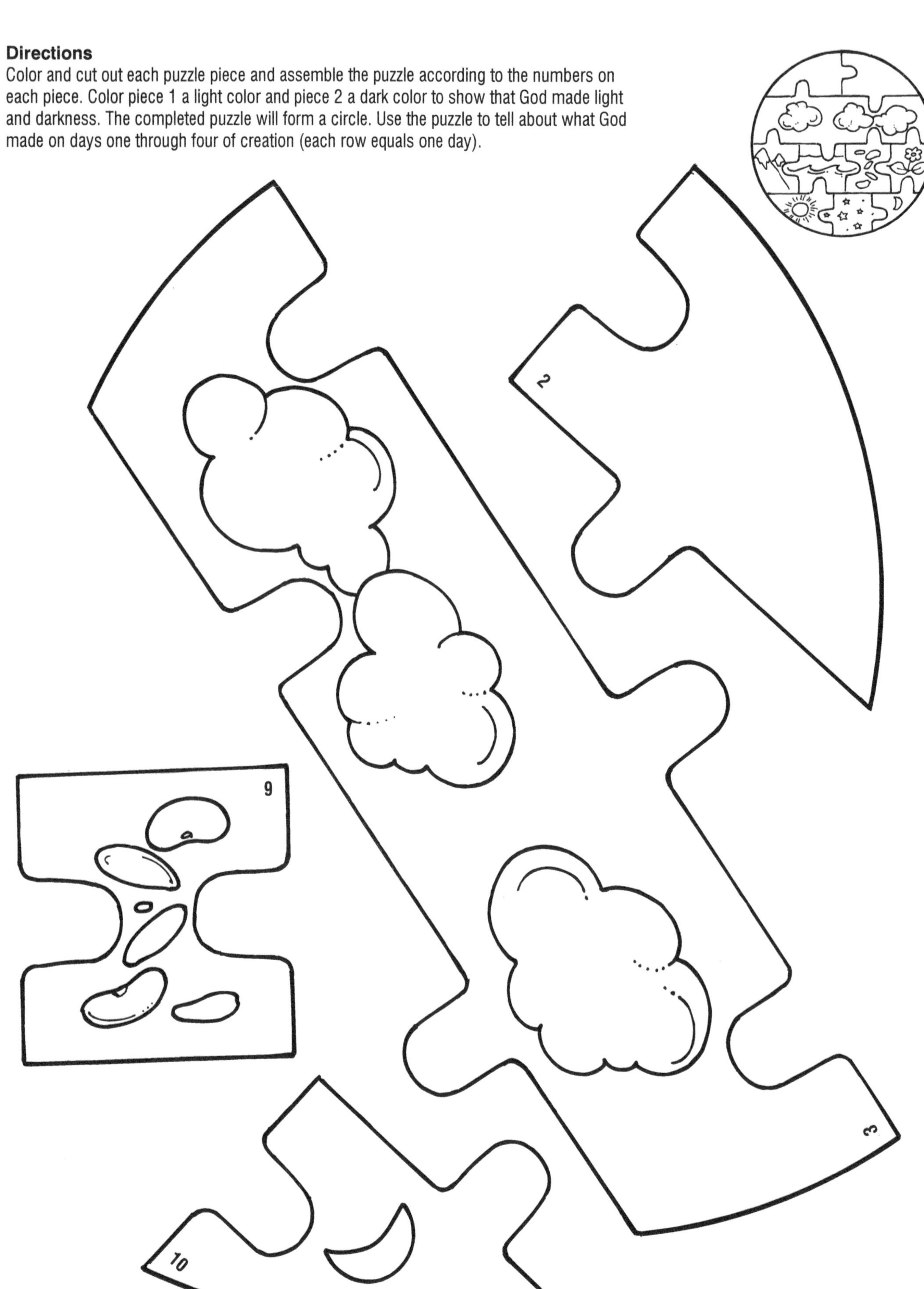

God Makes the Animals

Genesis 1: God Makes the Animals

Animal Mobile

Supplies

- copy of the Animal Mobile (preferably on white card stock) for each child
- crayons or markers
- scissors
- hole punch
- varying lengths of yarn (5 per student, any color)

Directions

Color the word strip and the three mobile pieces that show animal pictures. On the fourth mobile piece, draw and color your favorite animal. Cut out all the mobile pieces. Punch five holes in the word strip where the small circles are shown. Punch one hole at the top of each of the mobile pieces. Using varying lengths of yarn, tie each mobile piece to the word strip. Tie the fifth piece of yarn to the top center hole of the word strip and loop it at the top so the mobile can be hung. Use the mobile to tell about what God made on days five and six of creation.

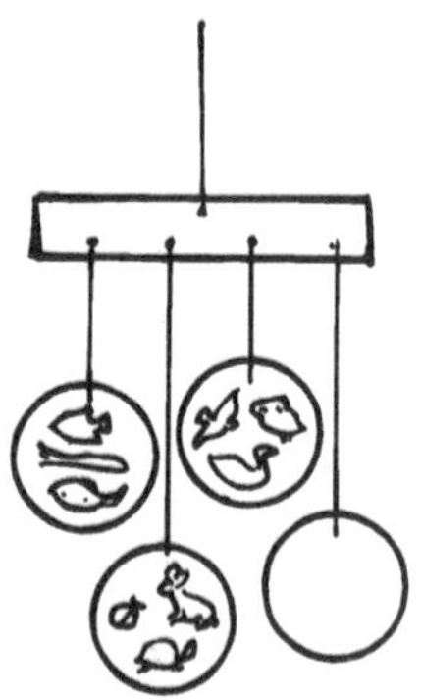

God Makes the Animals

God Makes People

Genesis 1–2: God Makes People

God Makes People Story Strips

Supplies

- copy of the God Makes People Story Strips for each child
- copies of the God Makes People coloring picture for each child (p. 15)
- 7 sheets of card stock or construction paper (6 white, 1 any color) per child
- scissors
- glue
- crayons or markers
- hole punch
- 3 pieces of yarn (4" long, any color) for each child

Directions

Cut out the six story strips and attach each one to the bottom of a separate sheet of white card stock or construction paper. Draw a picture above each strip. For example, for the first strip, draw something we see with our eyes, such as the sun and clouds. Color the God Makes People coloring picture and attach it to a sheet of card stock or construction paper (any color) to make a book cover. Assemble the cover and story pages to make a book. Punch two holes along the left side of all seven pages. Tie the book together using yarn. Use the book to tell about God making all people.

God made my eyes.

God made my ears.

God made my nose.

God made my mouth.

God made my arms and legs.

God made my mind.

Noah Trusts and Obeys God

Genesis 6–7: Noah Trusts and Obeys God

Floating Ark Puppet

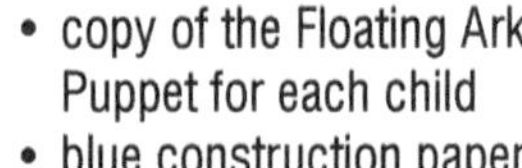

Supplies

- copy of the Floating Ark Puppet for each child
- blue construction paper
- crayons or markers
- craft sticks (2 per child)
- scissors
- glue

Directions

Color and cut out the ark puppet. Fold the ark puppet in half along the dotted line and glue a craft stick to the bottom of the ark puppet between the two halves. Glue the two halves of the ark together. Cut a piece of blue construction paper to look like waves and attach it to a craft stick. Hold the water in front of the ark as you retell the story (see the example).

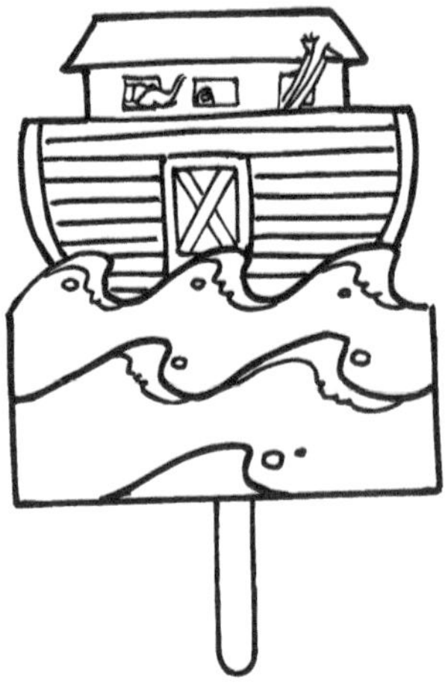

God Keeps His Promise to Noah

Genesis 8–9: God Keeps His Promise to Noah

Rainbow Peel-a-Picture

Supplies

- copy of Rainbow Peel-a-Picture sentence strips for each child (enlarge to 120%)
- copy of the God Keeps His Promise to Noah coloring picture (p. 19) for each child
- scissors
- crayons
- glue

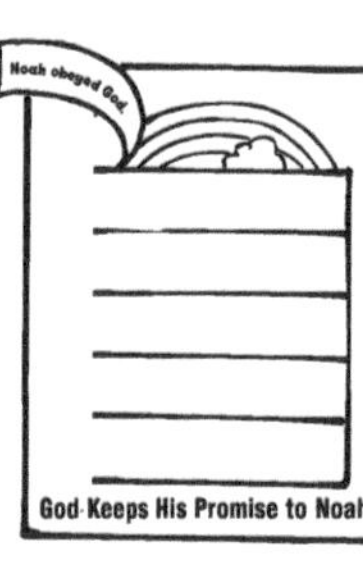

Directions

Cut around the outside edge of the sentence strips rectangle (do not cut along the dotted line or dividing lines between strips). Color the back of the rectangle (the blank side), using various rainbow colors. Then cut along the dividing lines between each strip, being careful to stop cutting at the dotted line. Color the God Keeps His Promise to Noah coloring picture. Apply glue to the sentence strips rectangle between the dotted line and edge only (do not apply any glue to the sentence strips themselves). Turn the rectangle over and attach the sentence strips over the coloring page (sentence side down) by pressing along the glued section. Peel back each strip in order to reveal the picture underneath; then read and tell that part of the Bible story.

Noah obeyed God.

God promised to keep Noah's family safe.

God kept His promise to Noah.

Noah worshipped God.

We can trust God to keep His promises.

We can tell others about God's promises.

Glue here

Abraham's New Home

Genesis 12–13: Abraham's New Home

Picture Pack Slide-a-Scene

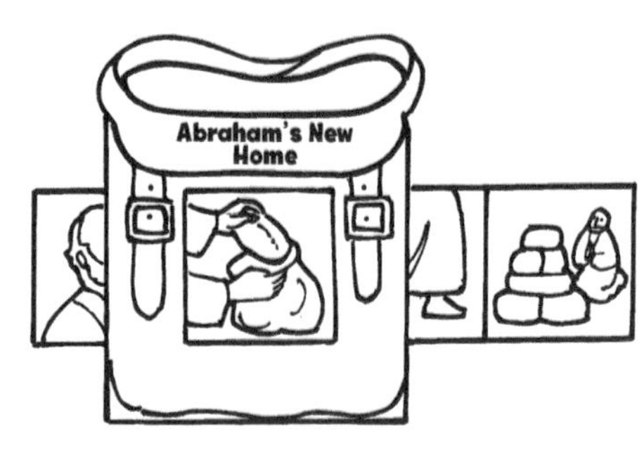

Supplies

- copy of the Picture Pack Slide-a-Scene for each child (preferably on white card stock)
- crayons or markers
- scissors
- glue

Directions

Color the pack and four story scenes. Cut out the story scenes strip along the outside border only (do not cut apart each individual scene). Cut out the pack around the outside edge. Cut two slits in the pack, one on either side of the center square. Slide the scene strip through the two slits in the picture pack (as shown in the example) as you retell the story of Abraham traveling to his new home.

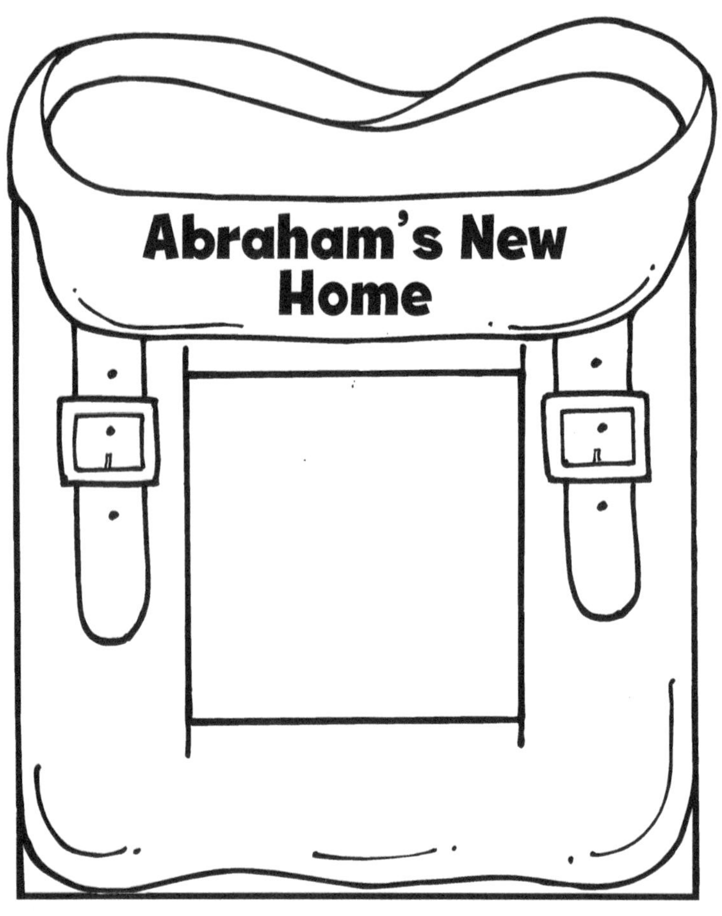

Abraham Follows God

Genesis 13: Abraham Follows God

Choose and Pull

Supplies

- copy of background scene (preferably on card stock) for each child (p. 25)
- copy of the Abraham and Lot figures (on construction paper) for each child
- crayons or markers
- scissors
- glue
- 2 strips of construction paper for each child (¾" wide and 6" long, preferably green or brown)

Directions

Color and cut out the background scene (p. 25). Cut along the two solid, vertical lines near the bottom edge of the scene to make two slits (do not cut through to the bottom of the picture). Color and cut out the Abraham and Lot figures. Attach a precut strip of construction paper to the back of each figure's feet. (Abraham's strip should extend out to the left, and Lot's strip should extend to the right.) Insert the strips through the slits (Abraham's in the left slit, Lot's in the right) and pull the figures across the scene in opposite directions as you tell how Abraham followed God and let Lot choose his land first.

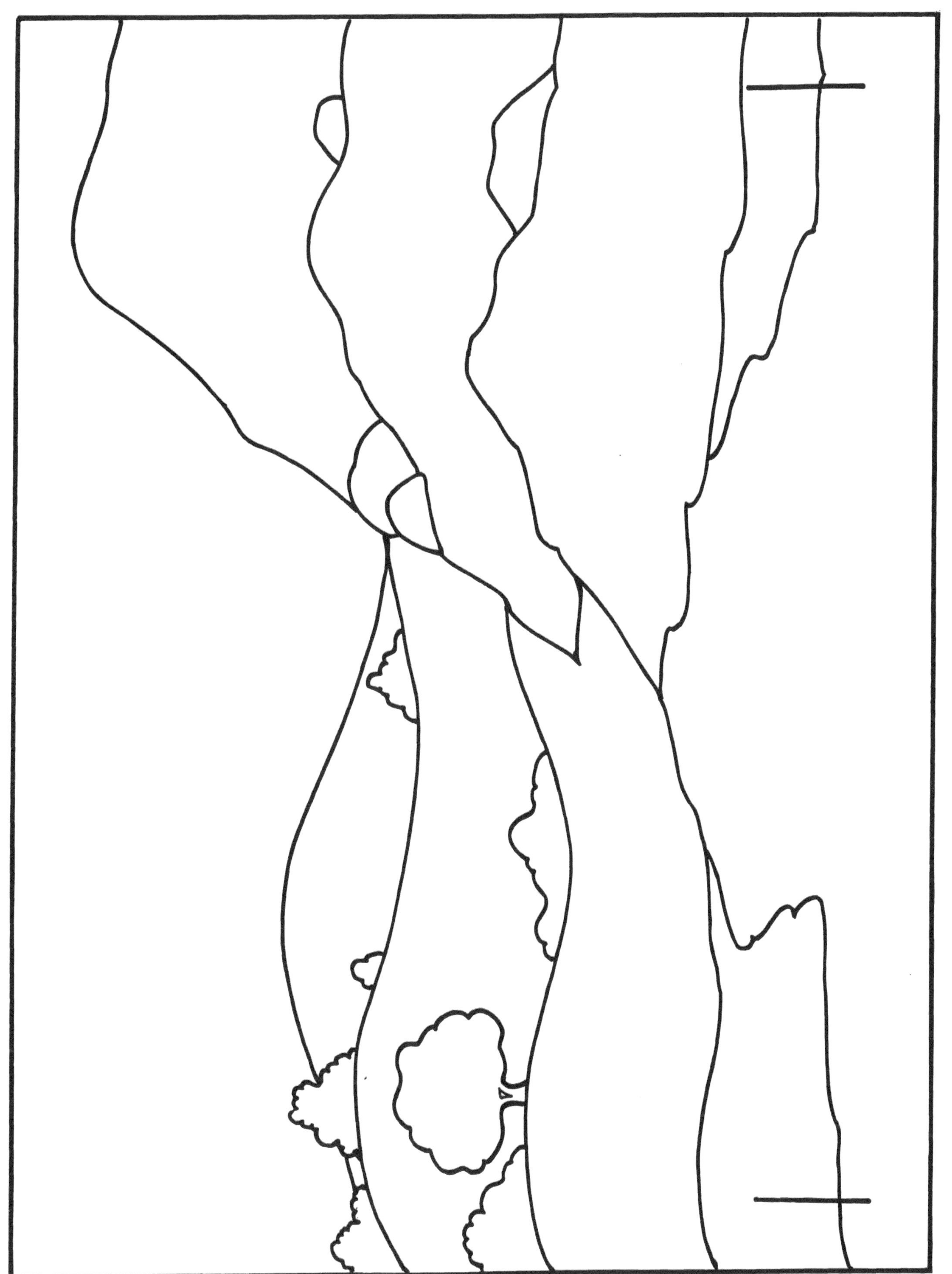

The Birth of Isaac

Genesis 15, 17–18, 21: The Birth of Isaac

Stand-Up Puppets

Supplies

- copy of the Stand-Up Puppets for each child
- crayons or markers
- scissors

Directions

Color and cut out each puppet along the outside border. Do not cut along the dotted lines on the bases. Fold along the dotted lines so the puppets stand up. Use the puppets to retell the story of the birth of Isaac. Attach Sarah's outfit over the Sarah puppet to show her holding baby Isaac when you retell that part of the story.

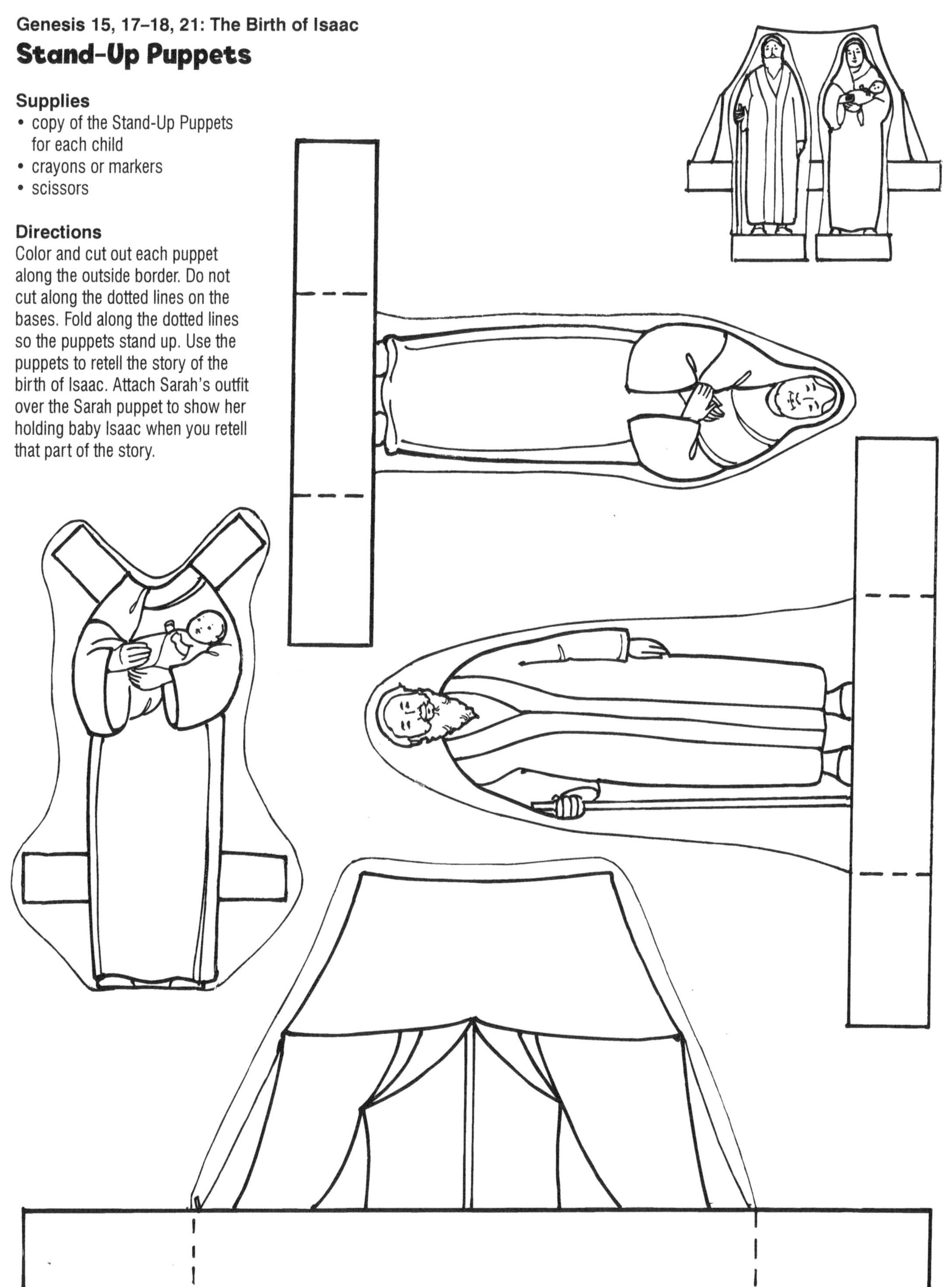

Abraham's Servant Asks for God's Help

Genesis 24: Abraham's Servant Asks for God's Help

God Provides Travel Map

Supplies

- copy of the map and figures (preferably on card stock) for each child (map continued on p. 30)
- crayons or markers
- scissors
- tape

Directions

Color and cut out the map and the two story figures. Attach the map at the seams using tape. Move the figures of Abraham's servant and Rebekah along the road on the map as you tell how God answered the prayer of Abraham's servant.

Isaac Listens to God

Genesis 26: Isaac Listens to God

Isaac's Wells

Supplies

- copy of Isaac's Wells for each child
- crayons or markers
- scissors

Directions

Color and cut out the six wells around the outside edge (do not cut along the dotted lines—all six wells should remain as one piece). Fold the wells back along the center dotted line so the wells are back-to-back with three on each side. Lay the wells down with scenes 1, 2, and 3 facing up. Fold scene 1 in on top of scene 2. Fold scene 3 back behind scene 2. (The wells should form an accordion pattern when finished.) Use the six wells as you tell what happened when Isaac chose to trust and obey God, rather than fight.

God Cares for Jacob

Genesis 28–33: God Cares for Jacob

Jacob's Journey Story Wheel

Supplies

- copy of the Jacob's Journey Story Wheel for each child
- copy of the Story Wheel Cover (p. 243) for each child
- crayons or markers
- scissors
- hole punch
- paper fasteners (1 per child)

Directions

Color the scenes on the story wheel. Cut out the wheel around the outside edge. On the Story Wheel Cover, write: "God Cares for Jacob." Then color the rest of the cover. Place the wheel cover on top of the story wheel and punch a hole through the center of both the cover and the wheel. Use a paper fastener to loosely attach the cover to the wheel. Rotate the cover to reveal each scene as you retell the story of how God cared for Jacob.

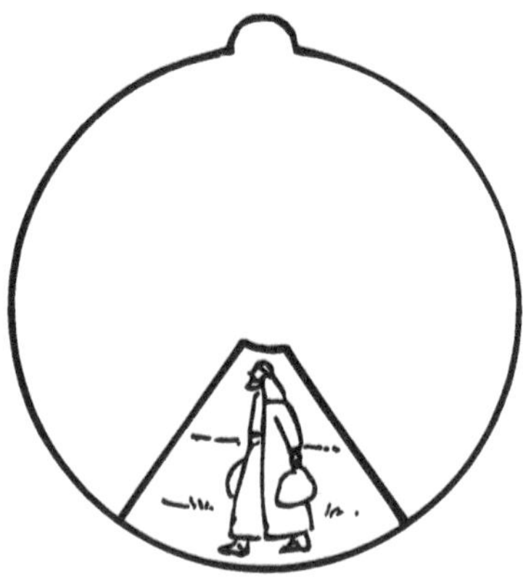

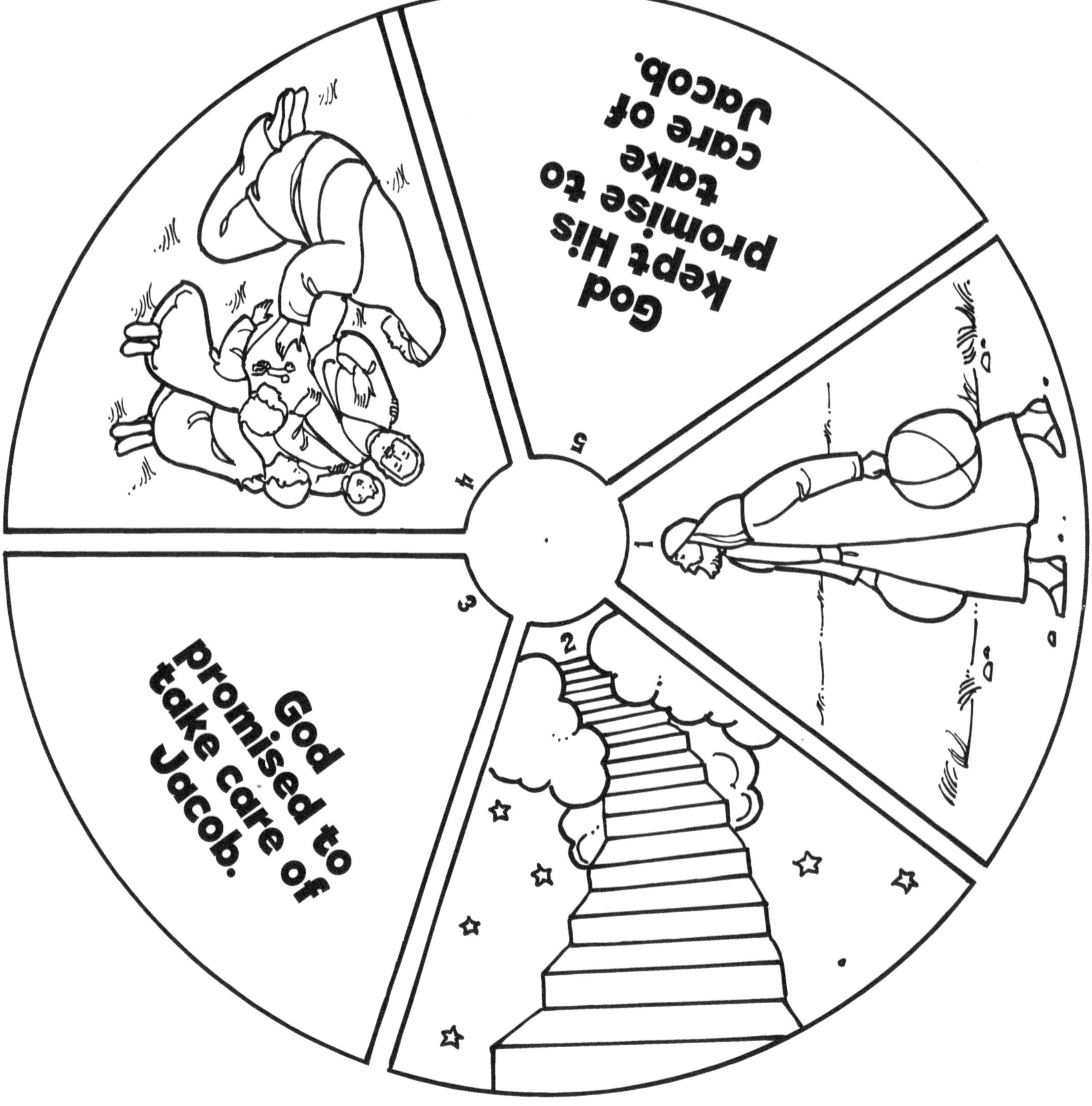

1

2

3

God promised to take care of Jacob.

4

5

God kept His promise to take care of Jacob.

Joseph Moves from Canaan to Egypt

Genesis 37, 39: Joseph Moves from Canaan to Egypt

Joseph's Many Robes

Supplies

- copy of the Joseph's Many Robes activity for each child
- crayons or markers
- scissors
- craft sticks (6 per child)
- tape (or glue sticks)

Directions

Color and cut out the figure of Joseph and each of his five robes. Attach each robe and the Joseph figure to a separate craft stick. Place each robe in front of Joseph as you tell what happened when Joseph was living with his father (Colorful Robe), sold as a slave (Slave Robe), put in charge of Potiphar's household (Servant Robe), thrown into prison (Prison Robe), and chosen as a leader (Leader Robe).

Slave Robe

Leader Robe

Colorful Robe

Prison Robe

Servant Robe

Joseph Forgives and Helps His Family

Genesis 39, 41–43, 45: Joseph Forgives and Helps His Family

Joseph and Brother Puppets

Supplies

- copy of the Joseph and Brother Puppets for each child
- crayons or markers
- scissors
- brown paper lunch bags (2 per child)
- glue

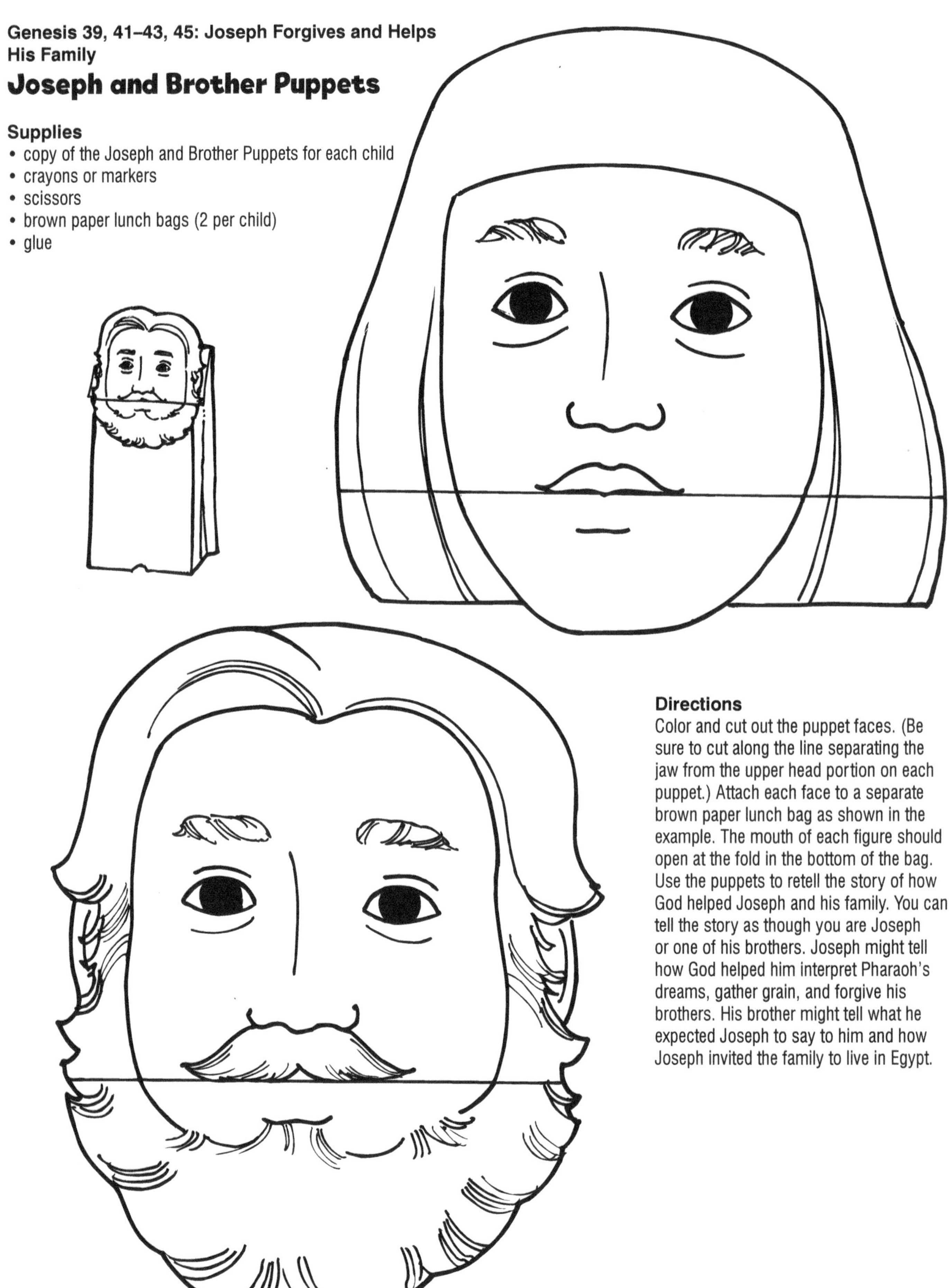

Directions

Color and cut out the puppet faces. (Be sure to cut along the line separating the jaw from the upper head portion on each puppet.) Attach each face to a separate brown paper lunch bag as shown in the example. The mouth of each figure should open at the fold in the bottom of the bag. Use the puppets to retell the story of how God helped Joseph and his family. You can tell the story as though you are Joseph or one of his brothers. Joseph might tell how God helped him interpret Pharaoh's dreams, gather grain, and forgive his brothers. His brother might tell what he expected Joseph to say to him and how Joseph invited the family to live in Egypt.

God Cares for Moses

Exodus 1–2, 6: God Cares for Moses

Moses Story Smush Book

See page 7 for supplies and directions for this activity.
Use the book to tell how God cared for baby Moses.

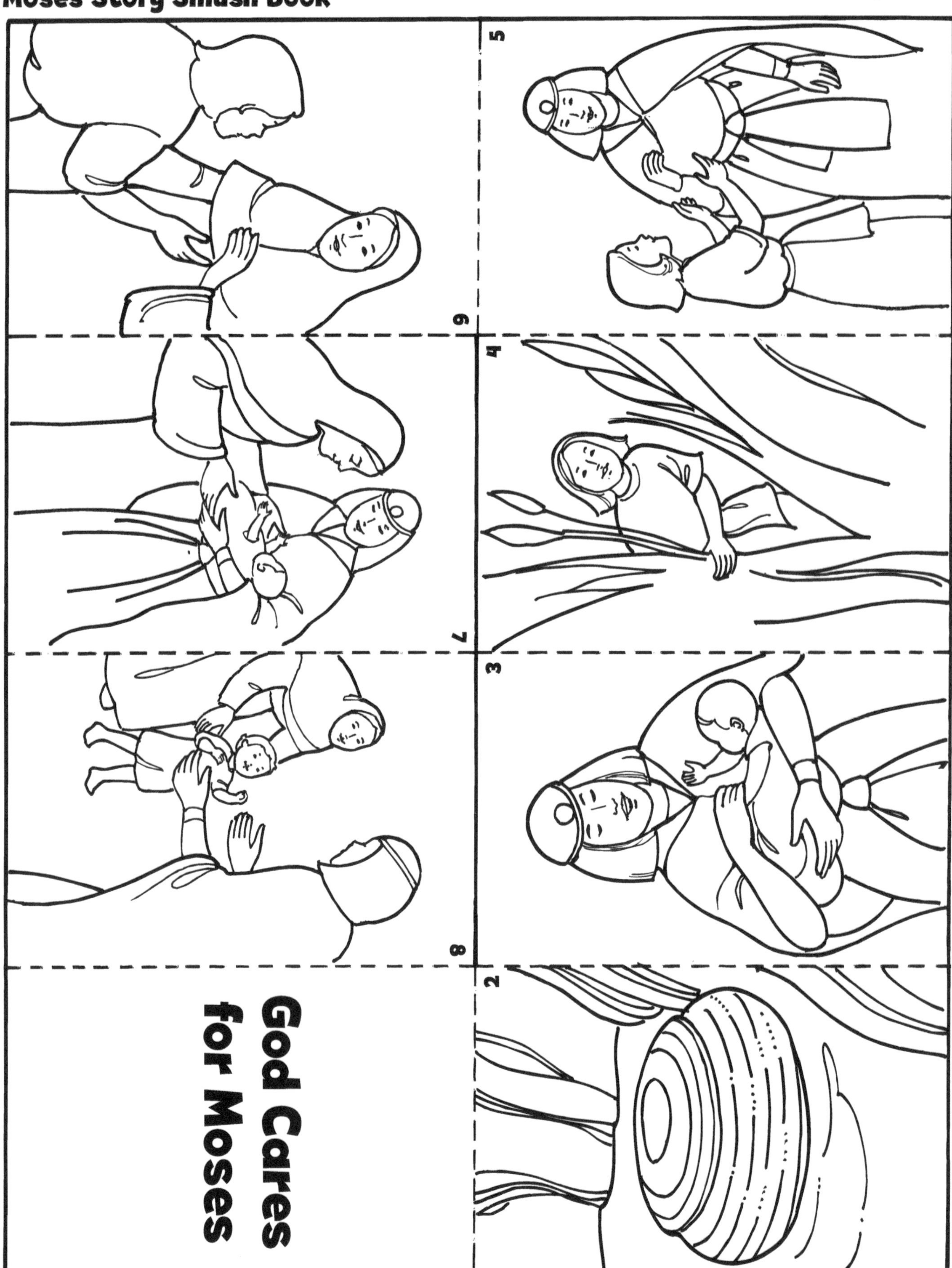

God Cares for His People

Exodus 7–13: God Cares for His People

Memory Plagues

Supplies

- 2 copies of the Memory Plagues cards (preferably on card stock) for each child
- crayons or markers
- scissors

Directions

Color and cut out both copies of the Memory Plagues cards. (Color card number 9 a dark color for the plague of darkness.) Use the cards to play a game of memory. Place all the cards facedown on the floor or a table. Turn over two cards at a time, trying to find a match. When a match is made, remove those two cards from the playing area. Play the game in teams of two for more fun. Use the cards to review the ten plagues and tell how God showed that He can do anything!

God's People Cross the Red Sea

Exodus 13–15: God's People Cross the Red Sea

Red Sea Pamphlet

See page 7 for supplies and directions for this activity.
Use the pamphlet to tell how God showed His power.

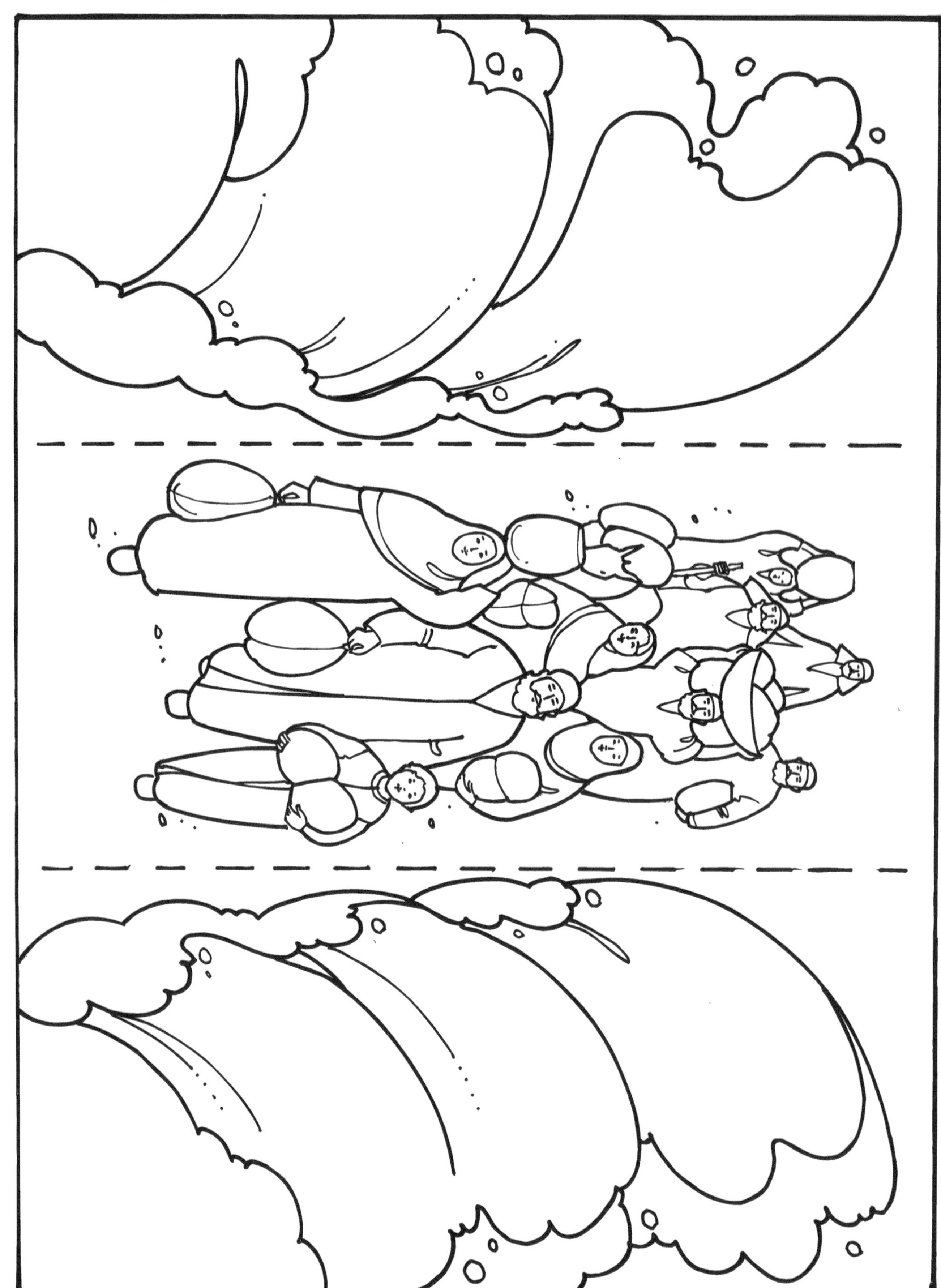

God Gives Food and Water

Feed Your Family Board Game

Supplies

- copy of the Feed Your Family Board Game and corresponding figures (preferably on card stock) for each child (continued on p. 47)
- white paper (or card stock)
- black permanent marker
- crayons or markers
- tape
- scissors

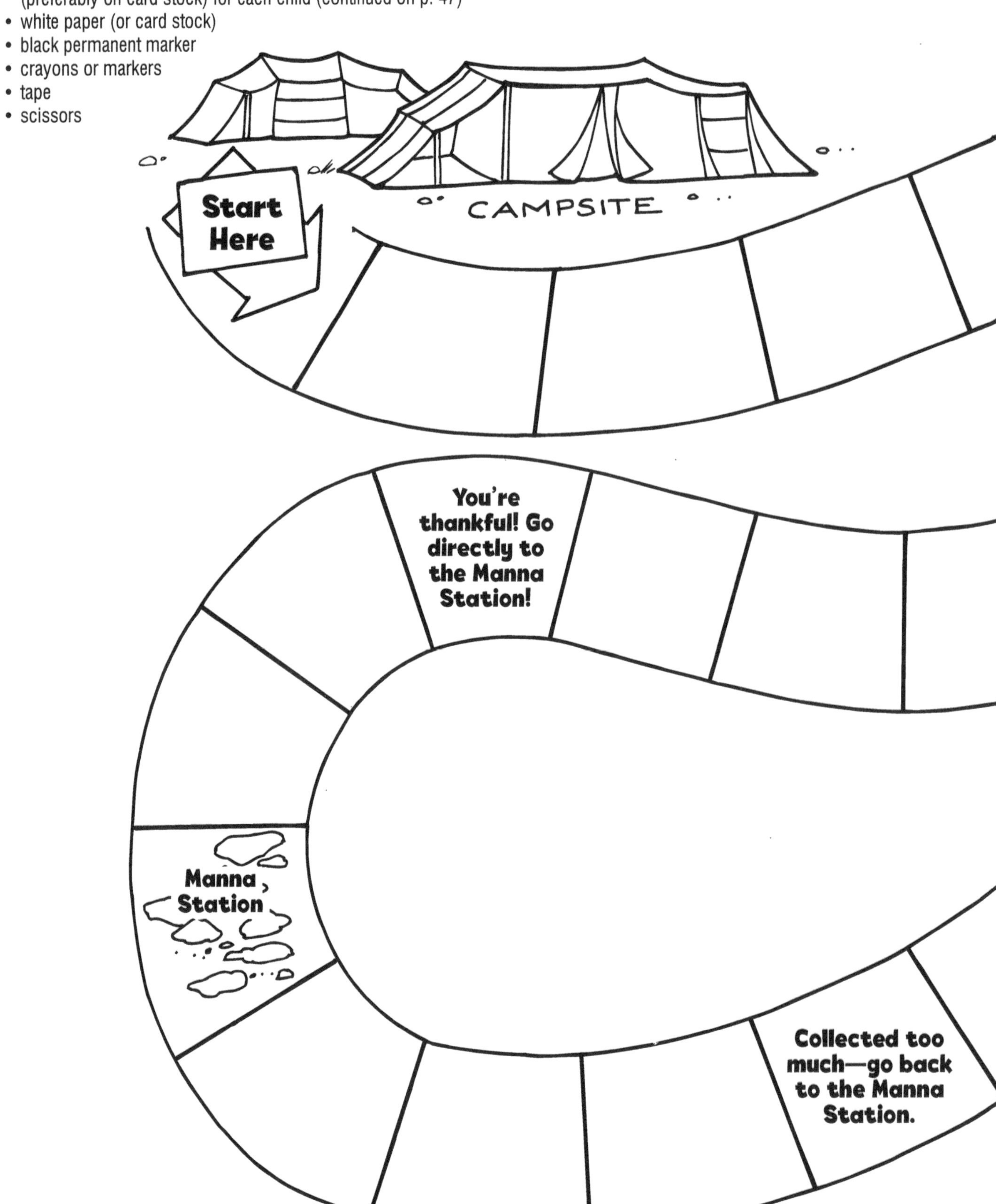

Directions

Before class, make a stack of numbered cards. Each card should have a number 1, 2, 3, or 4 written on it. Children will draw cards from the stack to determine how many spaces they can move forward on the game board.

Color the game board. Cut out the game pieces (the boy and girl). Use tape to attach the two pages of the game board at the seam. Place the stack of numbered cards facedown near the game board. Play this game in teams of two or more players. Draw a card from the stack and move your game piece forward on the board as many spaces as the card allows. If you land on a word space, follow the instructions on that space. To win the game, move your game piece from the campsite, through the quail and manna collection stations, to the home tent. Play this game as a reminder that God gave His people what they needed, and He always knows what we need too!

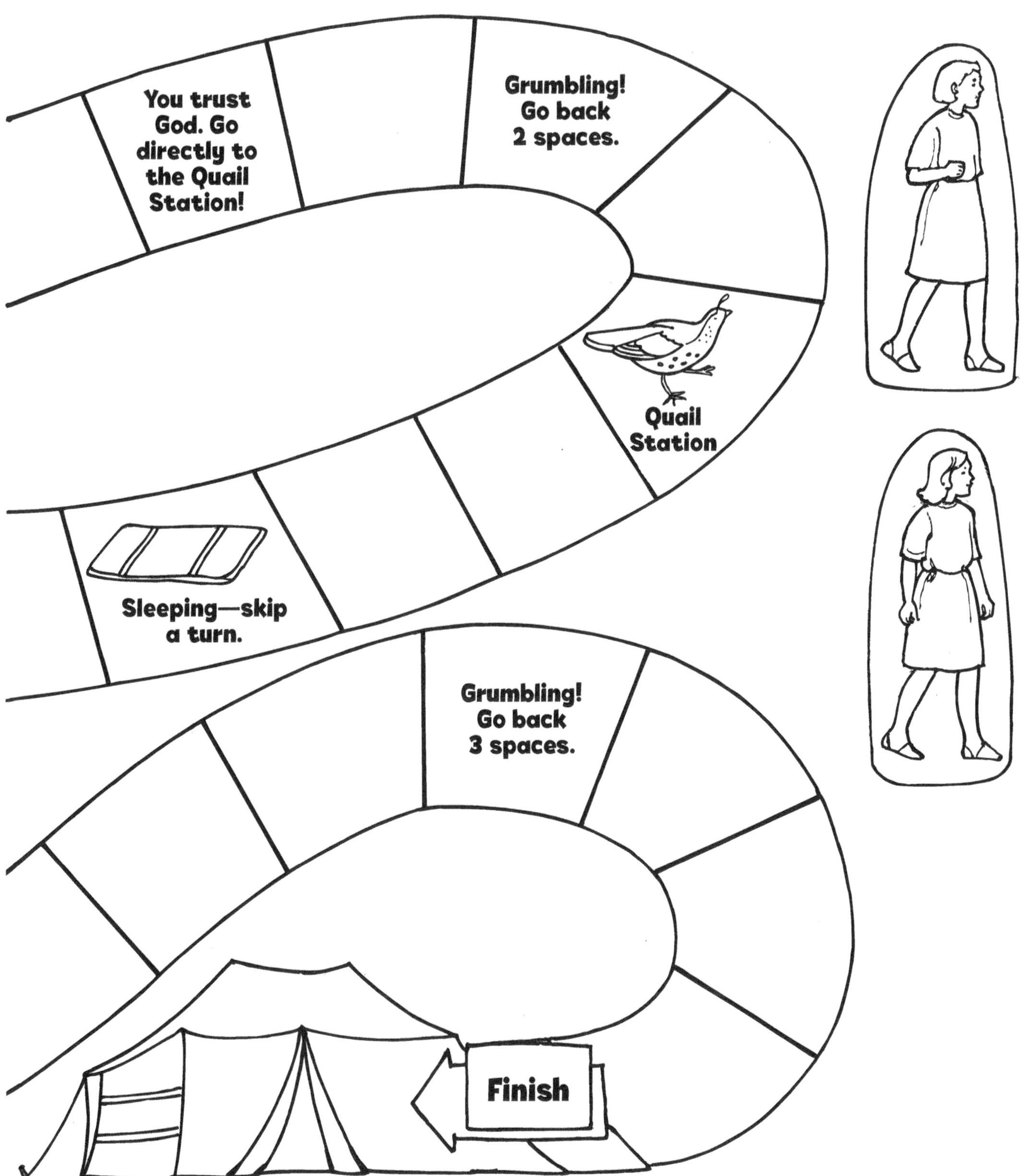

God Gives Ten Rules

Exodus 19–20, 24, 31–32: God Gives Ten Rules

3-D Mount Sinai

Supplies

- copy of the 3-D Mount Sinai for each child
- crayons or markers
- scissors
- glue or double-sided tape

Directions

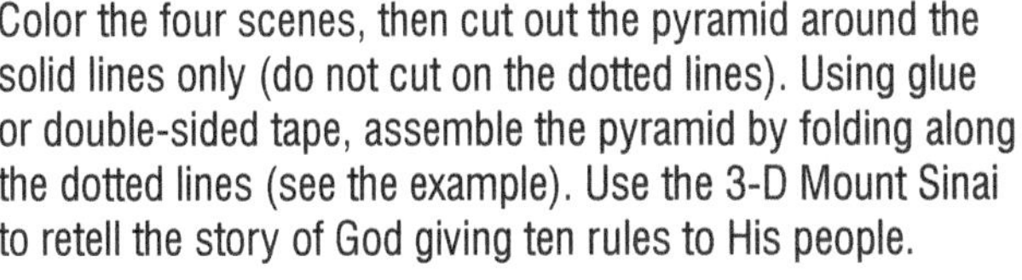

Color the four scenes, then cut out the pyramid around the solid lines only (do not cut on the dotted lines). Using glue or double-sided tape, assemble the pyramid by folding along the dotted lines (see the example). Use the 3-D Mount Sinai to retell the story of God giving ten rules to His people.

12 Spies Explore Canaan

Numbers 13–14: 12 Spies Explore Canaan

Promised Land Pennant Scenes

Supplies

- copy of the Promised Land Pennant Scenes for each child (continued on p. 52)
- crayons or markers
- scissors
- hole punch
- brown yarn or twine

Directions

Color the scenes inside the four grape clusters. Cut out each cluster along the outside edge. Color the back of each cluster purple. Punch two holes in each cluster as indicated by the open circles. String brown yarn or twine through the holes so the scenes appear in the correct order (as numbered on each scene); see the example p. 51.

Fold the clusters along the dotted lines so the scenes are folded inside. Use the Promised Land Pennant Scenes as you retell the Bible story. Explain what the 12 spies found in the land of Canaan and how Joshua and Caleb believed what God said.

God Is with Moses and Joshua

Deuteronomy 31, 34; Joshua 1:
God Is with Moses and Joshua

Pop-Up Promised Land

Supplies

- copy of the Pop-Up Promised Land card for each child
- crayons or markers
- scissors

Directions

Color and cut out the Pop-Up Promised Land card. Fold the card in half along the horizontal dotted line so the bottom two word boxes are folded behind the top two scenes. Fold the pop-up piece down along the dotted lines as you fold the card in half so that when the card is opened, the center piece pops up. Use this card to tell about the promises God made to Moses, Joshua, and the people.

God Was with Moses and Joshua

God Is Always with Us

Joshua Obeys God at Jericho

Joshua 5–6: Joshua Obeys God at Jericho

Jericho Folds!

Supplies

- copy of the Jericho Folds! activity for each child
- crayons or markers
- scissors

Directions

Color and cut out the Jericho picture as one piece (do not cut along the dotted lines). Fold the page back along the top dotted line, showing what Jericho looked like before the walls fell. As you retell the story, fold the scene down along the bottom dotted line (see the example) to show what Jericho looked like after God's people marched around the city one time for six days and seven times on the seventh day. Use the activity to show how Joshua and the Israelites obeyed God at Jericho.

God's People Choose to Serve Him

Joshua 24: God's People Choose to Serve Him

Serving Box

Supplies

- copy of the Serving Box (preferably on white card stock) for each child
- crayons or markers
- scissors
- tape
- tissue paper *(optional)*

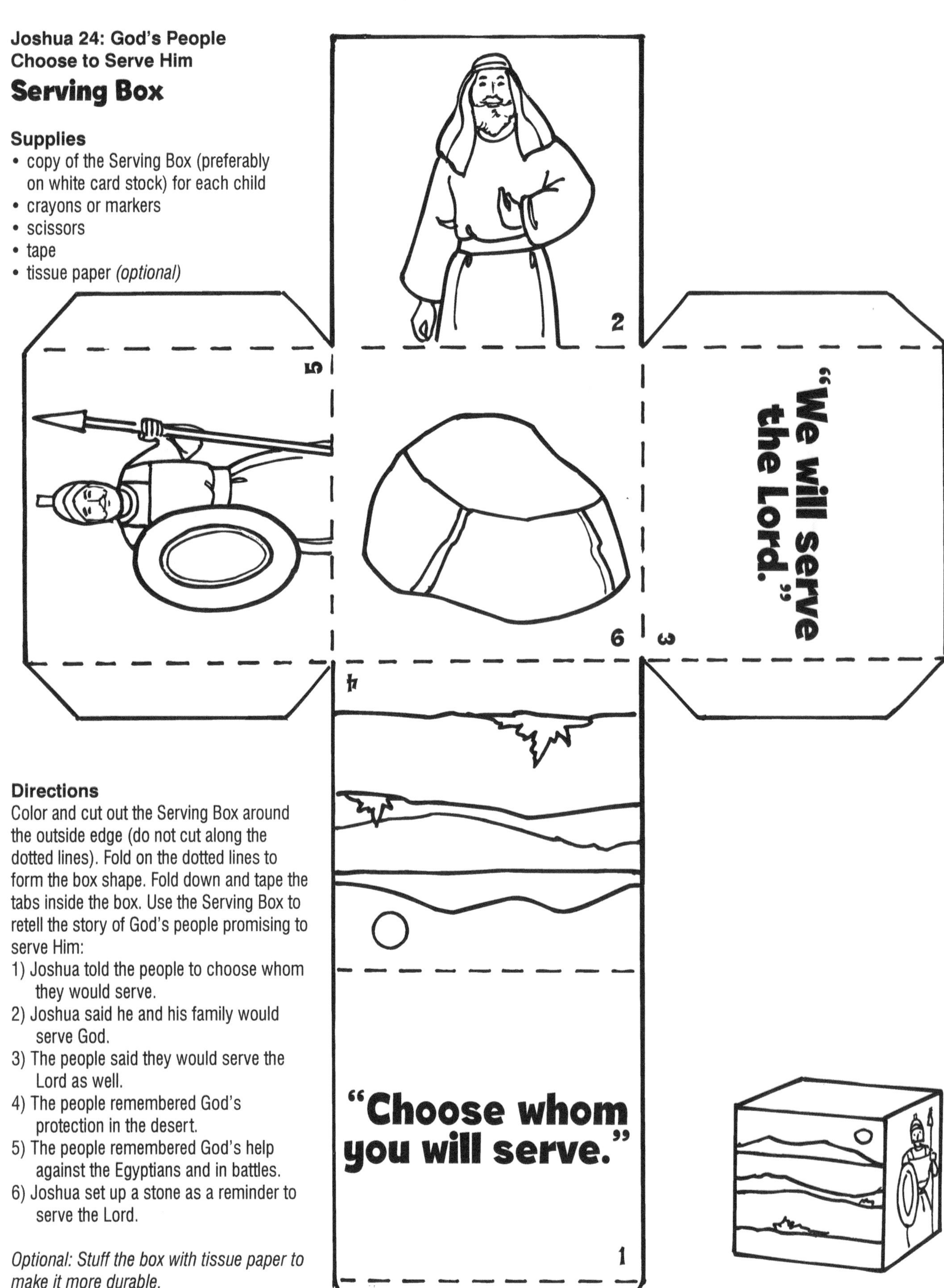

Directions

Color and cut out the Serving Box around the outside edge (do not cut along the dotted lines). Fold on the dotted lines to form the box shape. Fold down and tape the tabs inside the box. Use the Serving Box to retell the story of God's people promising to serve Him:

1) Joshua told the people to choose whom they would serve.
2) Joshua said he and his family would serve God.
3) The people said they would serve the Lord as well.
4) The people remembered God's protection in the desert.
5) The people remembered God's help against the Egyptians and in battles.
6) Joshua set up a stone as a reminder to serve the Lord.

Optional: Stuff the box with tissue paper to make it more durable.

Deborah and Barak

Judges 4: Deborah and Barak

Shield Scenes

Supplies

- copy of the Shield Scenes for each child
- crayons or markers
- scissors
- dark-colored card stock *(optional)*
- glue or glue sticks *(optional)*

Directions

Color and cut out the Shield Scenes as one piece (do not cut the scenes apart individually). Use the Shield Scenes to tell how Deborah and Barak worked together to do what God told them to do:

1) King Jabin was cruel to God's people.
2) God sent a message to Deborah, who was a judge.
3) Deborah sent a message to Barak telling him what God said.
4) Deborah and Barak went together to defeat King Jabin's army.

Optional: Mount the shield on card stock for a more durable shield.

Gideon

Judges 6–7: Gideon

Gideon's Horn

Supplies

- copy of Gideon's Horn for each child
- crayons or markers
- scissors
- tape

Directions

Color and cut out Gideon's Horn as one piece. Roll the horn into the shape of a megaphone and tape the tab behind the first scene. Use the horn to act out the Bible story, or use the three scenes to tell how Gideon trusted and obeyed God:

1) An angel appeared to Gideon to tell him that God was sending him to save God's people from the Midianites.
2) Gideon took an army of just 300 men to fight along with him.
3) Gideon's army blew their trumpets, broke their jars, held up their torches, and shouted. And God helped them defeat the Midianites!

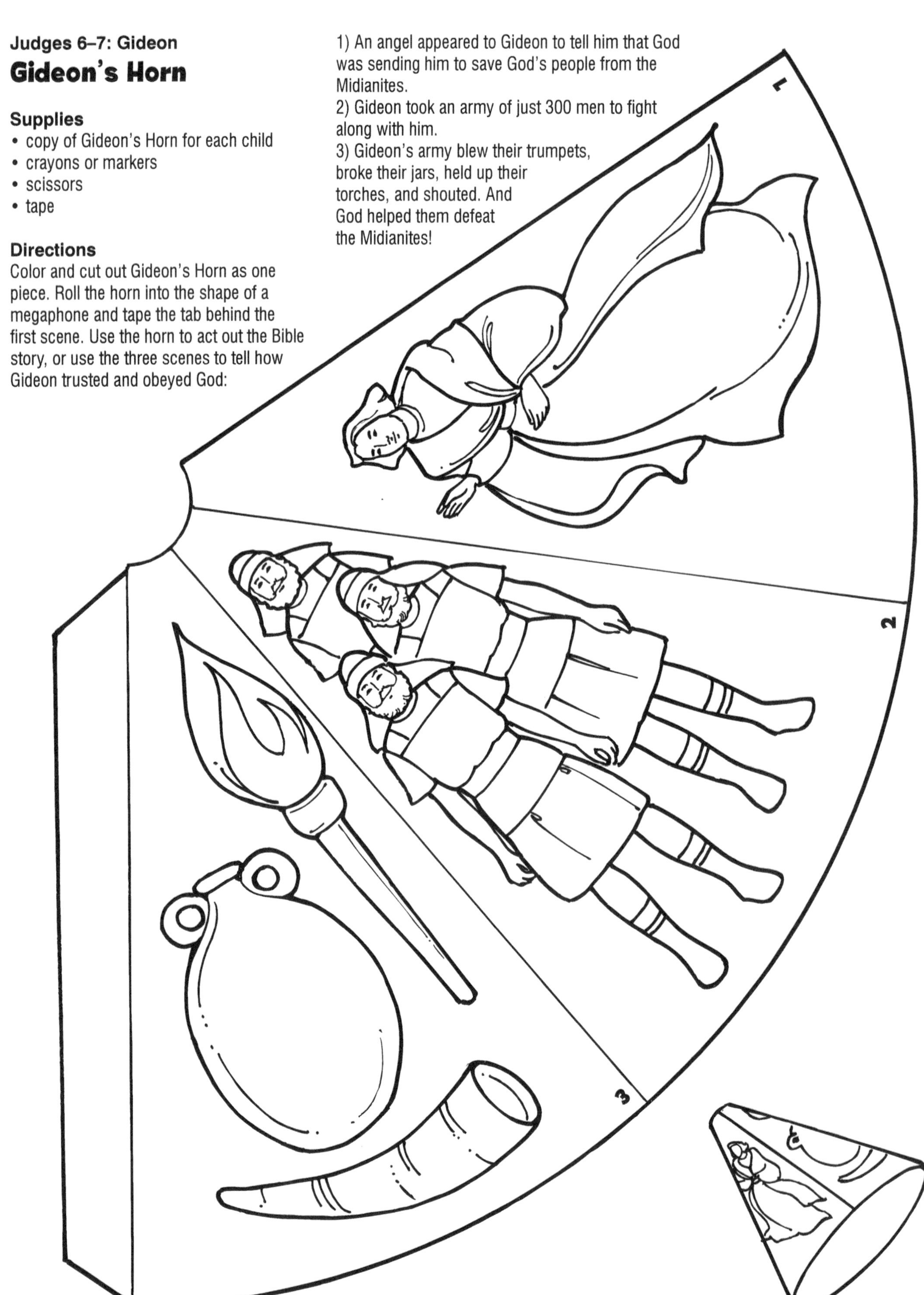

Naomi and Ruth

Ruth 1–2: Naomi and Ruth

Ruth Rebus

Supplies

- copy of the Ruth Rebus for each child
- crayons or markers

Directions

Color the pictures in the rebus. Use the rebus to retell the story of how Naomi and Ruth were faithful to God and each other.

 **Ruth**
 **Naomi**
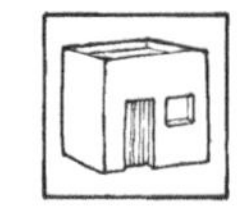 **home**
 **food**
 **fields**
 **grain**
 **Boaz**

 **was married to**  **'s son.**  **'s husband and**  **'s husband died.**  **decided to stay with**  **.**  **took**  **to Bethlehem to her** 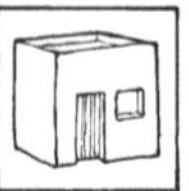 **in Judah.**  **was sad.**  **and**  **did not have much**  **.**  **offered to go work in the**  **and gather**  **.**  **collected**  **that the other workers left behind.**  **owned the**  **and was kind to**  **. let**  **pick**  **from his** 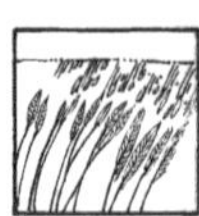 **as often as she wanted to.**  **and**  **had plenty of**  **. worked in the**  **every day from morning until night.**  **and**  **were faithful to God and to each other.**

Hannah

1 Samuel 1: Hannah

Kneel-and-Walk Puppets

Supplies

- copy of the Kneel-and-Walk Puppets (preferably on card stock) for each child
- crayons or markers
- scissors
- hole punch *(optional)*

Directions

Color and cut out the puppets. Cut out the circles where the legs are missing (or use a hole punch to punch out the areas). Insert fingers into the holes to make the puppets walk and kneel. Use the puppets to retell the story of Hannah keeping her promise to God and bringing Samuel to Eli the priest to be raised in God's house. Hannah can kneel as she prays for a son and can walk Samuel to meet Eli.

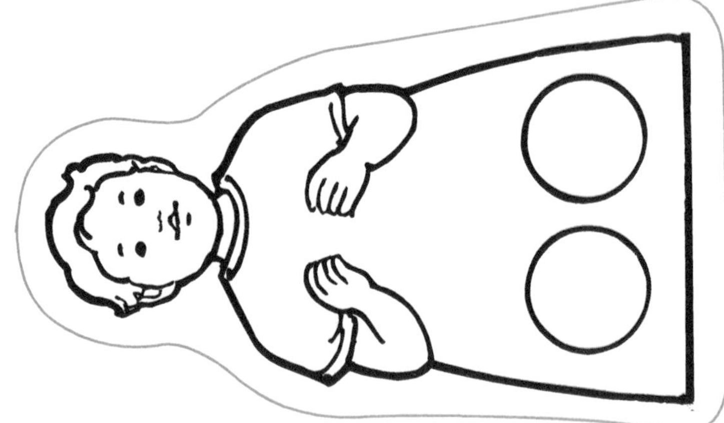

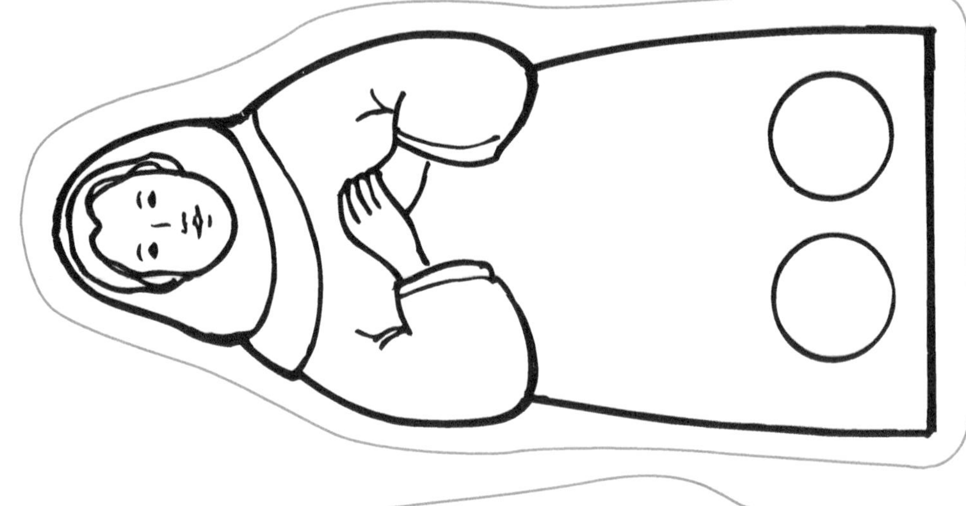

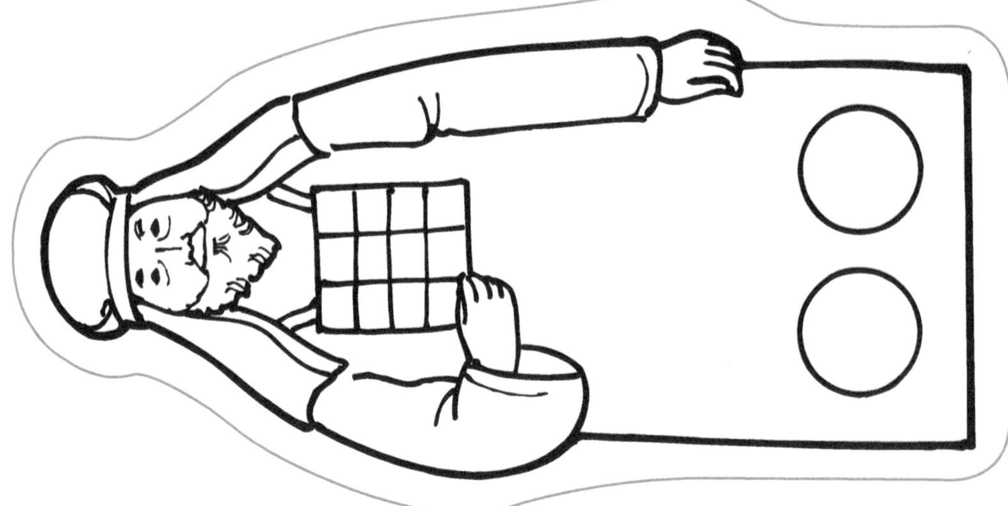

God Talks to Samuel

1 Samuel 2–4, 7: God Talks to Samuel

Samuel and Eli Stick Puppets

Supplies

- copy of the Samuel and Eli Stick Puppets for each child
- crayons or markers
- scissors
- glue (or tape)
- craft sticks (2 per child)

Directions

Color and cut out the puppets around the outside edges (do not cut on the dotted lines). Fold the puppets on the dotted lines and attach a craft stick to each puppet, using glue or tape. The craft stick should be glued between the two sides near the bottom of the puppet. You may also want to glue around the inside edges of the puppet to attach the two sides together. Use the puppets as you retell the story of Samuel listening and obeying when God spoke to him. When you tell about Samuel and Eli sleeping, show the sides with their eyes closed. Turn the puppets around to tell about them waking up each time.

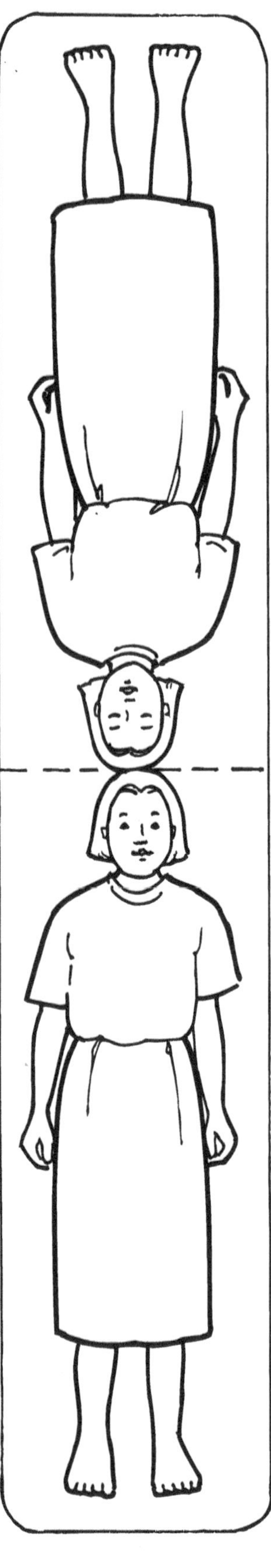

Samuel Talks to God

1 Samuel 8–10:
Samuel Talks to God

Crown Scenes

Supplies

- copy of the Crown Scenes for each child
- 2" x 12" strips of construction paper (2 per child, any color)
- crayons or markers
- scissors
- stapler (or tape)

Directions

Color and cut out the crown as one piece. Attach a 2"-wide strip of construction paper to one side of the crown. Size the crown to fit the child's head and attach the other end of the construction paper strip to the crown to make a headband (see the example). Use the Crown Scenes to retell the story of Samuel anointing Saul as king, or wear the crown as you retell the story from Saul's point of view:

1) The people wanted a king.
2) Samuel talked to God, and God told Samuel to anoint Saul as king. Saul went to look for the man God had chosen.
3) Saul went looking for his father's lost donkeys. He met Samuel.
4) Samuel poured oil on Saul's head to show that God had chosen Saul to be king.

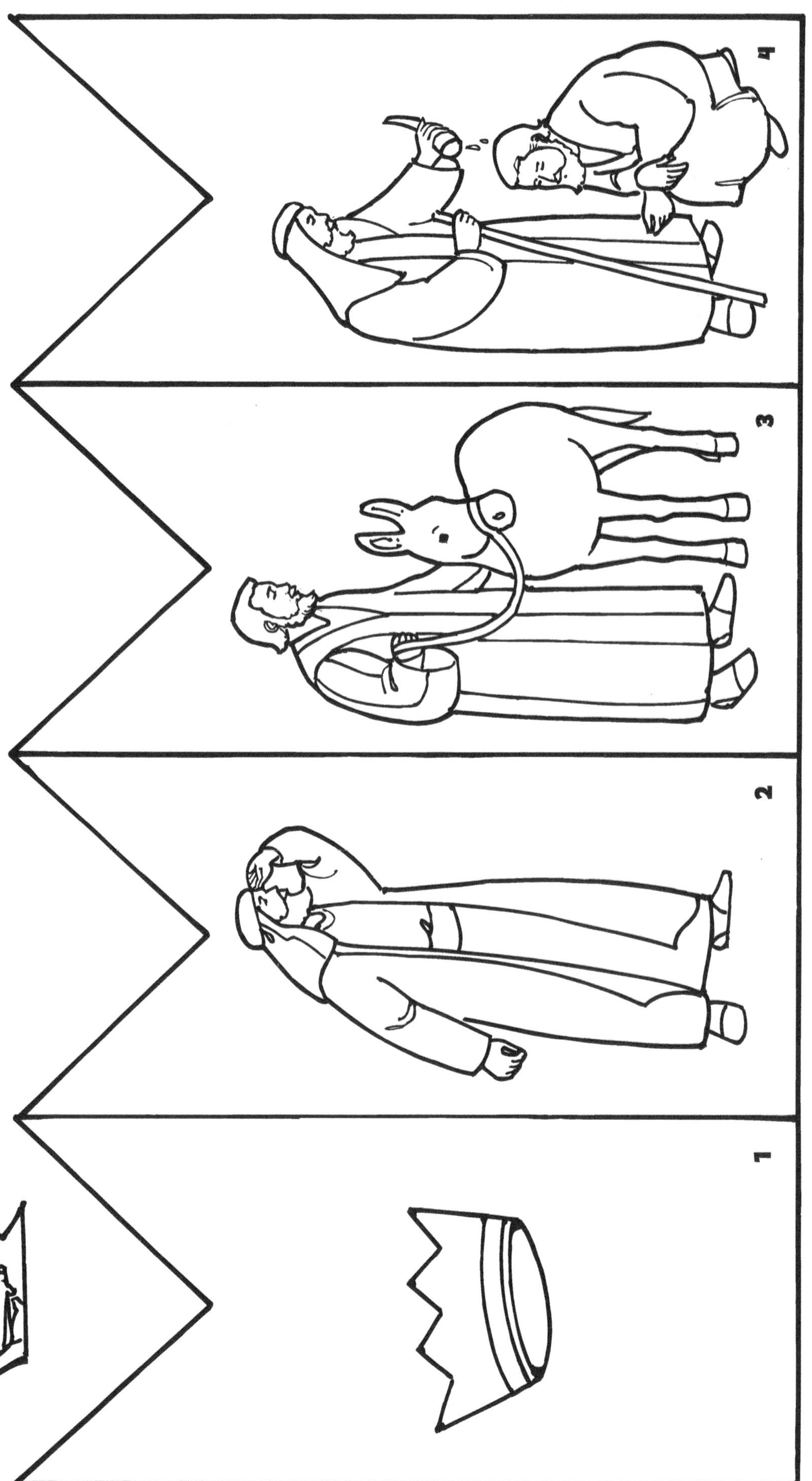

Saul Chooses Not to Listen

1 Samuel 15: Saul Chooses Not to Listen

Saul Disobeys Flip-Flap Book

Supplies

- copy of the Saul Disobeys Flip-Flap Book for each child
- crayons or markers
- scissors

Directions

Color and cut out the flip-flap book as one large rectangle (do not cut along the dotted lines or any other solid lines yet). Fold along the dotted line so the pictures are underneath the cover. Cut along the solid lines between the rectangles containing words, stopping when you reach the dotted line. Be careful not to cut between the picture scenes. Use the flip-flap book to retell the story of Saul disobeying God.

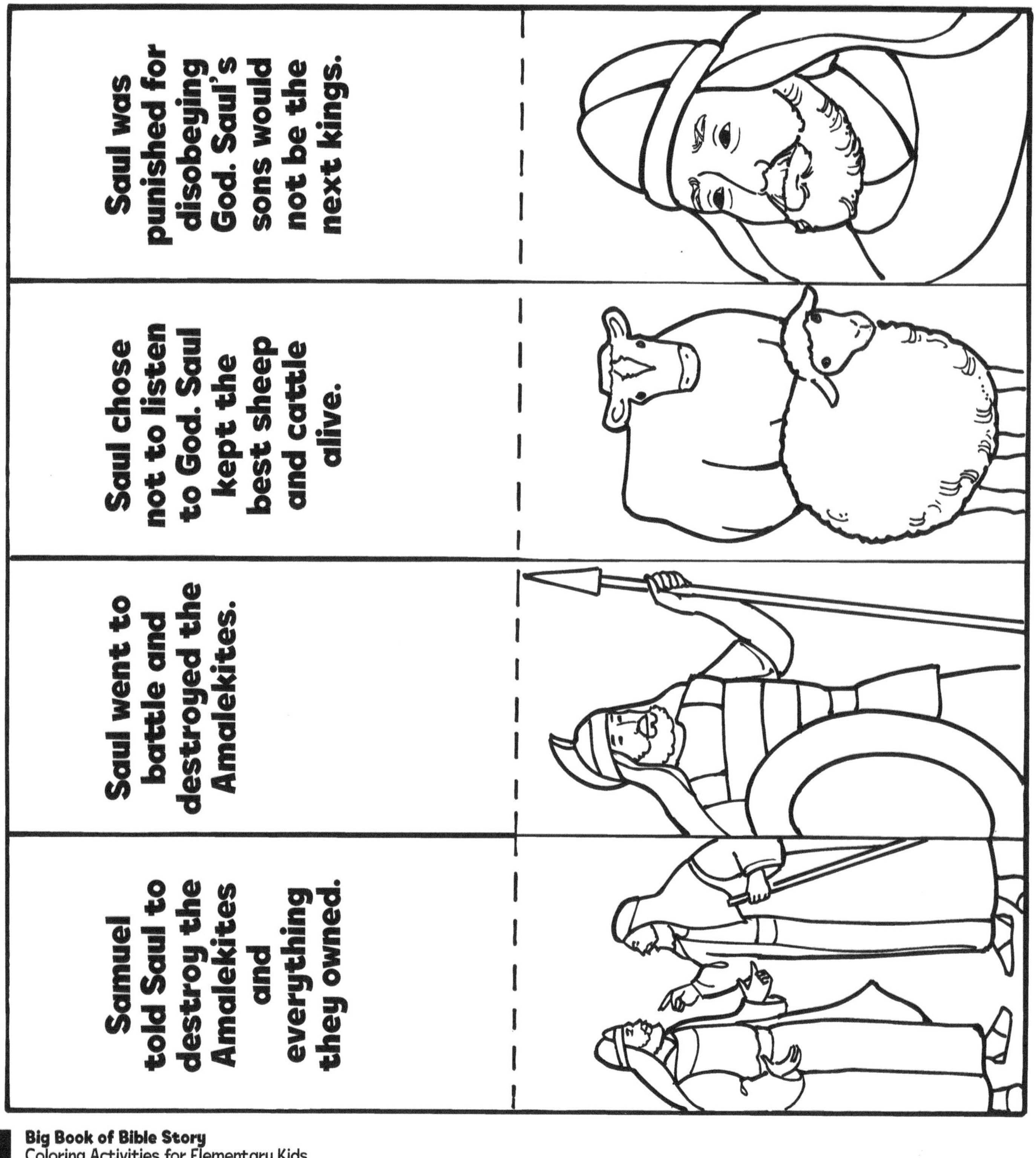

Samuel told Saul to destroy the Amalekites and everything they owned.

Saul went to battle and destroyed the Amalekites.

Saul chose not to listen to God. Saul kept the best sheep and cattle alive.

Saul was punished for disobeying God. Saul's sons would not be the next kings.

Samuel Anoints David as King

1 Samuel 16: Samuel Anoints David as King

Searching for David Card

Supplies

- copy of the card scenes for each child
- construction paper (any color, 1 sheet per child)
- crayons or markers
- scissors
- glue

Directions

Color and cut out the four scenes as one piece (do not cut along the dotted lines). Fold a sheet of construction paper in half widthwise to make a card. On the cover of the card, write: "God spoke to Samuel." Inside the card, top left, write: "Samuel did what the Lord said." Inside the card, top right, write: "The Lord looks at the heart." Fold the scenes along the dotted lines like an accordion. Position the scenes inside the card, carefully lining up the middle fold of the scenes with the center fold of the card. Glue the scenes to the card, gluing the back of the first scene onto the left side of the card and the back of the last scene onto the right side of the card. The two middle scenes should not be glued to the card (see the example). When the card is closed, the middle scenes will fold forward inside the card. The scenes will unfold as you open the card. Use the card to retell the story of Samuel anointing David as king.

God Helps David Do His Jobs

1 Samuel 16–17: God Helps David Do His Jobs

David's Job Book

Supplies

- copy of David's Job Book for each child (continued on p. 77)
- construction paper (any color, 1 sheet per child)
- crayons or markers
- scissors
- glue
- hole punch
- yarn or ribbon

Directions

Color the pictures of David; then cut out the pictures and the word strips. Cut a sheet of construction paper into four equal pieces. (You will use only three of the pieces for this activity.) Attach two story pictures to each piece of construction paper (front and back, in order per the number on each scene). Attach the word strips under their corresponding scenes (see the example). Place the book pages in order and punch two holes along the left side. Tie the book together using yarn or ribbon. Use the book to retell the story of David doing one of his jobs.

Optional: Use the remaining piece of construction paper as a cover for the book. Decorate this piece as you like and write "God Helps David Do His Job" on the front. Attach the cover to the front of the other pages.

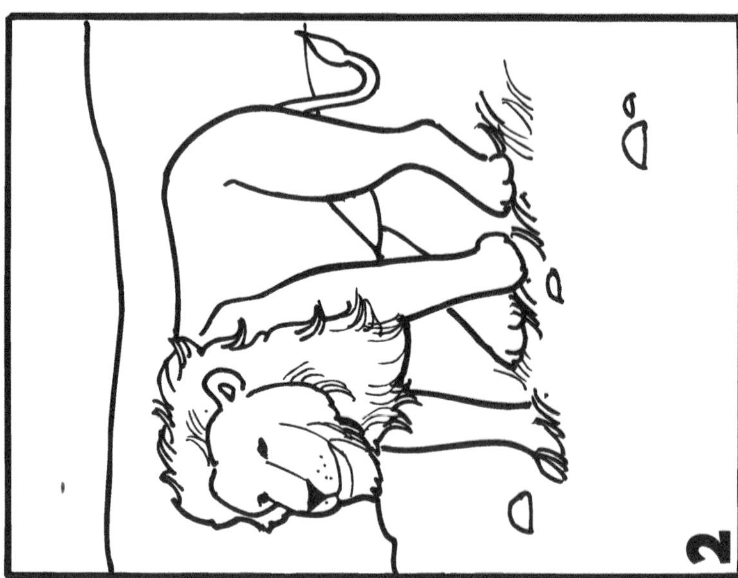

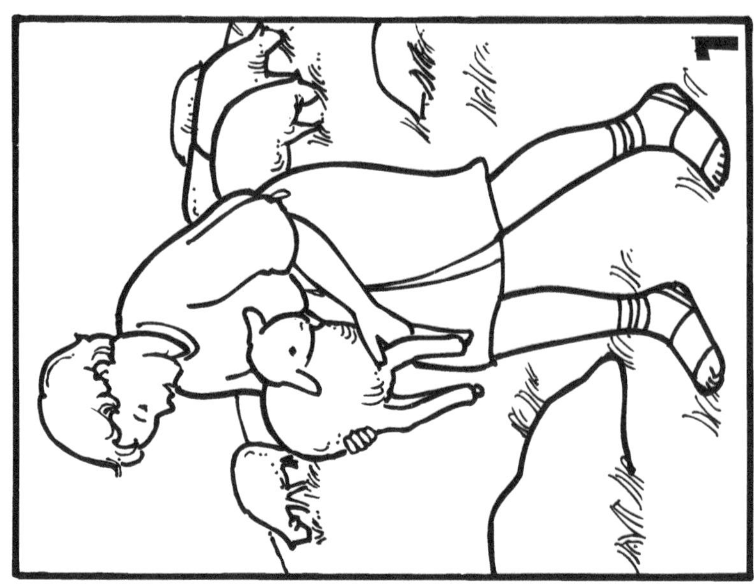

One of David's jobs was to care for his family's sheep.

A lion came to hurt the sheep.

David fought the lion and won.

David fought the bear and won.

A bear came to hurt the sheep.

God helped David do his job.

God Helps David Be Brave

1 Samuel 17: God Helps David Be Brave

David and Goliath Story Bag

Supplies

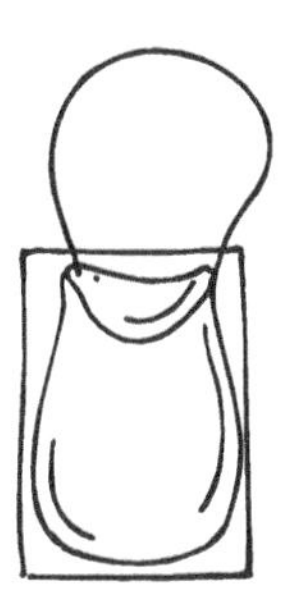

- copy of the David and Goliath Story Bag pieces for each child (continued on p. 80)
- brown paper lunch bags (1 per child)
- crayons or markers
- scissors
- glue
- twine
- tape

Directions

Color and cut out the story bag cover and the five stones. Color the back side of each stone brown or gray. Fold each stone along the dotted line so the scene is hidden inside. Cut 3$\frac{1}{2}$" off the top of a brown paper lunch bag. Attach the story bag cover to the front of the bag (see the example). Create a strap for the bag, taping the ends of a 24" piece of twine to opposite sides of the lunch bag. Place the five folded stones inside the bag. Pull the stones from the bag individually as you retell the story of David being brave when he fought Goliath:

1) Goliath was a mighty warrior, and everyone feared him.
2) David went to King Saul and offered to fight Goliath.
3) David chose five smooth stones from a stream.
4) Taking his shepherd's staff, his sling, and the stones, David went to fight Goliath.
5) David slung one stone from his sling. The stone struck Goliath in the forehead, and he fell. God helped David be brave.

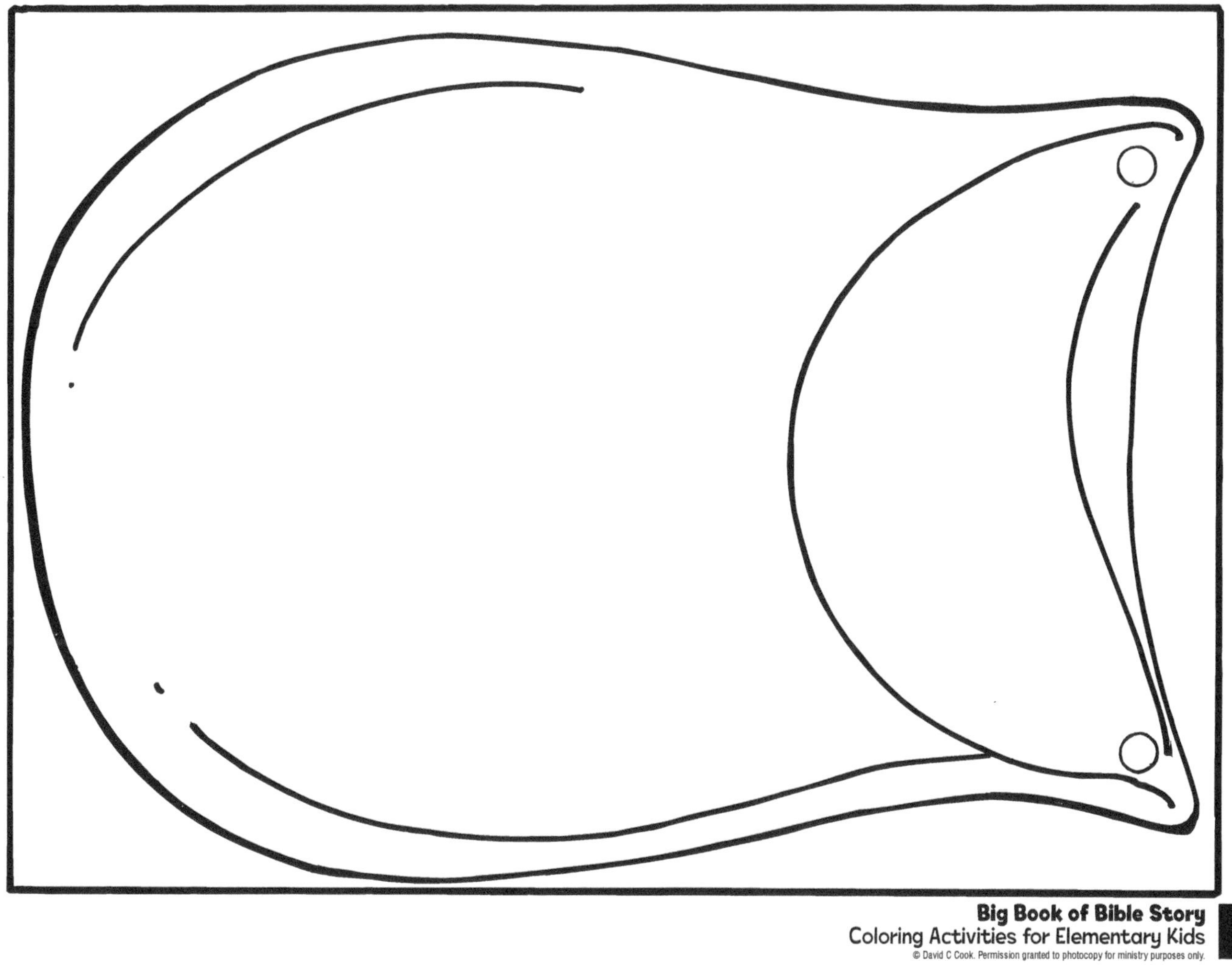

Story Bag Cover

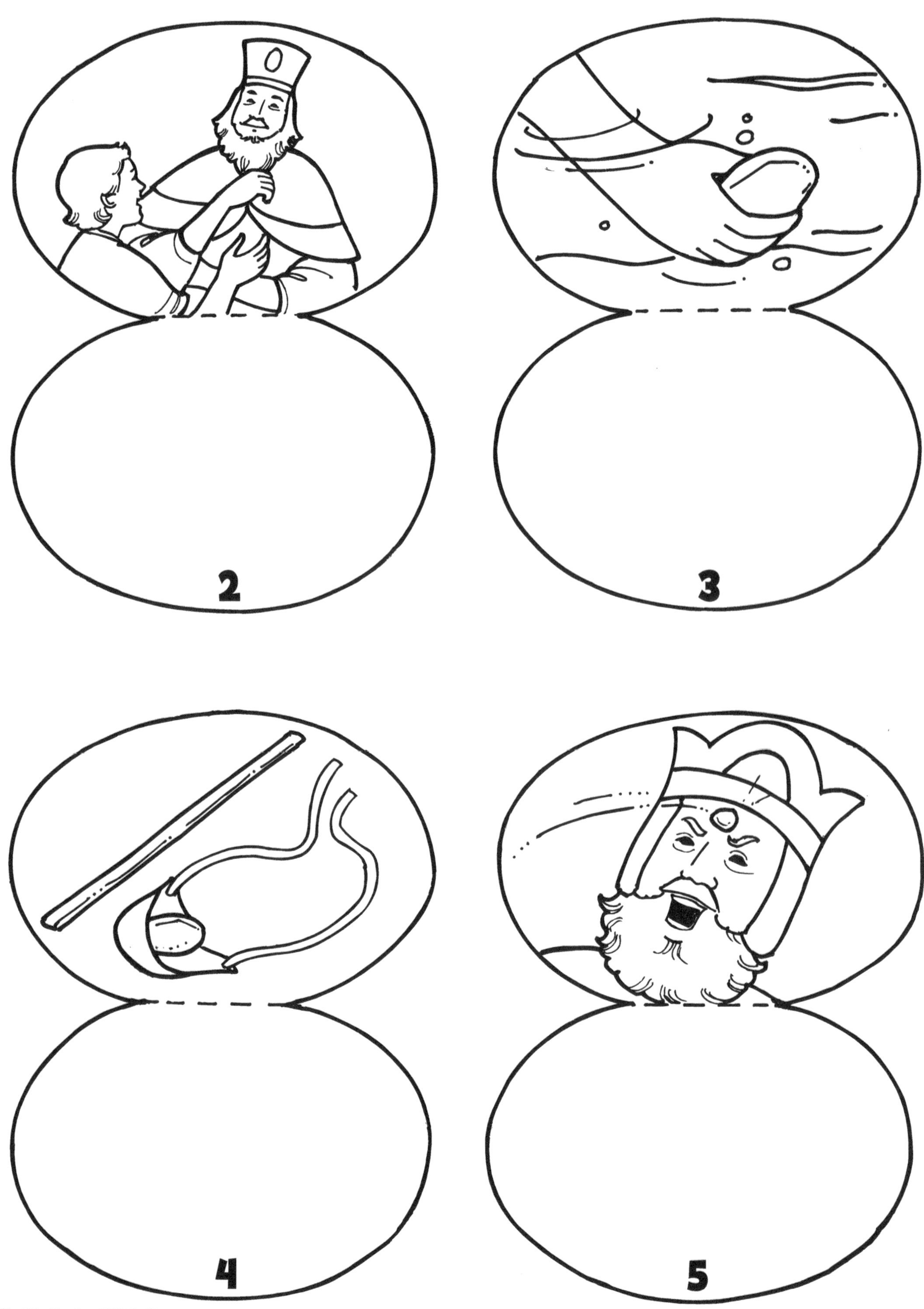
2
3
4
5

Jonathan Is a Good Friend to David

1 Samuel 18–20: Jonathan Is a Good Friend to David

Friendship Book

Supplies

- copy of the Friendship Book for each child
- crayons or markers
- scissors

Directions

Color and cut out the Friendship Book around the outside edge (do not cut on the dotted lines). Fold along the vertical dotted line so scenes 1 and 4 are behind scenes 2 and 3. Fold the book along the remaining dotted line so scenes 2 and 3 are folded inside the book. Use the Friendship Book to retell the story of how God helped Jonathan be a good friend to David.

David Chooses God's Way

1 Samuel 26: David Chooses God's Way

David's Decision Story Wheel

Supplies

- copy of the David's Decision Story Wheel for each child
- copy of the Story Wheel Cover (p. 243) for each child
- crayons or markers
- scissors
- hole punch
- paper fasteners (1 per child)

Directions

Color the scenes on the story wheel. Cut out the wheel as one piece (do not cut between scenes). On the Story Wheel Cover, write: "David Chooses God's Way." Cut out and decorate the cover. Place the wheel cover on top of the story wheel and punch a center hole through both pieces. Use a paper fastener to loosely attach the cover to the wheel. Rotate the cover to reveal each scene as you retell the story of David choosing to act in a way that honored God.

Solomon Asks God for Wisdom

1 Kings 3–4: Solomon Asks God for Wisdom

Solomon's Prayer Peel-a-Picture

Supplies

- copy of the Solomon's Prayer Peel-a-Picture sentence strips for each child, enlarged to 120%
- copy of the Solomon Asks God for Wisdom coloring picture (p. 85) for each child
- scissors
- crayons
- glue

Directions

Cut around the outside edge of the sentence strips rectangle and along the dividing lines between each strip, being careful to stop cutting at the dotted line. Color the Solomon Asks God for Wisdom coloring picture. Apply glue to the sentence strips rectangle between the dotted line and the edge only (do not apply any glue to the sentence strips themselves). Turn the rectangle over and attach the sentence strips over the coloring page (sentence side down) by pressing along the glued section. Peel back each strip to reveal the picture underneath; then read and tell that part of the Bible story.

Solomon was king of Israel.

He wanted to follow and please God.

One night, God told Solomon in a dream to ask for whatever he wanted.

Solomon asked for help to know right from wrong.

God was pleased with Solomon's request.

God helped Solomon make wise decisions and also gave him riches and honor.

Glue here

Elijah Trusts and Obeys God

1 Kings 16–17: Elijah Trusts and Obeys God

God Provides Pamphlet

Supplies

- copy of the God Provides Pamphlet for each child
- crayons or markers
- scissors

Directions

Color and cut out the pamphlet as one piece (do not cut along the dotted lines). Fold the pamphlet along the dotted lines so the right panel folds in first, and the left panel folds over the right panel. Open the left panel and color the back of the right panel blue. Close the left panel. On the back of the left panel, write: "Elijah Trusts and Obeys God"; then color the rest of the panel brown to show the ground had dried up due to a drought. Use the pamphlet to retell the story of how God cared for Elijah when Elijah trusted and obeyed Him.

God Provides for Elijah and a Woman in Zarephath

1 Kings 17: God Provides for Elijah and a Woman in Zarephath

Jar Mobile

Supplies

- copy of the Jar Mobile (preferably on white card stock) for each child (continued on p. 91)
- crayons or markers
- scissors
- hole punch
- varying lengths of any color of yarn (5 per child)

Directions

Color and cut out the jar scenes and the word strip. Punch holes in the word strip and at the top of each jar. Attach each mobile piece to the word strip, using varying lengths of yarn (see the example). Use the last piece of yarn to tie a loop through the top center hole in the word strip so you can hang your mobile as you retell the story of how God gave Elijah and a woman from Zarephath the food they needed.

1

2

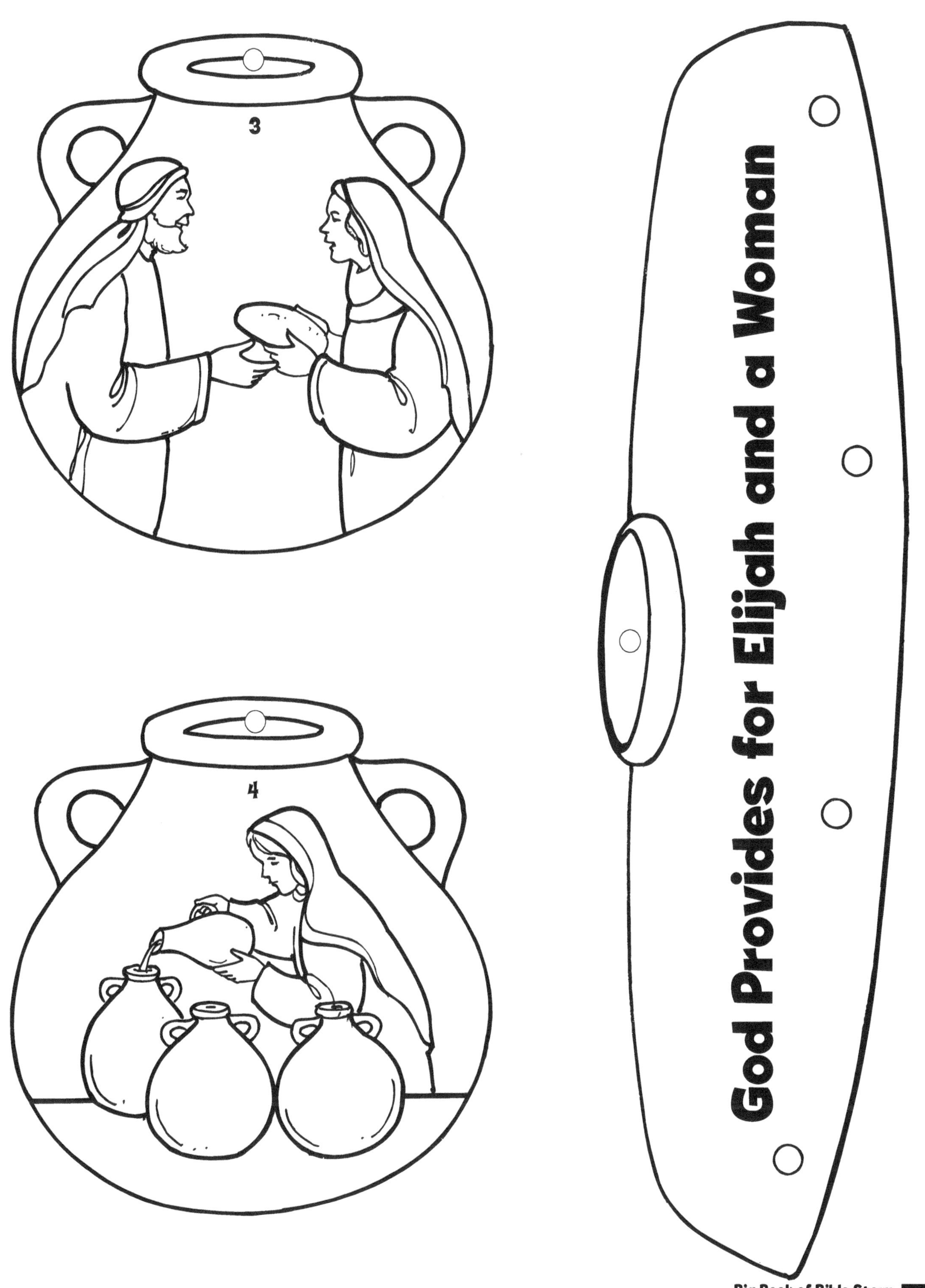
3
4
God Provides for Elijah and a Woman

God Shows His Power

1 Kings 18: God Shows His Power

Slide-a-Scene Altar

Supplies

- copy of the Slide-a-Scene Altar (preferably on card stock) for each child
- crayons or markers
- scissors

Directions

Color and cut out the altar and the four story scenes (do not cut the scenes apart individually—leave all four as one long strip). Cut two slits in the altar where indicated by the bold, vertical lines. Fold back the flame portion of the altar behind the stones so the fire is not showing. Slide the scene strip through the slits as you retell the story of God showing His power through Elijah:

1) Elijah challenged the prophets of Baal.
2) The prophets of Baal danced and shouted as they tried to get their god to answer.
3) Elijah poured water on his altar to make it harder to catch on fire.
4) Elijah prayed for God to show His power and send fire.
5) God sent fire from heaven, and the fire consumed Elijah's altar.

When you come to this part of the story, lift up the fire piece so it appears on top of the altar.

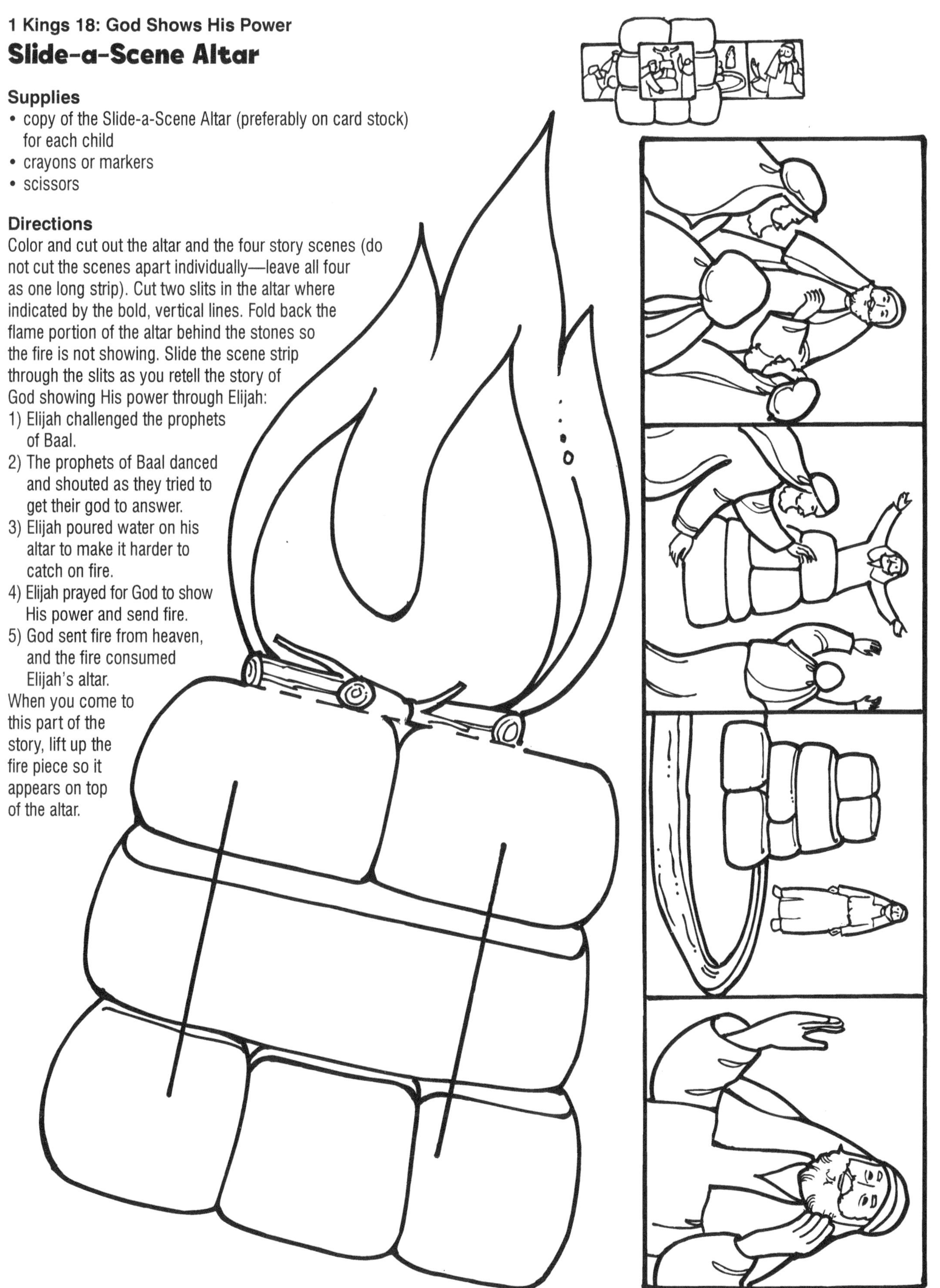

God Helps Elisha and a Family in Shunem

2 Kings 4: God Helps Elisha and a Family in Shunem

Back-to-Life Smush Book

See page 7 for supplies and directions for this activity.
Use the book to tell how God provided help in a surprising way.

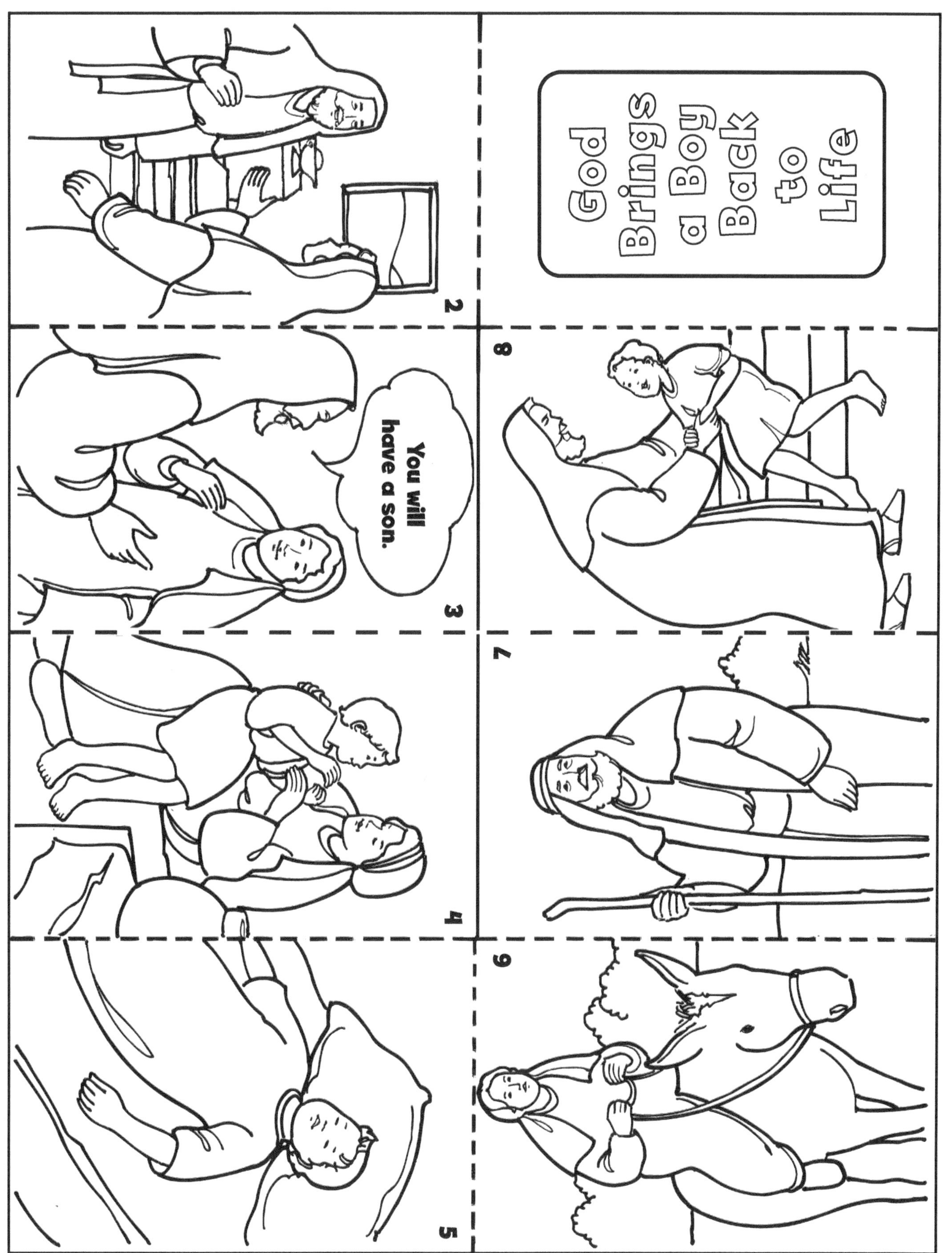

Naaman Learns to Obey God

2 Kings 5: Naaman Learns to Obey God

Naaman Story Puppets

Supplies

- copy of the puppets for each child
- crayons or markers
- blue construction paper
- scissors
- craft sticks (4 per child)
- tape

Directions

Color and cut out the puppets and the outfits. Attach a craft stick to each of the puppets (but not the outfits) by taping the stick near the bottom on the back of each figure. Cut a piece of blue construction paper to look like water. Attach a craft stick to the back of the water piece (see the example). Use the puppets and the water piece to retell the story of what happened when Naaman obeyed God.

1) Naaman had a terrible disease. He told the king of Aram about a prophet in Israel who could heal him (show Naaman and king #1).
2) The king sent Naaman to another king closer to where the prophet lived (put king #2 outfit on the king puppet to show this was a different king).
3) The prophet Elisha sent a message to the king, asking for Naaman to come to him. Naaman went to see Elisha (show Naaman and Elisha puppets).
4) Elisha told people what God wanted them to do. Elisha said Naaman was to go and dip in the Jordan River seven times, and then he would be healed. Naaman didn't want to dip in the river, but a servant talked to him and he obeyed (show Naaman going behind the water piece seven times).
5) When Naaman came out of the water the seventh time, he was healed (put the outfit on Naaman to show that his skin was healed)!

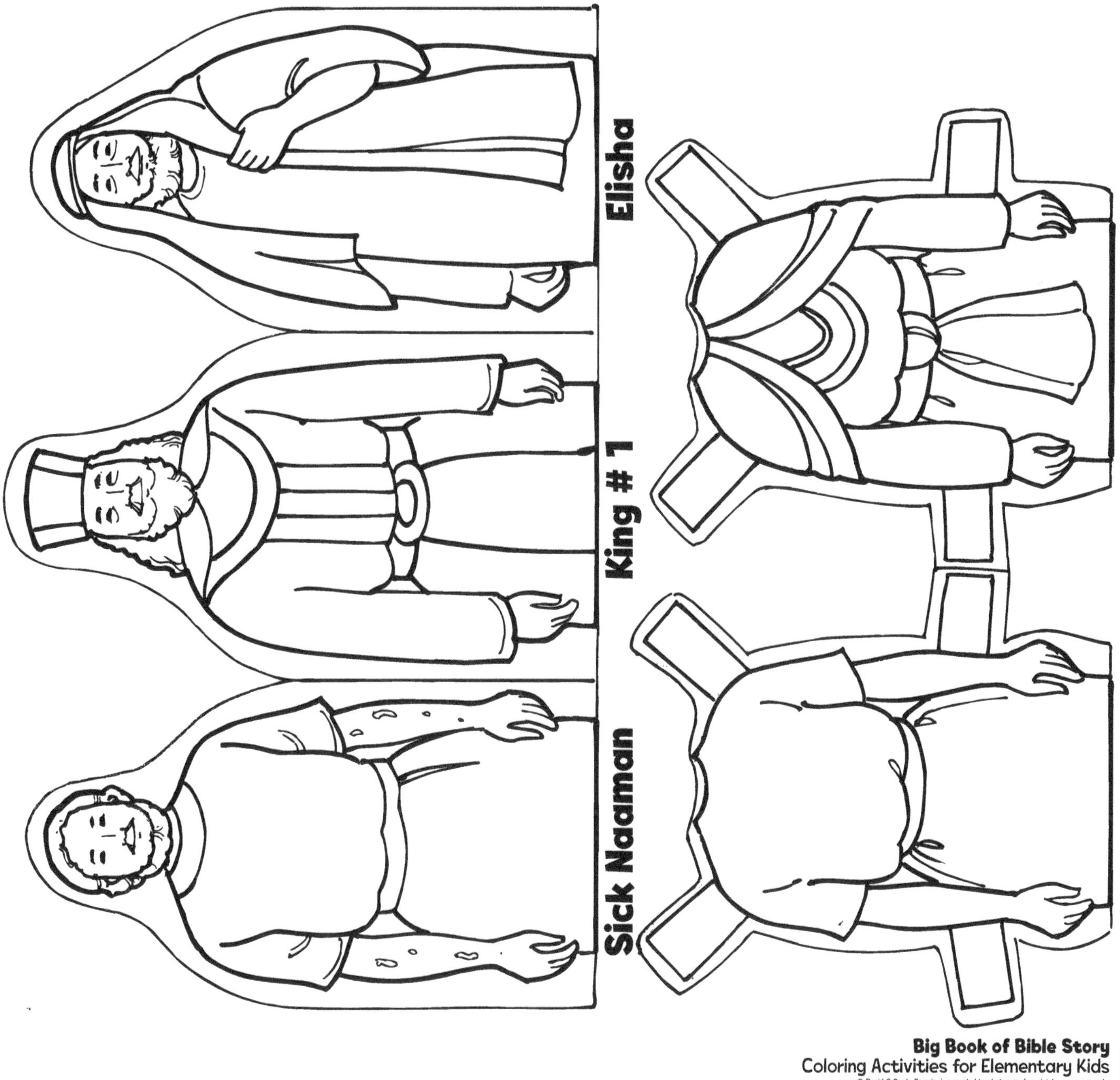

Elisha

King # 1

Sick Naaman

King # 2

Healed Naaman

Hezekiah Asks for God's Help

2 Kings 19–20; 2 Chronicles 29–30:
Hezekiah Asks for God's Help

Hezekiah and Isaiah Puppets

Supplies

- copy of the puppets for each child
- crayons or markers
- scissors
- brown paper lunch bags (2 per child)
- glue

Directions

Color and cut out the puppet faces. Cut along the solid line that appears across each mouth (each face should have two separate pieces). Glue the top piece of each face to the bottom of a brown paper lunch bag. Glue the bottom portion of each face to the lunch bag, directly below where the top portion ends (see the example). Use the puppets to retell the story of how Hezekiah prayed and asked God to help the people of Israel. Tell what happened when Hezekiah became sick and Isaiah came to visit him. You can tell the story from each character's point of view.

King Josiah Hears God's Word

2 Kings 22–23: King Josiah Hears God's Word

King Josiah Rebus

Supplies

- copy of the rebus for each child
- crayons or markers

Directions

Color the pictures in the rebus. See the picture descriptions that tell what each picture stands for. Use the rebus to retell the story of King Josiah obeying the law, how the Book of the Law was found later in the temple, and what King Josiah did when the book was read to him.

King Josiah

God

Shaphan

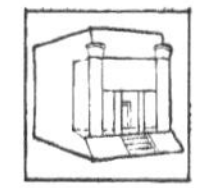
Temple

Book of the Law

People

was eight years old when he became king. He was a good king who always did what was right in the eyes of . When was 26 years old, he sent to the . wanted workers  to repair the  . Hilkiah, the high priest, told  that he had found the  in the 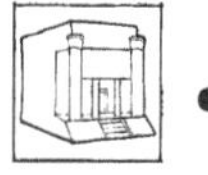 . read the  , and then  read the  to  . When heard the words of the , he was sad because he knew that he and his had not been doing what  wanted.  called the high priest, , and some other men together and asked them to ask  about the  . Then called his together and read them all the words in the . and the agreed to obey .

Jehoshaphat and God's People Pray and Worship God

2 Chronicles 20: Jehoshaphat and God's People Pray and Worship God

Prayer Box

Supplies

- copy of the Prayer Box for each child
- crayons or markers
- scissors
- tape

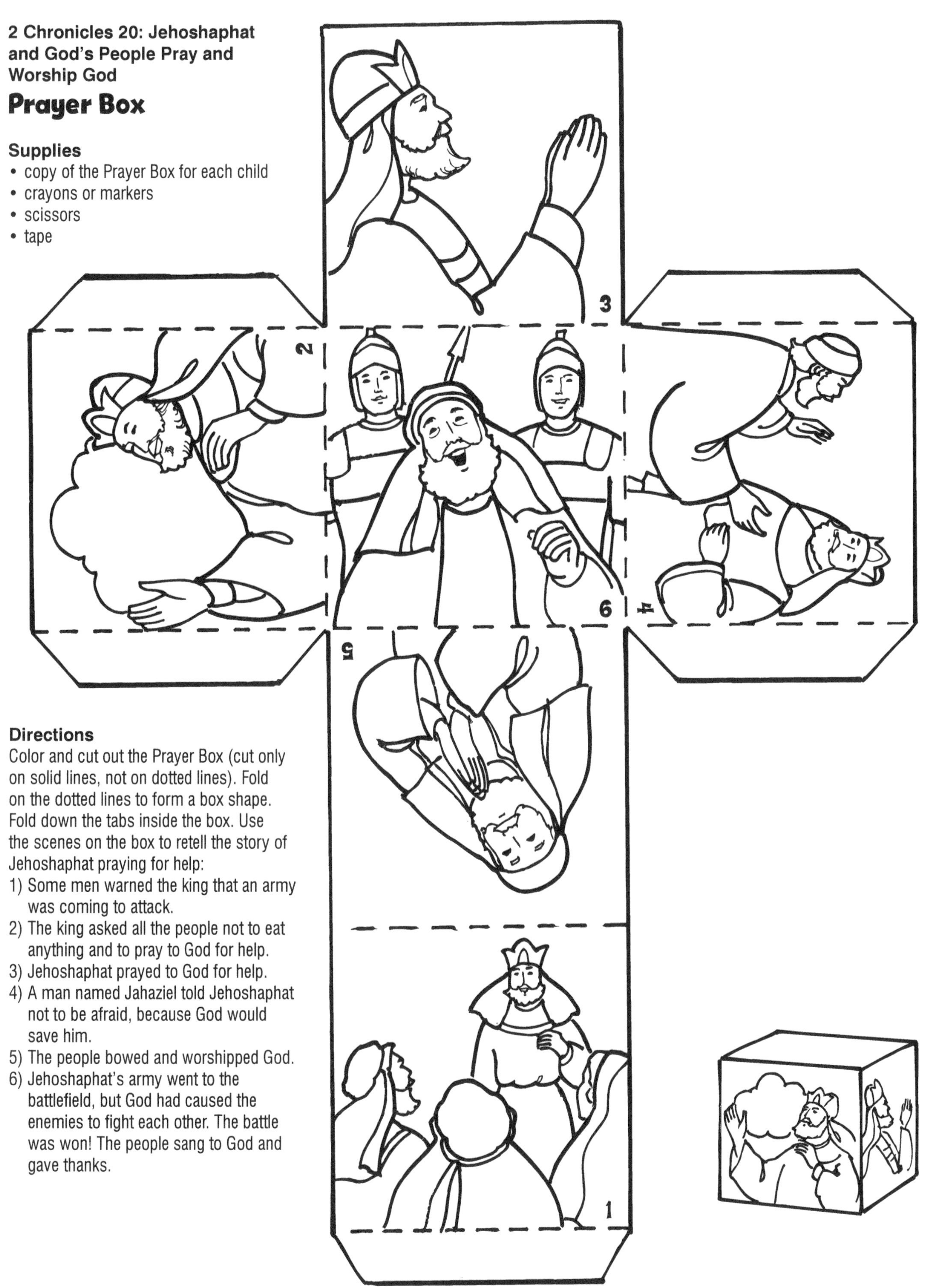

Directions

Color and cut out the Prayer Box (cut only on solid lines, not on dotted lines). Fold on the dotted lines to form a box shape. Fold down the tabs inside the box. Use the scenes on the box to retell the story of Jehoshaphat praying for help:

1) Some men warned the king that an army was coming to attack.
2) The king asked all the people not to eat anything and to pray to God for help.
3) Jehoshaphat prayed to God for help.
4) A man named Jahaziel told Jehoshaphat not to be afraid, because God would save him.
5) The people bowed and worshipped God.
6) Jehoshaphat's army went to the battlefield, but God had caused the enemies to fight each other. The battle was won! The people sang to God and gave thanks.

Manasseh Asks God for Forgiveness

2 Chronicles 33: Manasseh Asks God for Forgiveness

Chain Mobile

Supplies

- copy of the Chain Mobile for each child
- 1"-wide strips of construction paper (any color, 6 per child)
- crayons or markers
- scissors
- tape
- hole punch
- varying lengths of yarn (4 pieces per child)

Directions

Color and cut out each mobile piece. Punch holes in the top of each piece where indicated. Using the construction paper strips, make a chain by taping the ends of each strip together in interlocking circles (see the example). Tie each mobile piece onto a separate link in the chain, using varying lengths of yarn. Use the scenes on the Chain Mobile to retell the story of how God answered Manasseh's prayer for forgiveness. Tell what Manasseh did when God forgave him.

Ezra Teaches God's Law

Ezra 7, 9–10; Nehemiah 8: Ezra Teaches God's Law

Ezra's Scroll Scenes

Supplies

- copy of the Ezra's Scroll Scenes (preferably on card stock) for each child
- crayons or markers
- scissors
- glue

Directions

Color the scroll and four story scenes. Cut out the story scenes along the outside border (do not cut apart each individual scene). Cut out the scroll around the outside edge. Cut two slits in the scroll where indicated by the bold, vertical lines in the center of the scroll. Slide the scenes through the slits in the scroll (as shown in the example) as you tell what happened when Ezra taught the people from God's Book of the Law:

1) Ezra spent many hours reading God's Book of the Law.
2) Ezra read to the people from God's Book of the Law.
3) The people listened carefully as Ezra read. They said, "Amen! Amen!"
4) The people built houses to live in during a special celebration.

God's Book of the Law

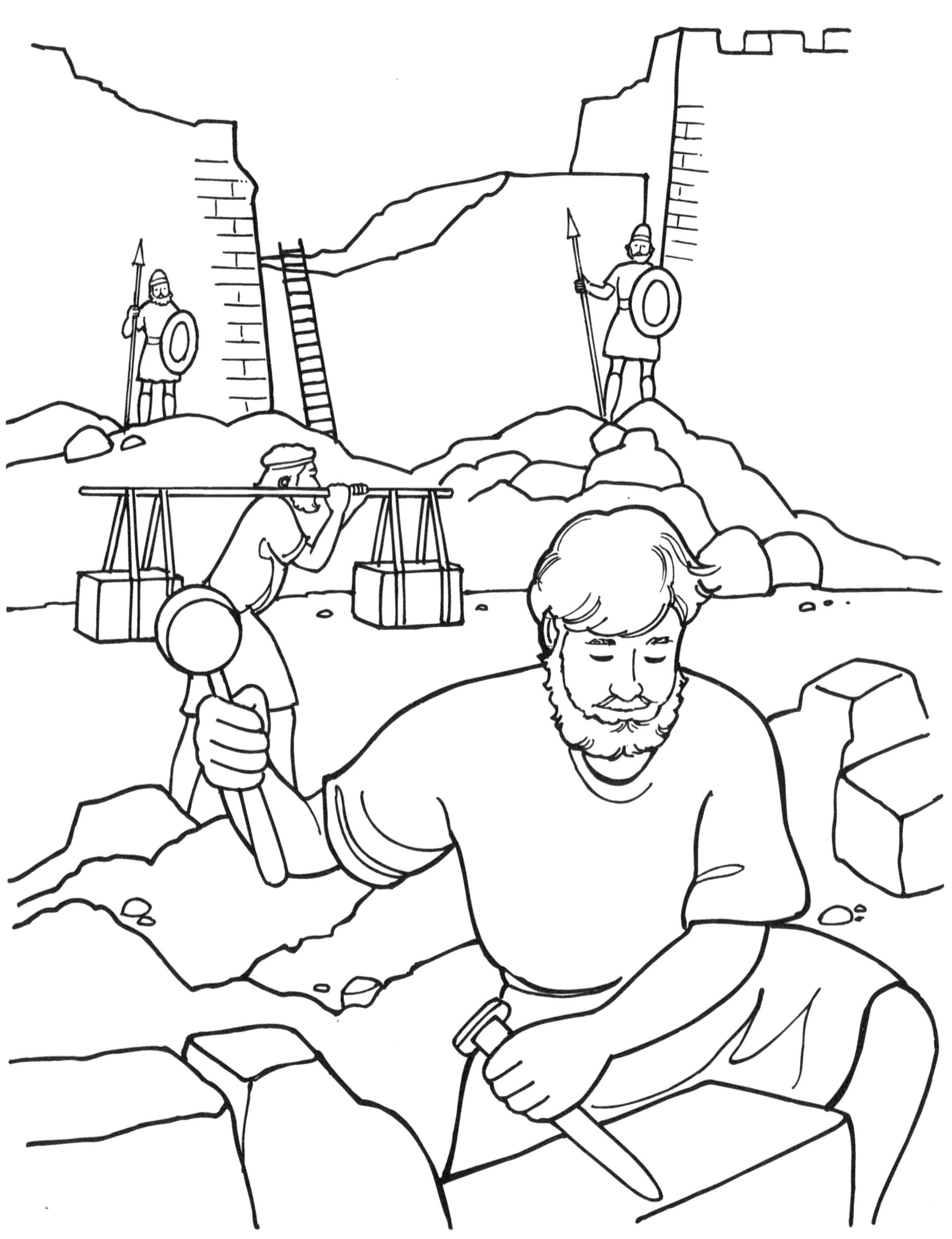

Nehemiah and God's People Rebuild the Wall

Nehemiah 1–2, 4, 6, 8: Nehemiah and God's People Rebuild the Wall

Nehemiah Maze

Directions

Color the maze. Draw a line through the maze as you retell the story of Nehemiah rebuilding the wall. Make sure you pass all the markers, in order, along the way.

Supplies

- copy of the Nehemiah Maze for each child
- crayons or markers

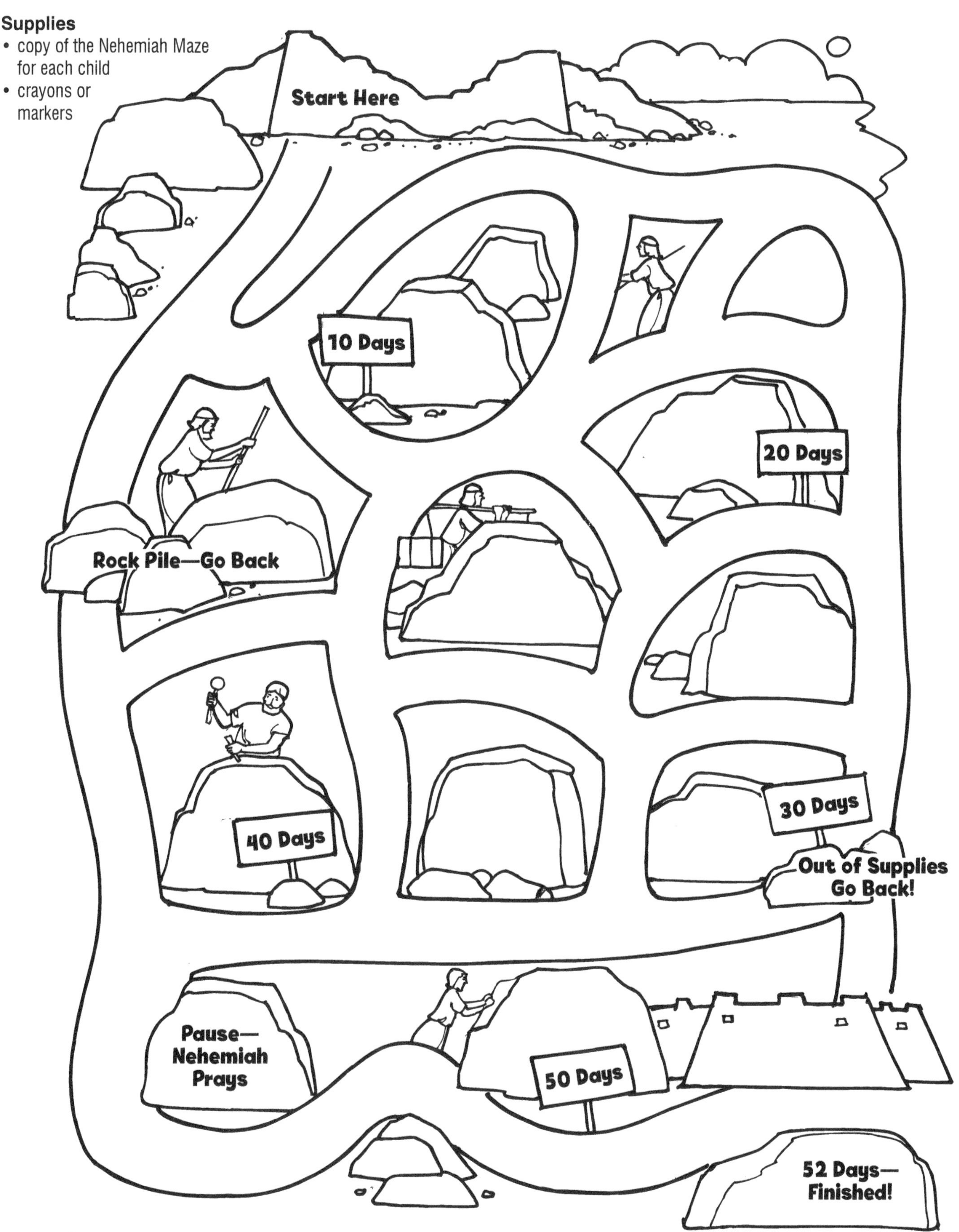

God's People Pray for Queen Esther

Esther 2–5, 7–8: God's People Pray for Queen Esther

Esther Crown and Mordecai Hat

Supplies

- copy of the crown and hat for each child
- crayons or markers
- scissors
- construction paper strips (2" x 12", 2 strips per child, any color)
- stapler (or tape)
- decorative embellishments such as glitter, sequins, beads, gems, stickers; glue *(optional)*

Directions

Color and cut out the crown and hat. (Decorate if desired.) Attach a construction paper strip to one side of each hat and crown. Adjust each hat and crown to fit the size of a child's head. Attach the other end of each construction paper strip to its hat or crown, making headpieces that fit well. Use the crown and hat to retell the story of how Queen Esther was encouraged by Mordecai and God's people. You can tell the story from the viewpoint of King Xerxes, Mordecai, or Queen Esther.

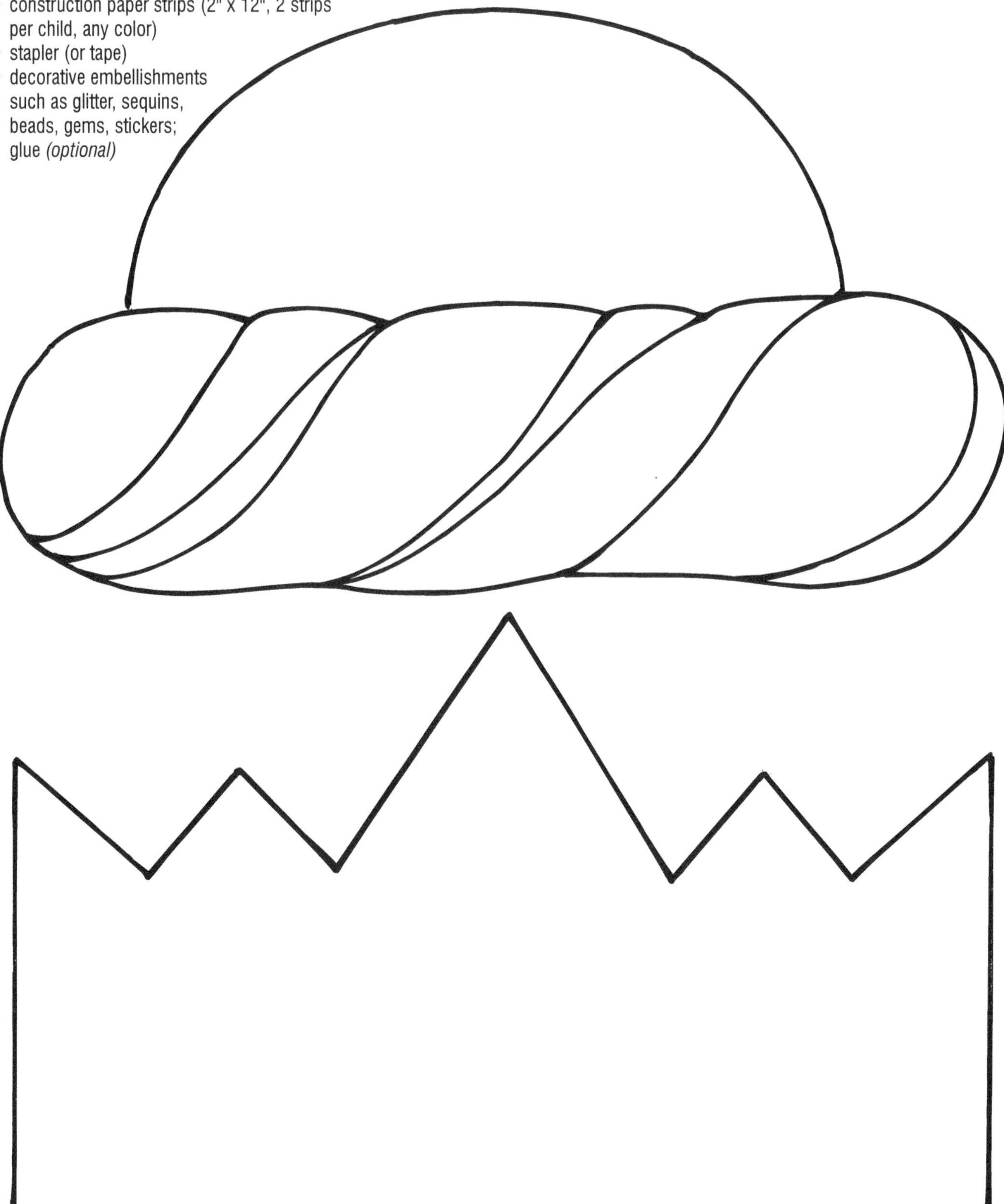

Job Trusts God

Job 1–2, 38, 42: Job Trusts God

Job Time Line

Supplies

- copy of the time line scenes and Job figure for each child (continued on p. 114)
- construction paper (2 sheets per child)
- crayons or markers
- scissors
- tape
- glue

Directions

Color and cut out each time line scene and the Job figure. Cut the two sheets of construction paper in half widthwise to have four pieces of paper (each 9" wide and 6" tall). Slightly overlapping the ends, tape three of the pieces together to form one long strip (approx. 6" x 26"). Glue the time line scenes, in order, onto the long construction paper strip so the ends of the scenes are touching. From the extra piece of construction paper, cut a strip that is $1^1/_2$" wide and 9" long. Fold 1" of this strip down and tape the Job figure to the folded section (so the folded part is attached to the back, just above Job's feet). Hook the Job figure over the top of the time line with the strip running behind the time line (as shown), and move the figure along as you retell the story of what Job did when everything was taken from him:

1) Job was happy and healthy, with a large family and lots of animals.
2) Job lost most of his family, and he was sad.
3) Job got sick and was miserable.
4) Job worshipped God and never stopped praising Him.
5) God blessed Job and gave him even more than he had in the beginning.

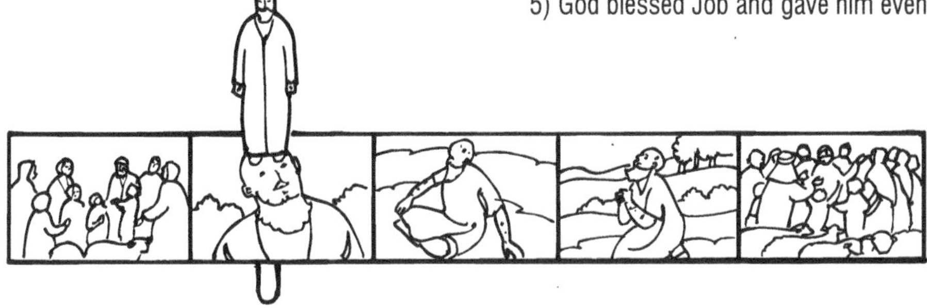

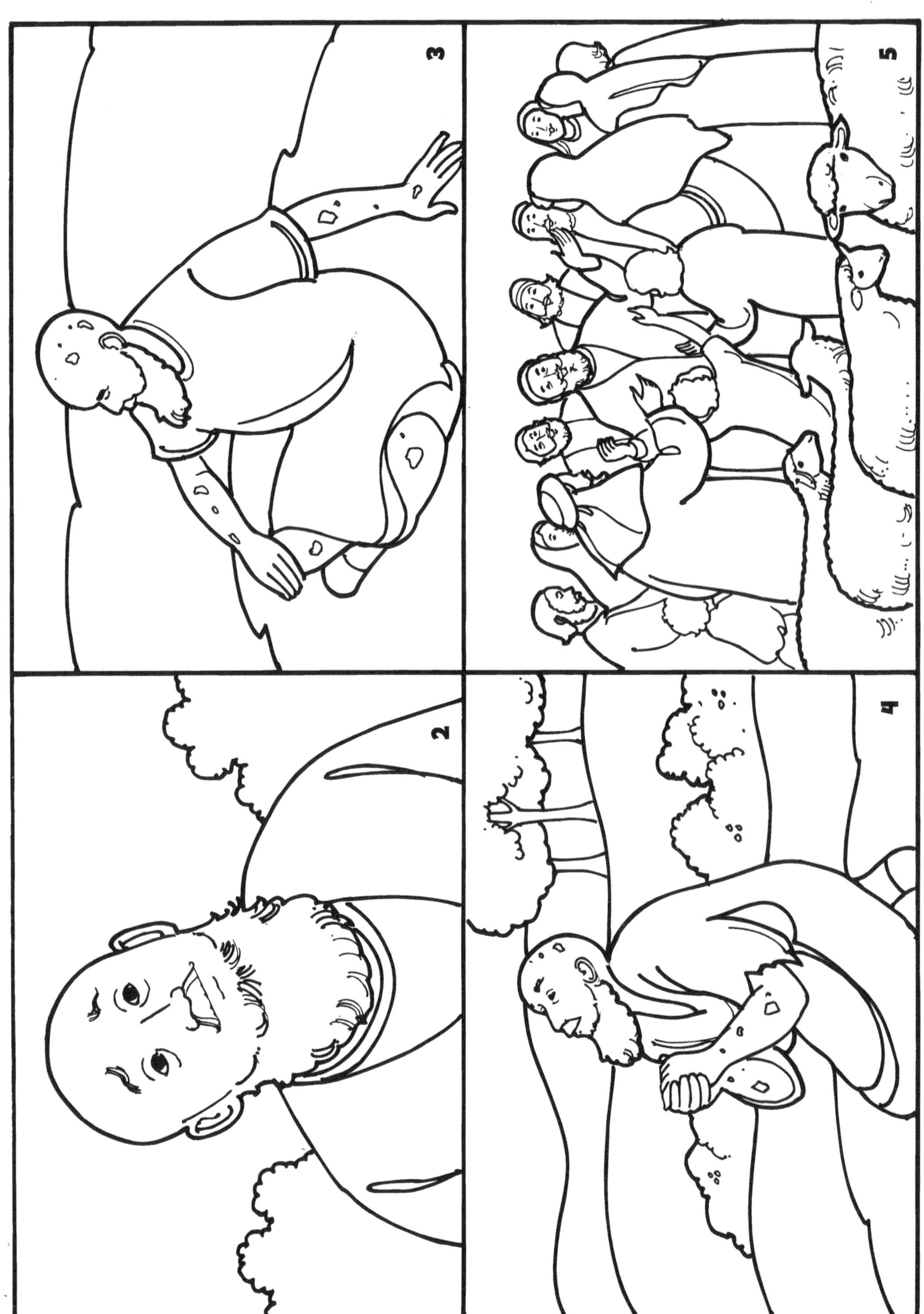
2
3
4
5

Daniel and His Friends Choose God's Way

Daniel 1: Daniel and His Friends Choose God's Way

Daniel's Grocery Bag

Supplies

- copy of the grocery bag cover and the vegetable scenes for each child (continued on p. 117)
- brown paper lunch bags (1 per child)
- crayons or markers
- scissors
- glue

Directions

Color and cut out the grocery bag cover and the vegetable scenes. Attach the bag cover to the front of a brown paper lunch bag (see the example). Place the vegetable scenes inside the bag. Use the grocery bag to retell the story of Daniel and his friends choosing to live God's way:

1) Daniel and his friends were preparing to be servants of the king (hold up the vegetable scene showing the four men).
2) Daniel and his friends did not want to disobey God and eat the king's food (hold up the scene showing meat and a cup), so they asked permission to eat only vegetables and drink only water (hold up the scene showing the plate with vegetables only).
3) Daniel and his friends ate only vegetables and drank only water for ten days (hold up the bag showing the cover).
4) At the end of ten days, Daniel and his friends looked healthier than all the other men (hold up the vegetable scene showing the four men). Daniel and his friends were later chosen to be the servants of the king. God blessed the four young men because they chose to live for Him.

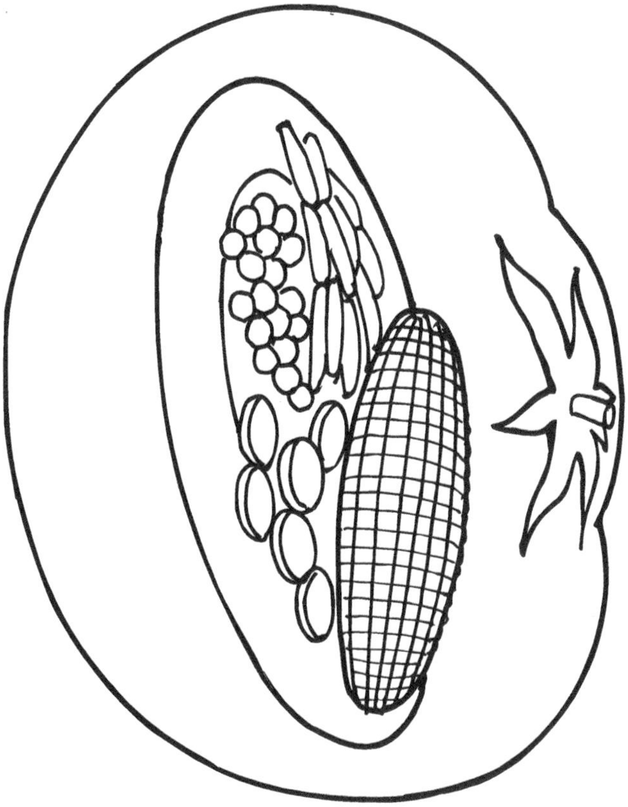

Daniel's Friends Face a Fiery Furnace

Daniel 3: Daniel's Friends Face a Fiery Furnace

3-D Fiery Furnace

Supplies

- copy of the 3-D Fiery Furnace pieces (preferably on card stock) for each child (continued on p. 120)
- construction paper (preferably gray for the furnace or orange to match the fire; 1 sheet per child)
- crayons or markers
- scissors
- glue

Directions

Color and cut out the 3-D Fiery Furnace pieces (be sure to cut out the center of the furnace piece). Fold a sheet of construction paper in half widthwise. Open the sheet of paper, with one half flat on the table and the other half standing (as a backdrop). Fold each figure and the fiery furnace piece back along the dotted lines to form bases. Glue each base to the bottom half of the sheet of construction paper (see the example). Use the 3-D scene to retell the story of what happened when Daniel's friends chose to serve and worship only God.

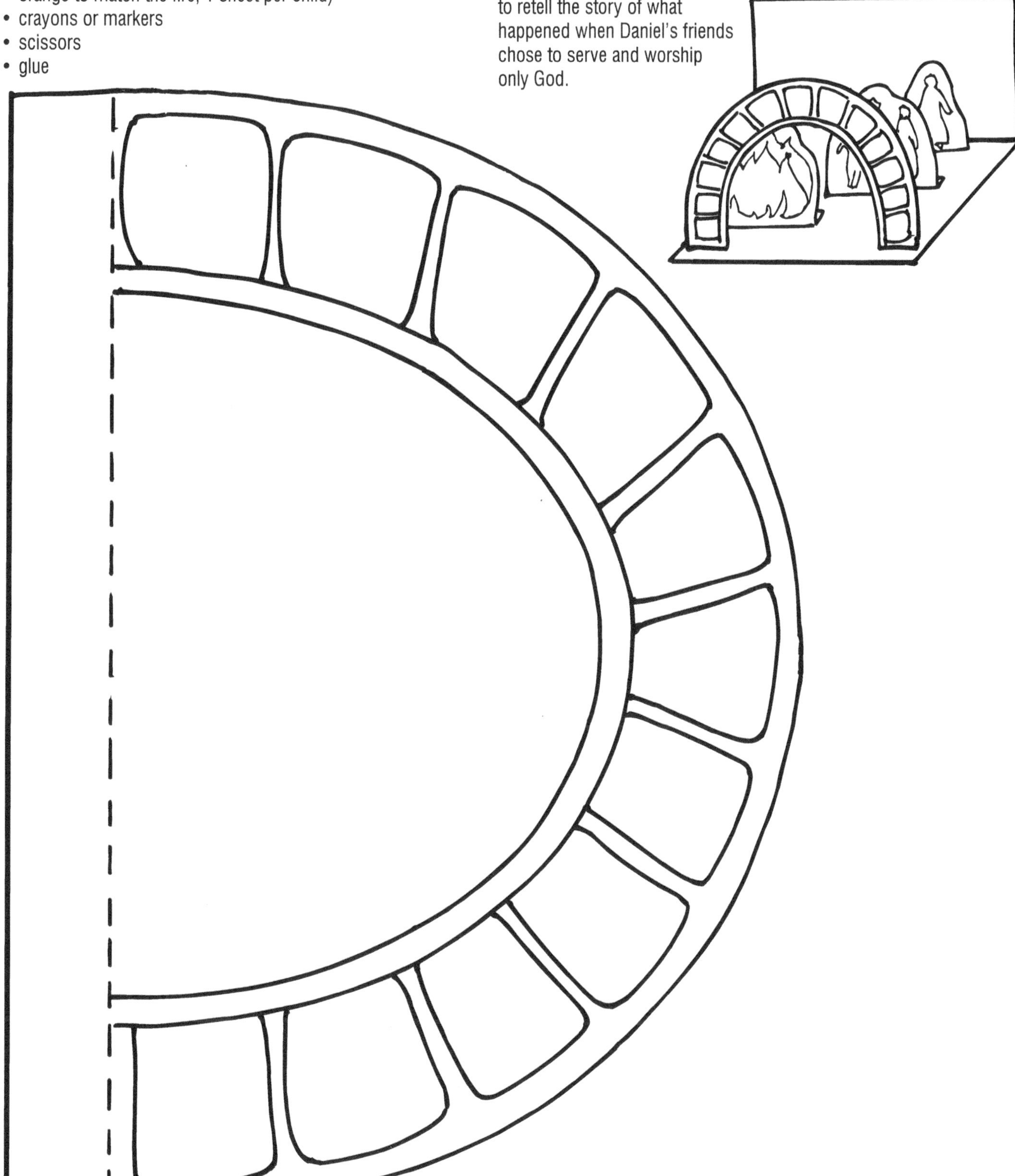

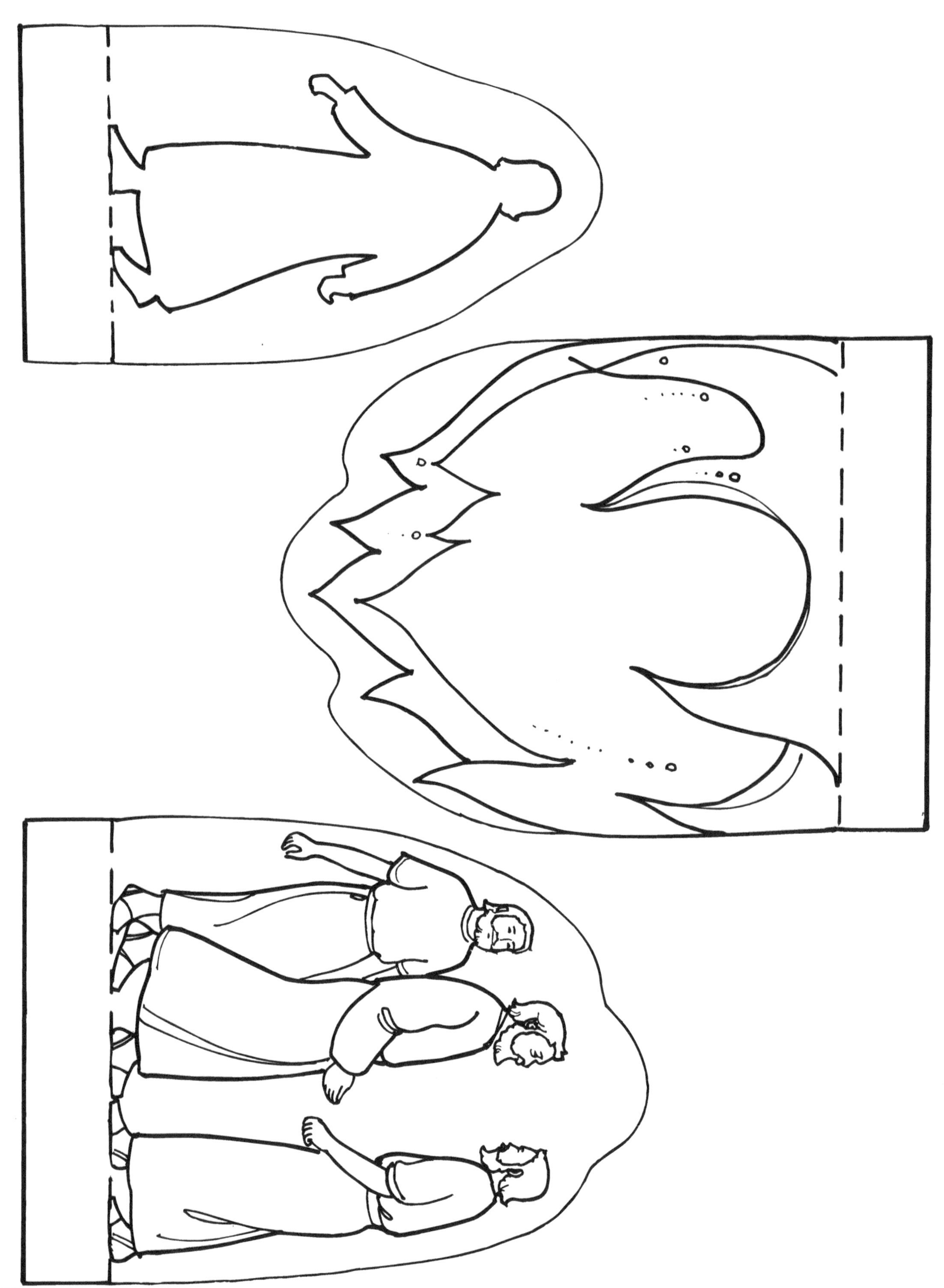

Daniel and the Lions' Den

Daniel 6: Daniel and the Lions' Den

Daniel's Flip-Flap Book

Supplies

- copy of the flip-flap book for each child
- construction paper (any color, 1 sheet per child)
- crayons or markers
- scissors and glue

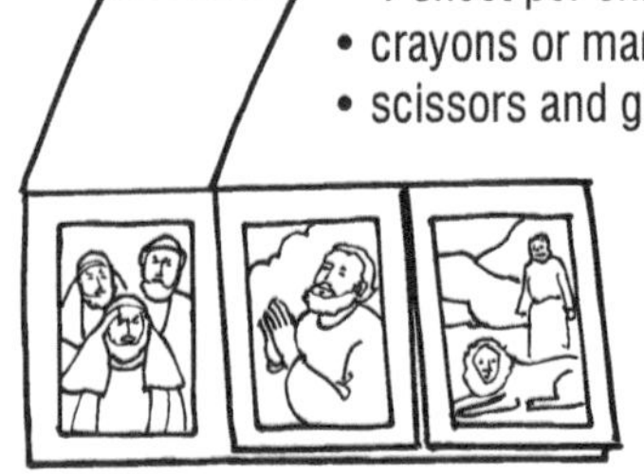

Directions

Color and cut out each of the six scenes separately. Fold a sheet of construction paper in half lengthwise. Cut the top half of the sheet into three equal sections, stopping at the fold line (see the example). Each flap should be about 4" wide. Attach scenes 1, 3, and 5 to the top of the flaps so the scenes show when the flaps are folded closed. Attach scenes 2, 4, and 6 under each flap so the scenes appear when the top flaps are lifted. Starting with the three flaps closed, use the book to tell what happened when Daniel prayed to God.

1) King Darius liked Daniel.
2) This made the other men who worked for the king very jealous (lift the first flap).
3) Daniel broke the king's law by praying to God.
4) The king realized he had to punish Daniel, even though he didn't want to (lift the center flap).
5) God kept Daniel safe in the lions' den by sending an angel to close the lions' mouths.
6) The king was very happy that Daniel was safe, and the king praised God (lift the third flap).

1

3

5

2

4

6

Jonah

Jonah 1–3: Jonah

Map of Jonah's Travels

Supplies

- copy of the Jonah figure and map (preferably on card stock) for each child (continued on p. 125)
- crayons or markers
- scissors
- tape

Directions

Color and cut out the Jonah figure and both halves of the map. Assemble the map, taping the halves together along the center seam. Move Jonah through the different locations on the map as you retell the story of Jonah.

1) Jonah heard God speak to him saying, "Go preach in Nineveh!"
2) Jonah went to Joppa to get on a ship and run away from God.
3) Jonah sailed toward Tarshish.
4) Jonah was thrown overboard when God sent a storm.
5) A large fish swallowed Jonah.
6) Jonah prayed to God, and the fish spit Jonah out onto dry land.
7) Jonah finally obeyed God and went to Nineveh to do what God said.

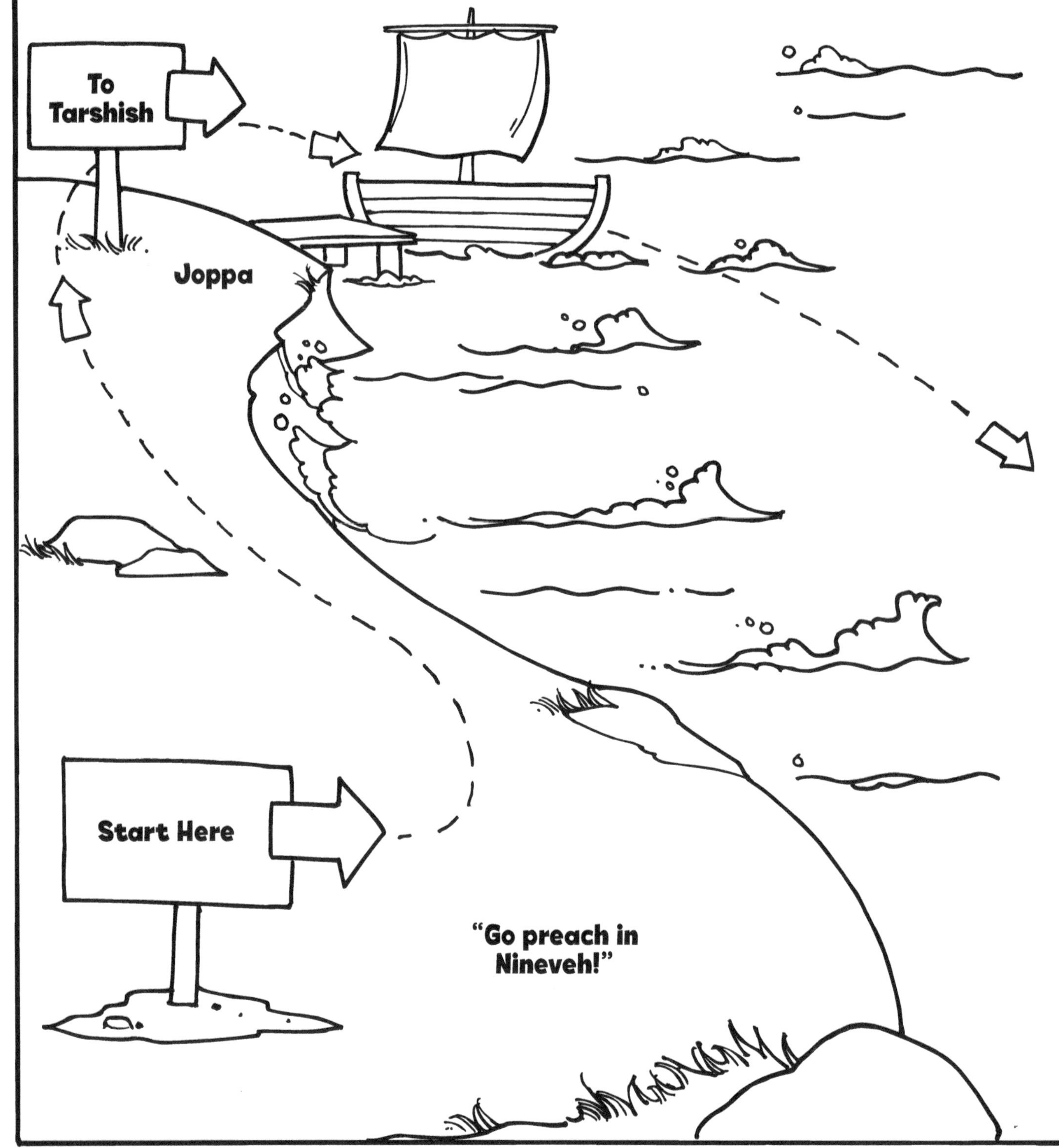

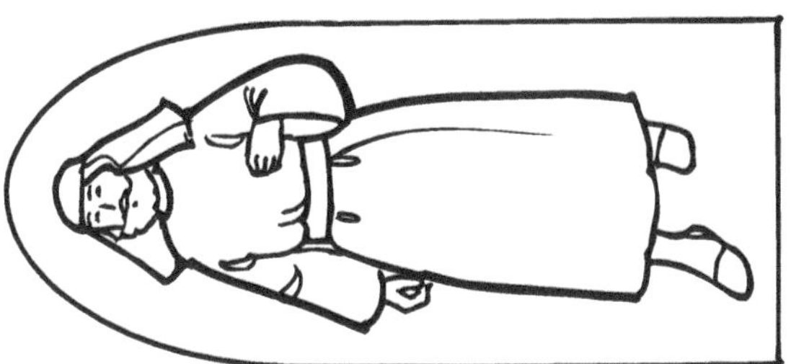

Nineveh

New Testament Bible Story Coloring Activities

Zechariah Praises God

Luke 1: Zechariah Praises God

Zechariah and Elizabeth Story Strips

Supplies

- copy of the Zechariah and Elizabeth Story Strips for each child
- copy of Zechariah Praises God coloring page (p. 127) for each child
- 7 sheets of card stock or construction paper (6 white, 1 any color) per child
- scissors
- glue
- crayons or markers
- hole punch
- yarn (any color)

Directions

Color the Zechariah Praises God coloring picture and attach it to a sheet of card stock or construction paper (any color) to make a book cover. Cut out the six story strips and attach each one to the bottom of a separate sheet of card stock or construction paper. Draw a picture above each strip. For example, for the first strip draw and color the sad faces of Zechariah and Elizabeth. Assemble the cover and story pages in order to make a book. Punch two holes along the left side of all seven pages. Tie the book together using yarn. Use the book to tell about Zechariah and Elizabeth's good news.

Zechariah and Elizabeth were very old but had no children.

1

Zechariah served God as a priest at the temple.

2

One day an angel appeared to Zechariah.

3

The angel told Zechariah that he and Elizabeth would have a son and should name him John.

4

Zechariah wasn't sure he could believe the angel. Because of Zechariah's uncertainty, he could not speak until the child was born.

5

Elizabeth gave birth to a boy. They named him John. Then Zechariah became able to speak. He praised God.

6

An Angel Visits Mary

Luke 1: An Angel Visits Mary

Angel and Mary Story Masks

Supplies

- copy of the Angel and Mary Story Masks for each child (preferably on card stock)
- crayons or markers
- scissors
- yarn or elastic
- hole punch
- glue and glitter (or glitter pens) for children to decorate the angel mask *(optional)*

Directions

Color each mask and cut them out, including the openings for the eyes. Punch a hole in both sides of each mask where indicated by the open circles. Attach yarn or elastic to one side of each mask. Size each mask to fit each child's head, and attach the other end of the yarn or elastic to the opposite side of the mask. Wear the masks as you retell the story of the angel visiting Mary. You can pretend to be either the angel or Mary as you retell the story.

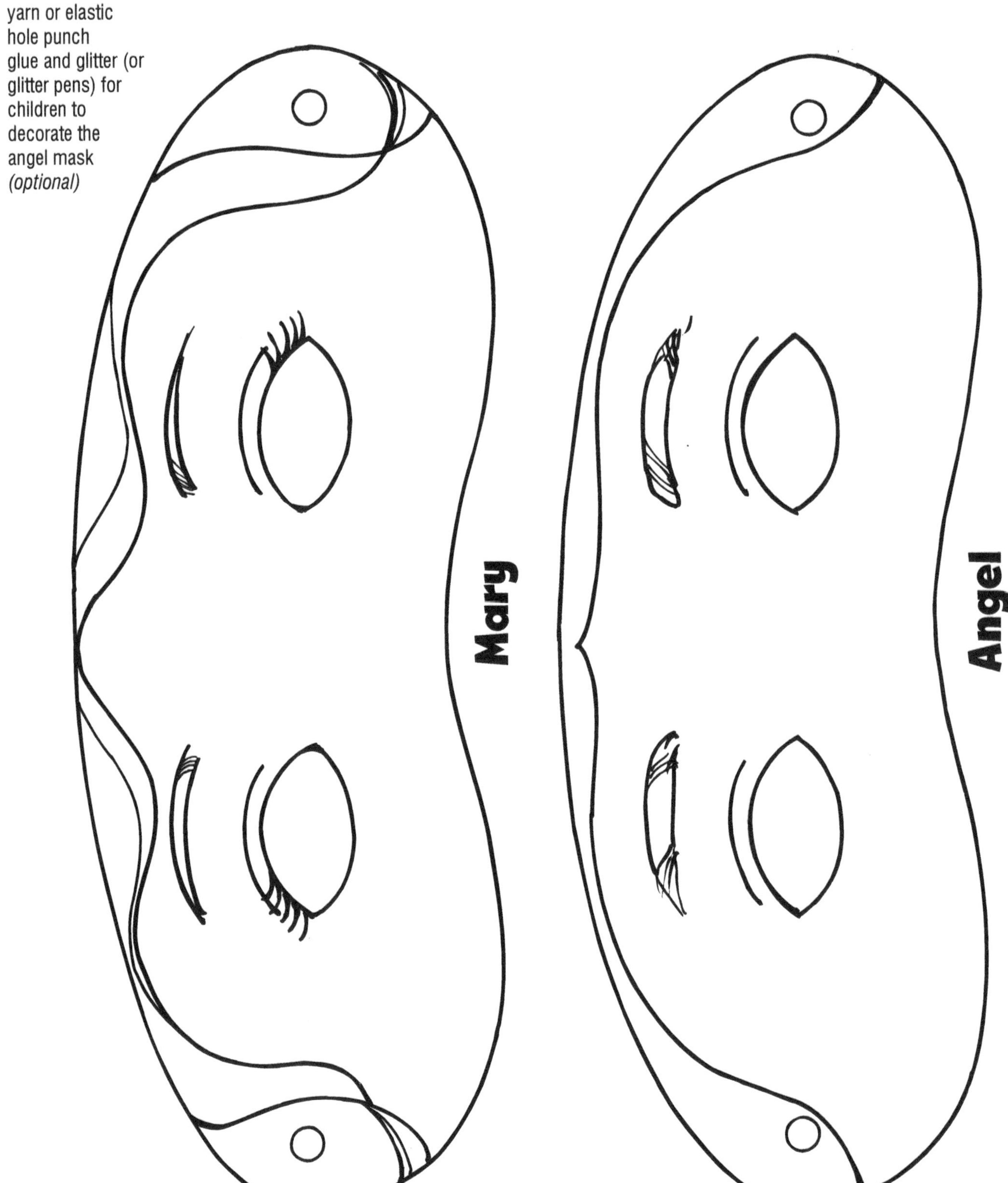

Mary Rejoices

Luke 1: Mary Rejoices

Mary Praises God Rebus

Supplies

- copy of the rebus for each child
- crayons or markers

Directions

Color the pictures in the rebus. Use the rebus to retell the story of Mary praising God after she received the news that she would be Jesus' mother. See the descriptions for the meaning of each picture.

Gabriel

Mary

Baby

Elizabeth

God sent the angel  to speak to .  told  that God was pleased with her. He said that she would have a  and should name Him Jesus.   told  the  would be the Son of God.  also told  that her cousin  was going to have a  too, even though  was old.  said nothing is impossible with God.  said she was the Lord's servant.  went to visit . When they greeted each other, the  inside  jumped for joy!  agreed that God had blessed .  praised God. She said, "I rejoice in God my Savior."

Jesus Is Born

Luke 2: Jesus Is Born

Jesus' Birth Pop-Up Card

Supplies

- copy of the Jesus' Birth Pop-Up Card for each child
- crayons or markers
- scissors

Directions

Color and cut out the pop-up card. Fold the card back along the horizontal dotted line so the scenes are back-to-back. Fold the center piece down along the dotted lines and fold the card in half so the pop-up piece is folded inside. Use the card to retell the story of Jesus' birth.

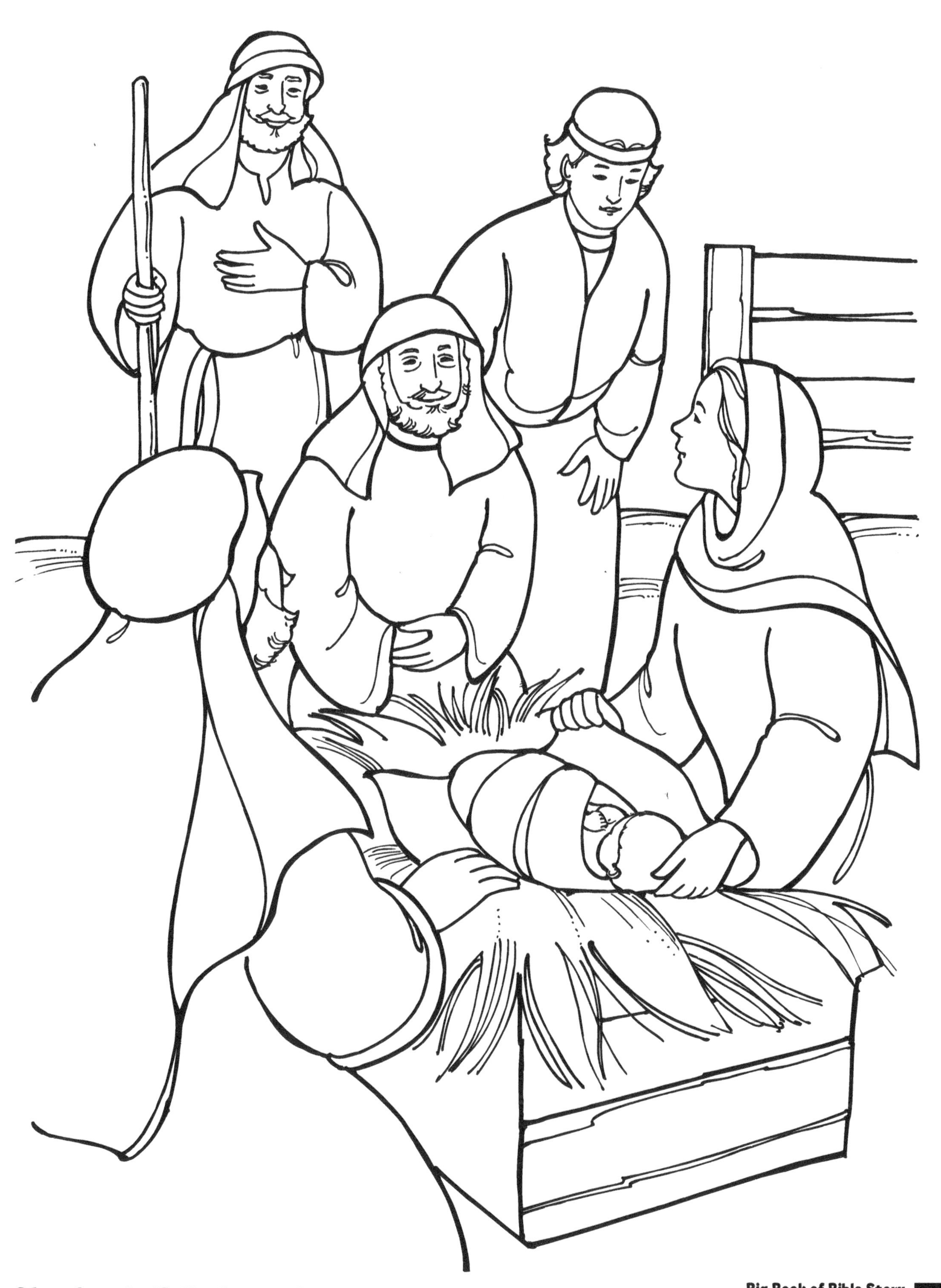

Shepherds Tell about Jesus

Luke 2: Shepherds Tell about Jesus

Sheep and Shepherd Scenes

Supplies

- copies of the Sheep and Shepherd Scenes (you will need 2 copies of the shepherd and 3 copies of the sheep per child, in addition to 1 copy of the story scenes per child) (continued on p. 137)
- crayons or markers
- scissors
- hole punch
- yarn
- other embellishments *(optional)*

Directions

Color and cut out the five scenes, two shepherds, and three sheep around the outside edges of the pieces. Place a shepherd on top of each of the tall scenes, and place a sheep over each of the short scenes. Place the scenes in the order they occurred (refer to the numbers on each scene). Punch holes in each scene and its cover piece, as indicated by the open circles. Use yarn to string the scenes together in order (see the example) and then hang the scenes on a wall or door. Lift the sheep and shepherd flaps as you retell the story of the shepherds telling others what the angel had told them about Jesus: "He is the Messiah, the Lord."

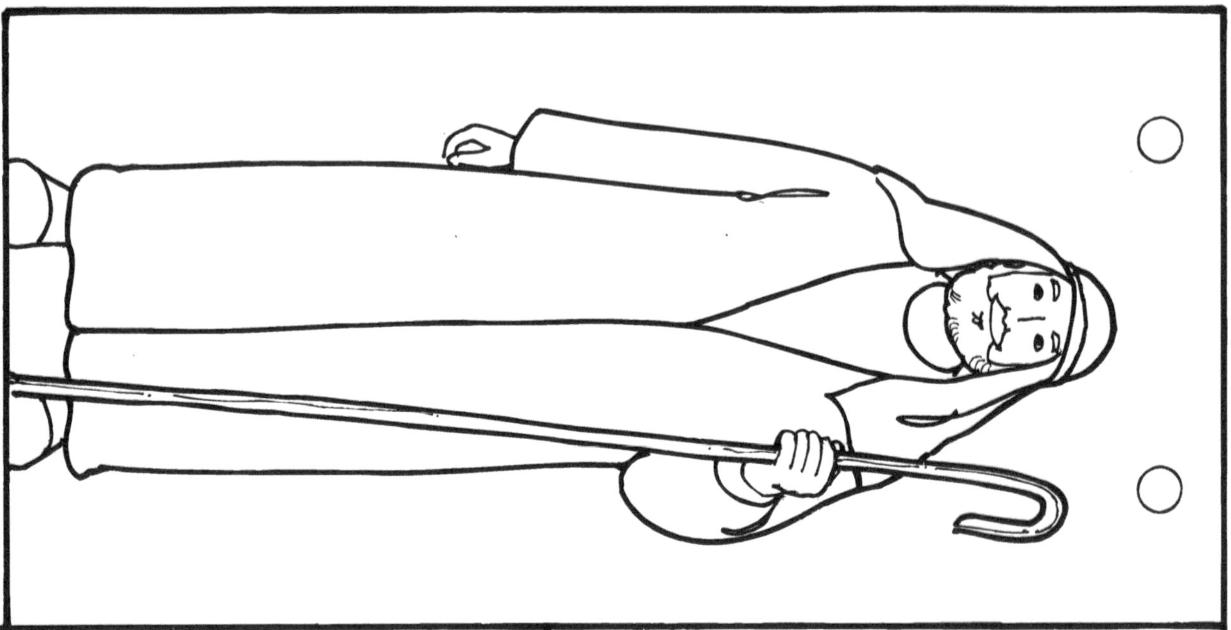

1

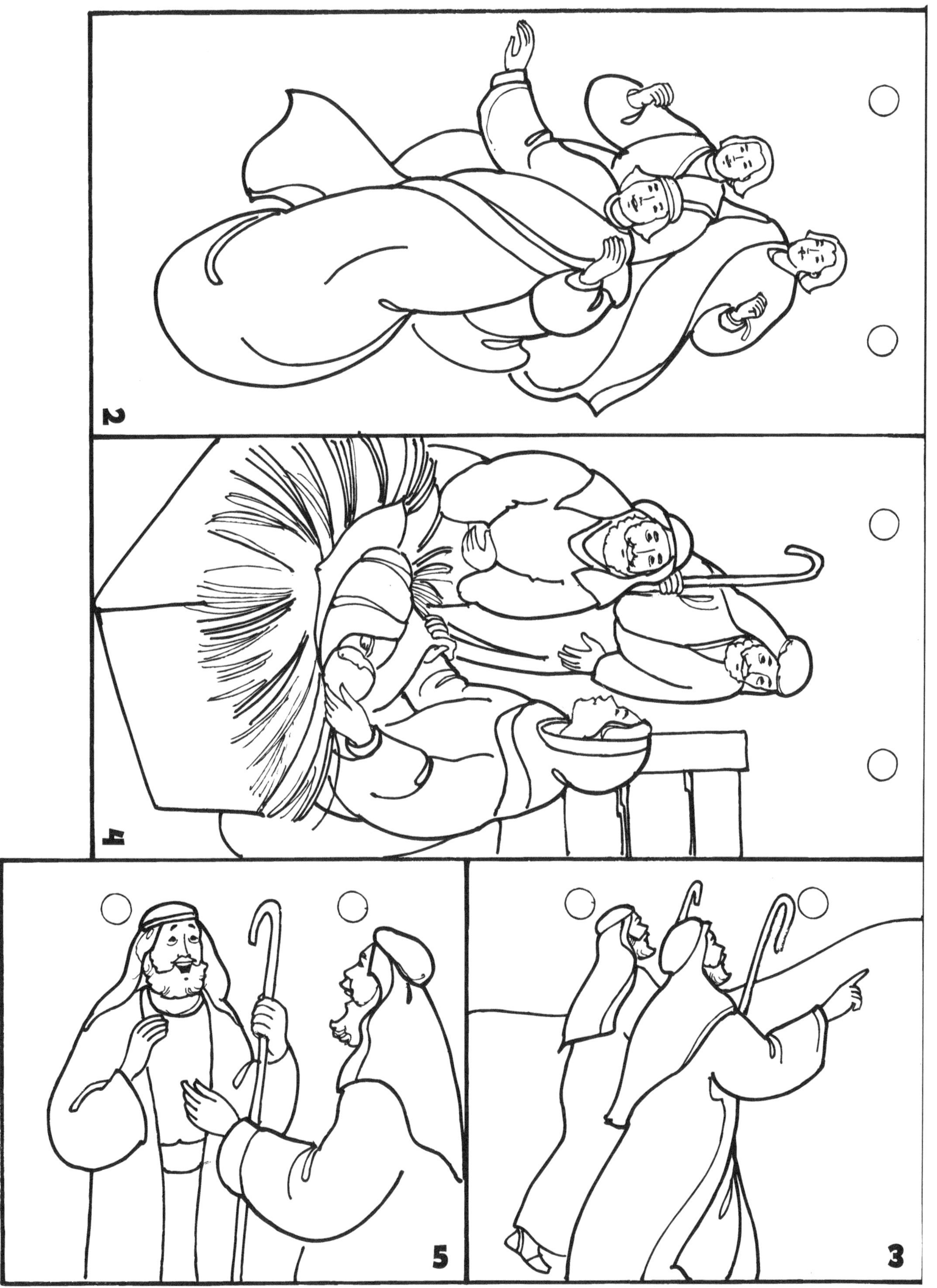
2
4
5
3

Shepherds Tell Others

Luke 2: Shepherds Tell Others

Sheep Book

Supplies

- copy of the Sheep Book pieces (on construction paper or cardstock) for each child
- crayons or markers
- scissors
- tape or glue

Directions

Color and cut out the sheep's head, tail, and feet. Cut out the story scenes as one long piece (do not cut along the dotted lines). Fold the book like an accordion along the dotted lines so that when it is folded, there are no scenes visible on the front or back. Attach the sheep's head to the inside of the first scene along the cut edge. Tape the tail to the back of the second scene along the first folded edge. Tape the feet to the inside of the first scene along the bottom (see the example). Use the Sheep Book as you retell the story of the shepherds telling others the good news they had heard and seen—God's Son, Jesus, had been born!

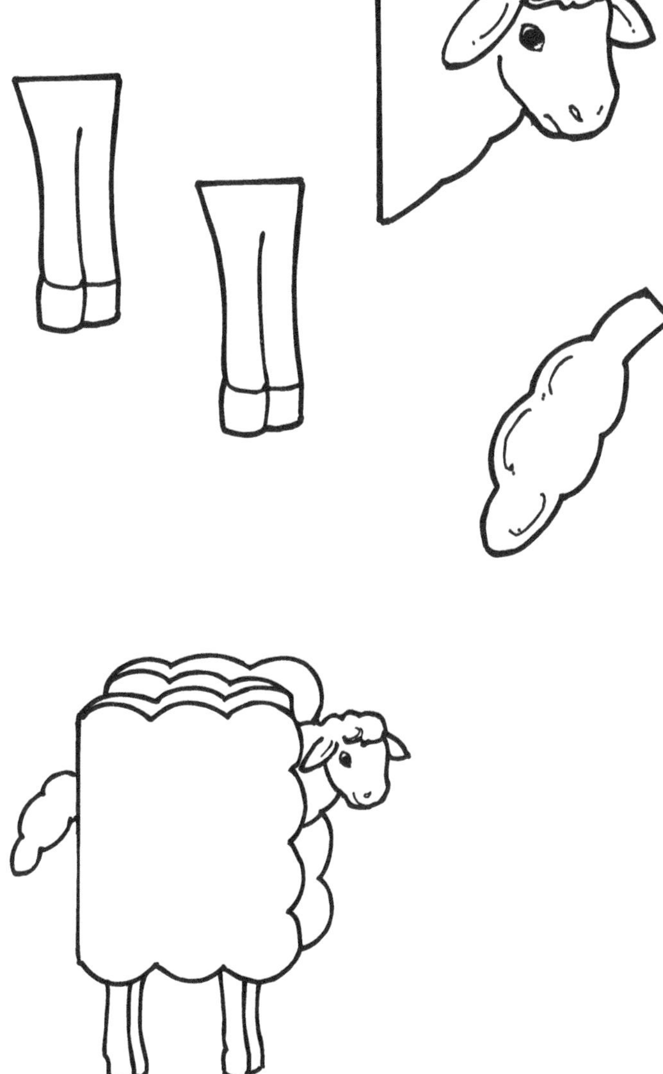

Simeon and Anna Thank God

Luke 2: Simeon and Anna Thank God

Simeon and Anna Fold-Out Card

Supplies

- copy of the card scenes for each child
- construction paper (any color, 1 sheet per child)
- crayons or markers
- scissors
- glue

Directions

Color and cut out the four scenes as one piece (do not cut along the dotted lines). Fold a sheet of construction paper in half widthwise to make a card. Write "Simeon and Anna Thank God" on the front of the card. Inside the card, draw a background scene showing what the temple courtyard might have looked like. Fold the card scenes along the dotted lines like an accordion. Position the scenes inside the card, carefully lining up the middle fold of the scenes with the center fold of the card (see the example above or on p. 74). Glue the scenes to the card, gluing the back of the first scene onto the left side of the card and the back of the last scene onto the right side of the card. The two middle scenes should not be glued to the card. When the card is closed, the middle scenes will fold forward inside the card. The scenes will unfold as you open the card. Use the card to retell the story of Simeon and Anna thanking God for Jesus.

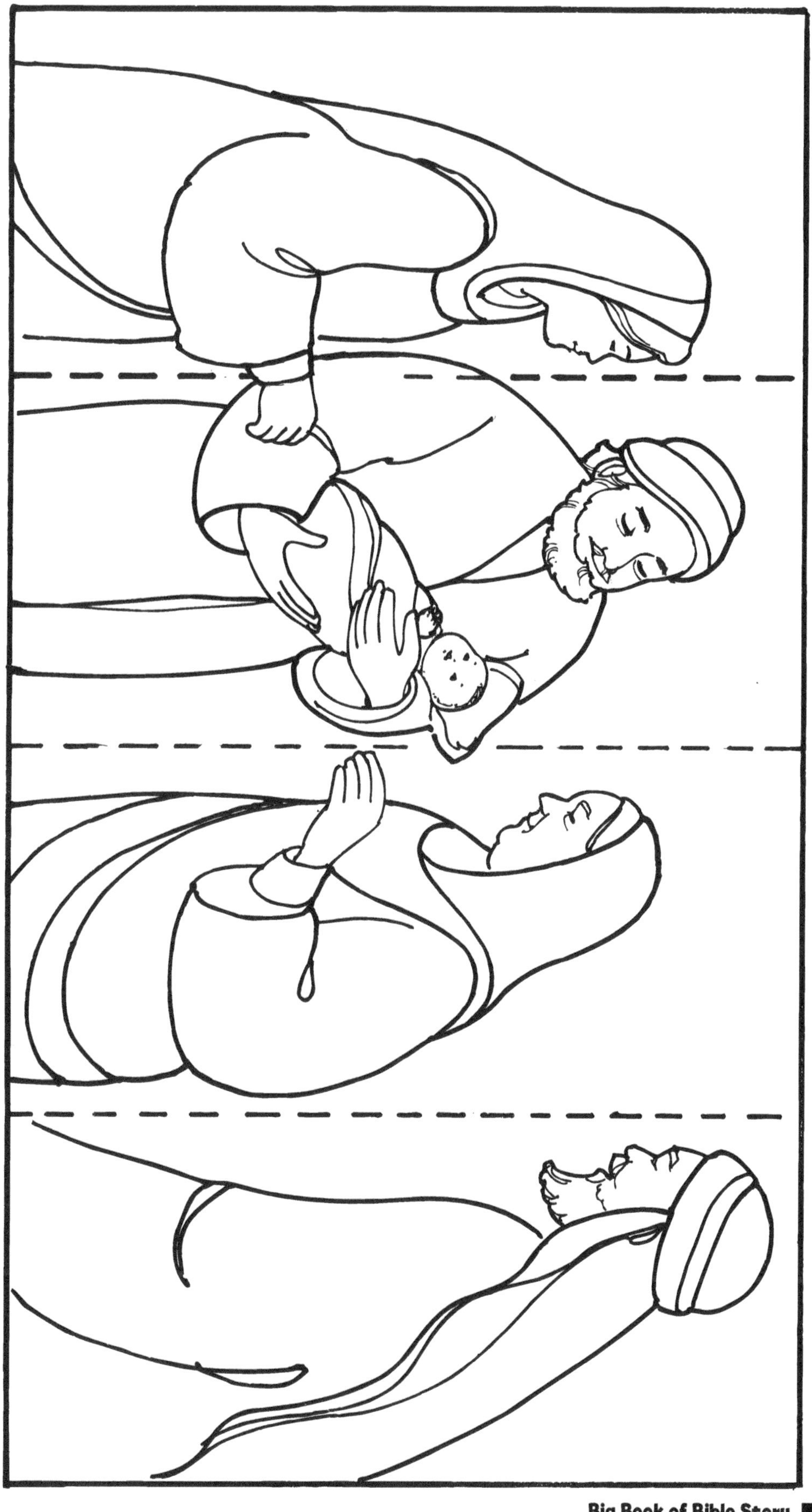

Wise Men Worship Jesus

Matthew 2: Wise Men Worship Jesus

Wise Men Matching Game

Supplies

- copy of the Wise Men Matching Game (preferably on card stock) for each child
- crayons or markers
- scissors

Directions

Color and cut out the eight cards. Use the cards to play a matching game. Lay the cards facedown on the floor or a table. Turn over one card and then try to find its match by turning over another card. You have a match if the two cards form one complete scene when placed together. Try to collect the matching scenes in story order: 1) The wise men talked to a king. 2) The wise men continued their journey. 3) One bright star in a sky full of stars showed the way. 4) The wise men found young Jesus and gave gifts to Him. As you play the game, retell the story. *Optional: You may want to use two sets of cards for added difficulty.*

Wise Men Worship Jesus

Matthew 2: Wise Men Worship Jesus

Stand-Up Star

Supplies

- copy of the Stand-Up Star (on construction paper or card stock) for each child (continued on p. 146)
- crayons or markers
- scissors
- glue

Directions

Color and cut out the four stars. Glue star number 2 to the back of star number 1. Glue star number 4 to the back of star number 3. Cut the stars along the solid dividing lines in the center of the stars, stopping the cut when the dividing line stops. Assemble the stars by sliding them together (see the example). As you slide the stars together, make sure the scenes match (see the example). Use the star scenes as you retell the story of the wise men worshipping Jesus:

1) The wise men visited King Herod. They told him about the star and that they were looking for Jesus. This made Herod angry.
2) Herod sent the wise men to find Jesus, but Herod had a bad plan in his mind.
3) The wise men found Jesus. They worshipped Him and gave Him gifts.
4) The wise men returned home a different way because God warned them not to go back to Herod.

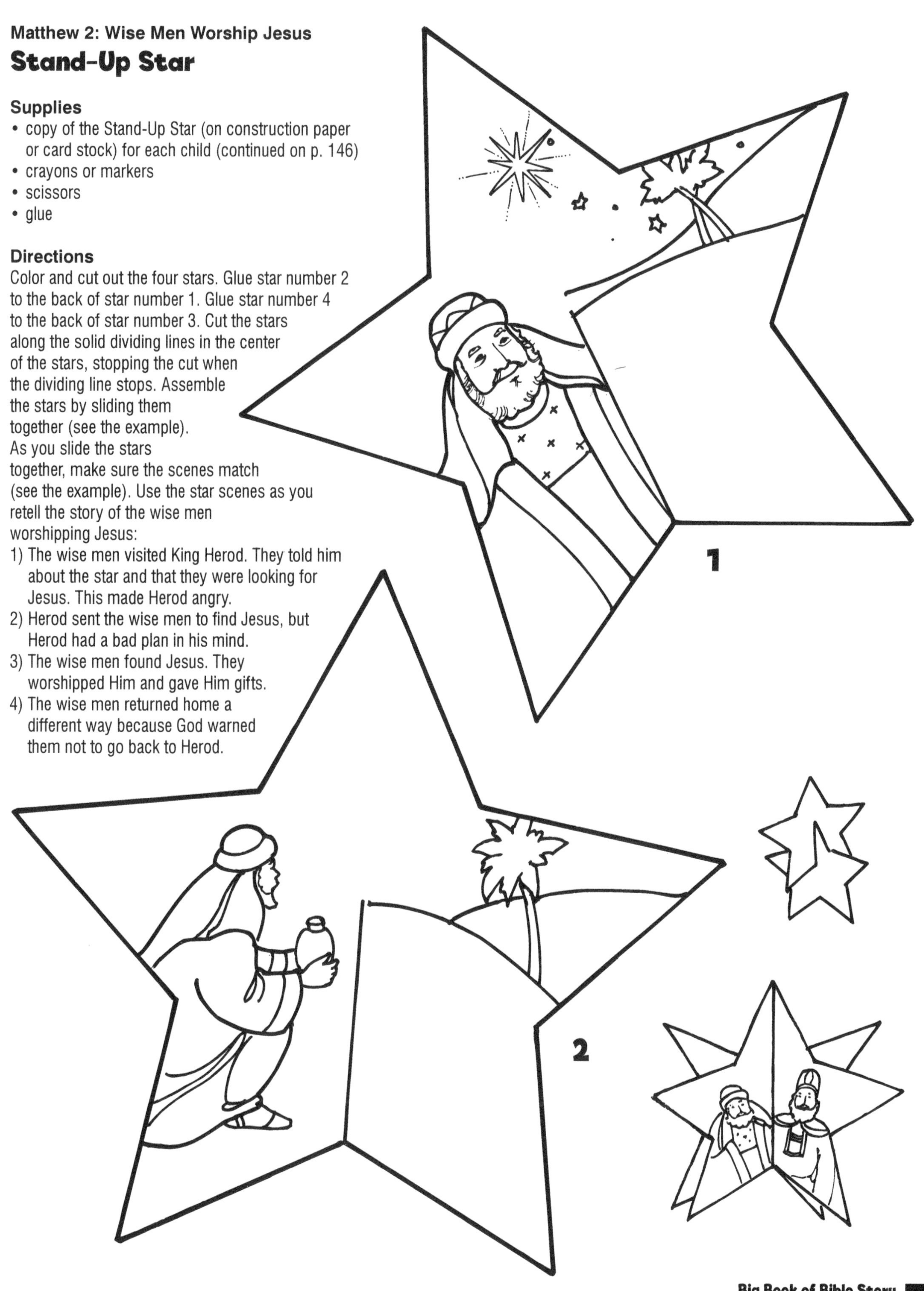

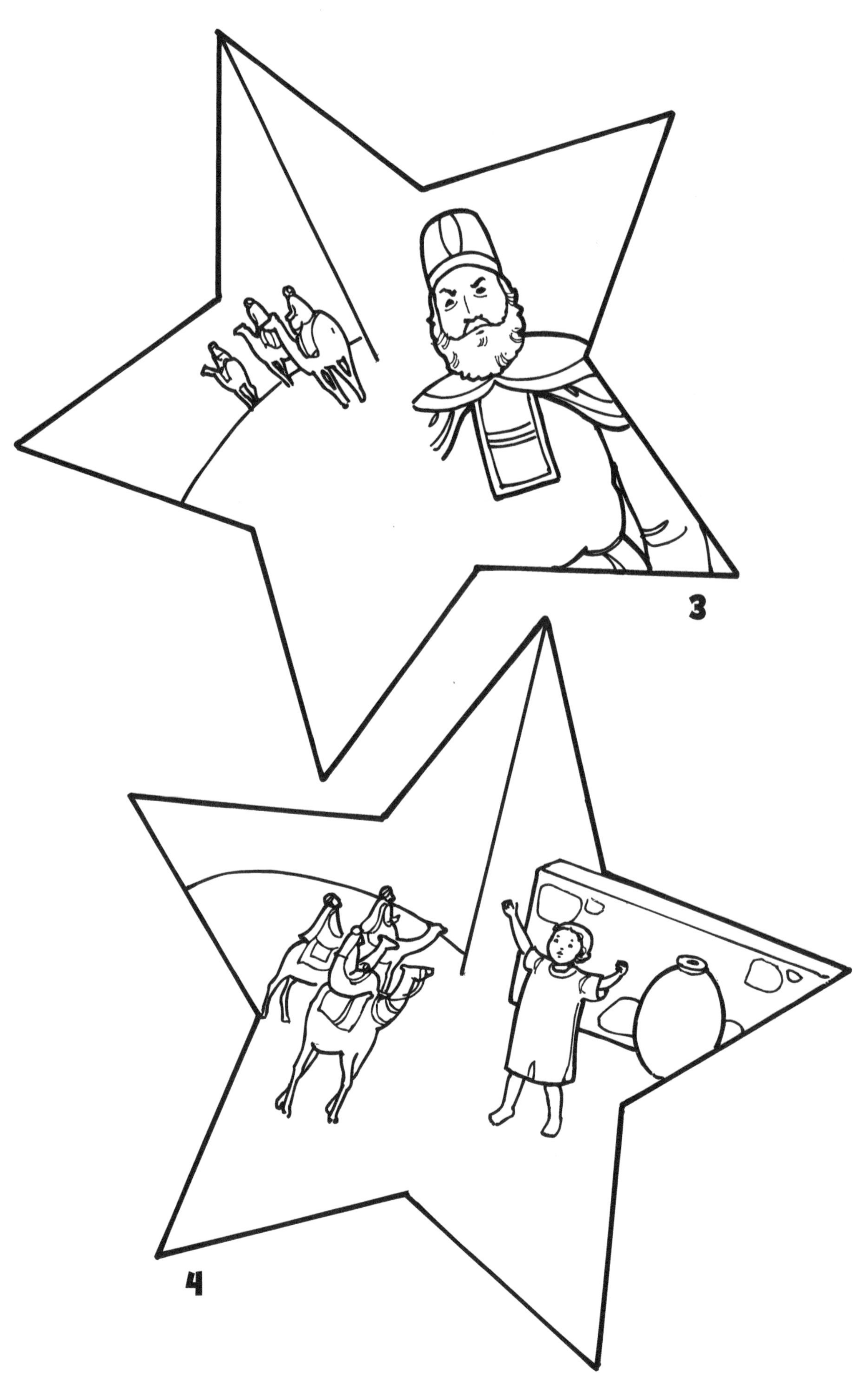
3
4

Jesus Grows Up

Luke 2: Jesus Grows Up

Jesus and Family Travel Map

Supplies

- copy of the map and stand-up figures (preferably on card stock) for each child (continued on p. 149)
- crayons or markers
- scissors

Directions

Color and cut out the map and stand-up figures. Fold each figure along the dotted lines at the base so the figures stand up. Use the map to retell the story of Joseph, Mary, and Jesus traveling to the temple when He was a boy:

1) Jesus was 12 years old and visiting the temple in Jerusalem with Joseph and Mary (move Joseph, Mary, and Jesus from their house in Nazareth to the temple in Jerusalem).
2) Joseph and Mary left to return home, but Jesus was not with them (move Joseph and Mary halfway down the path toward their home in Nazareth; leave Jesus in Jerusalem).
3) Joseph and Mary searched for Jesus for three days (move Joseph and Mary back to Jerusalem and around the city three times).
4) Joseph and Mary found Jesus in the temple talking with the teachers (move Joseph and Mary to the temple with Jesus. Set up the figure of the two teachers so they are looking in Jesus' direction).
5) Joseph and Mary were happy. Jesus explained that He had to be in His Father's house. They all went back to Nazareth together (move Joseph, Mary, and Jesus back to Nazareth).

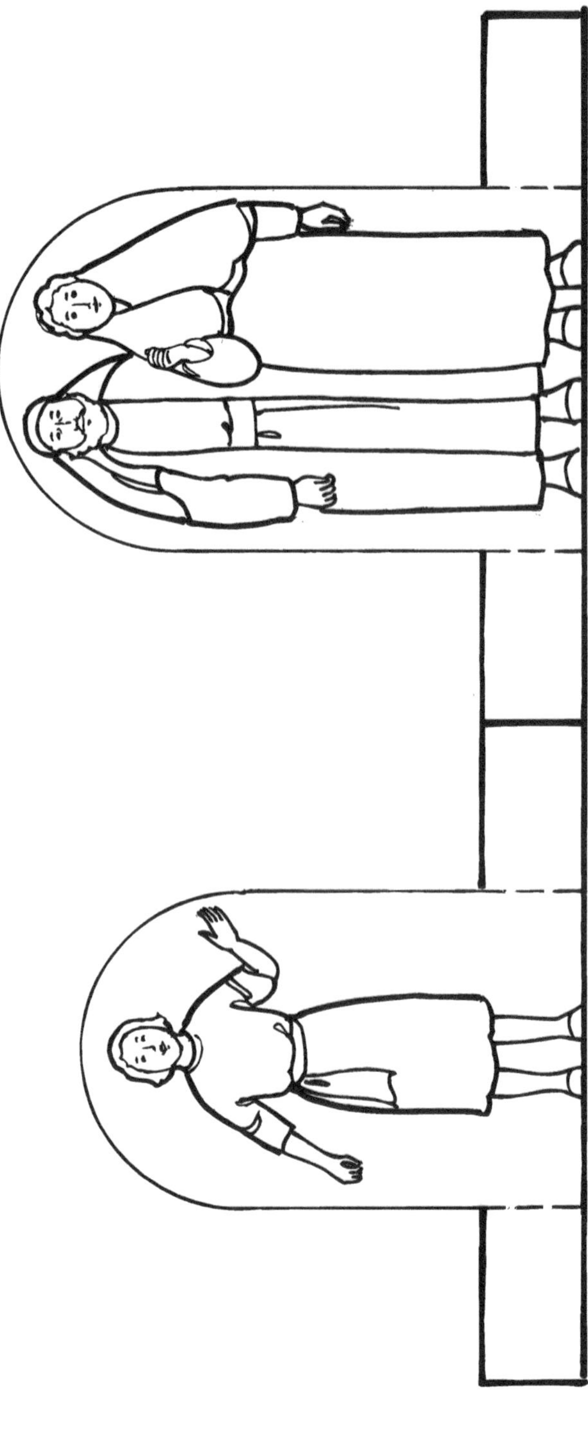

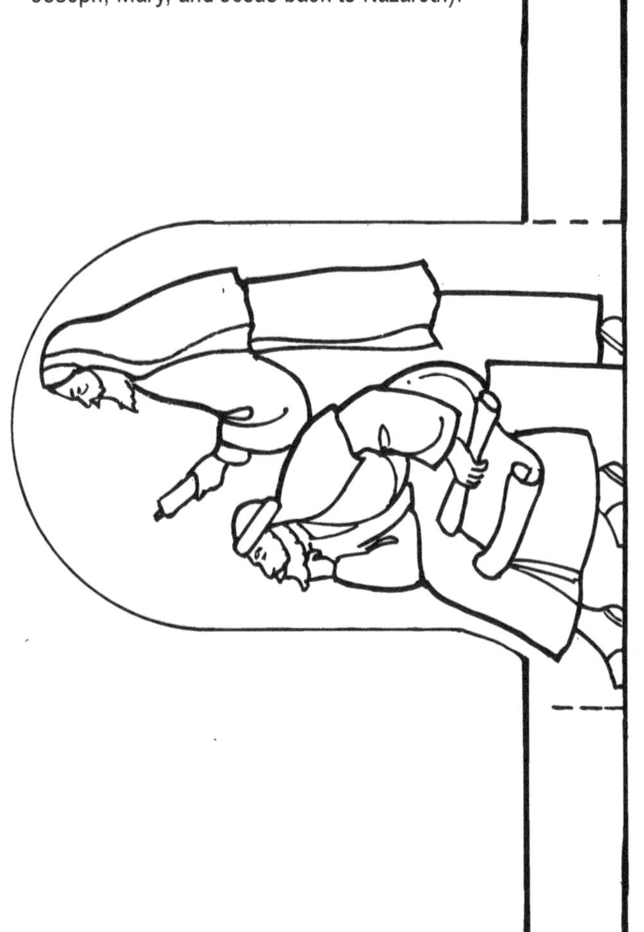

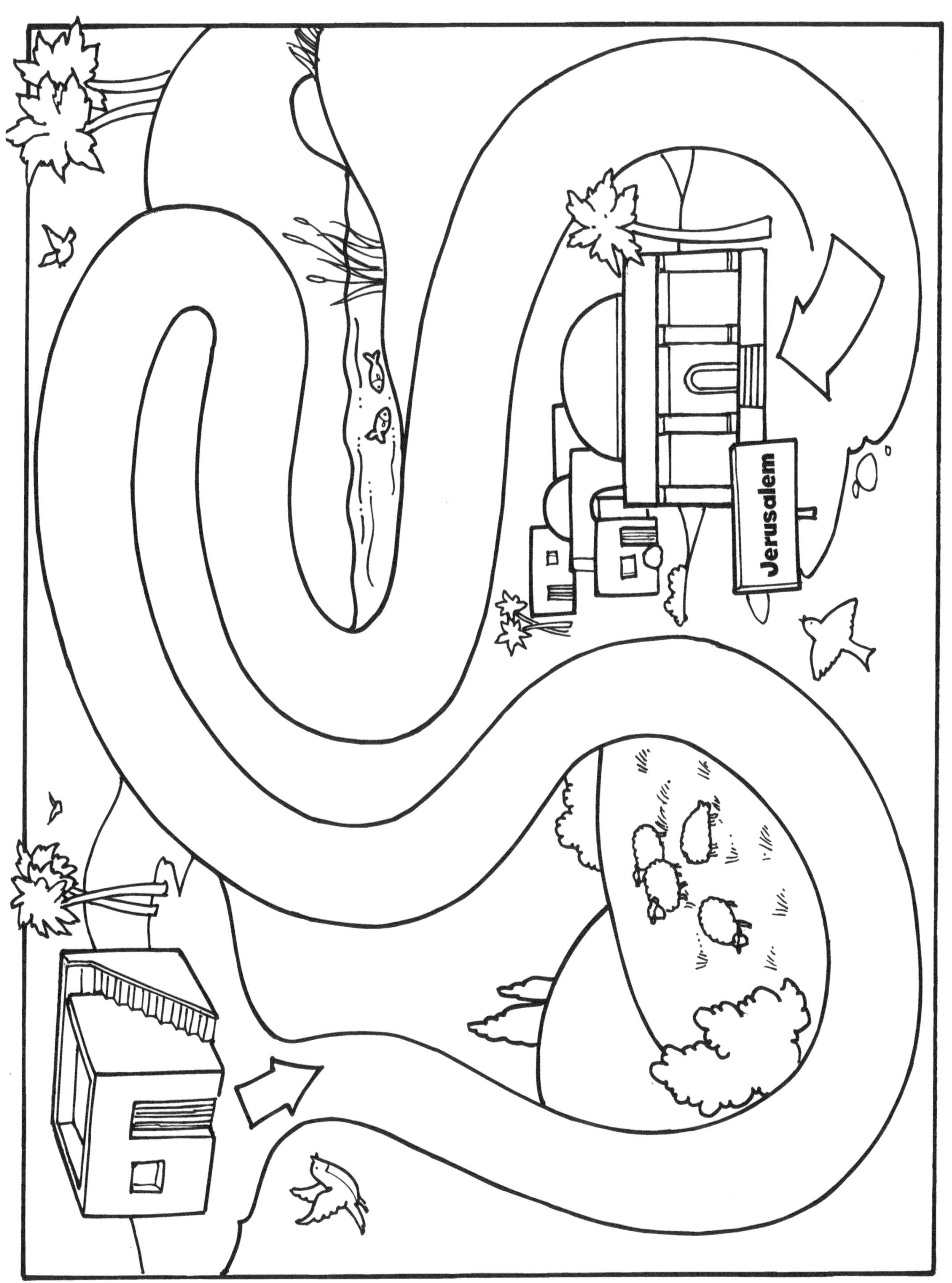
Jerusalem

John Baptizes Jesus

Matthew 3; John 1: John Baptizes Jesus

Fold-Down Baptism

Supplies

- copy of the Fold-Down Baptism activity for each child
- crayons or markers
- scissors

Directions

Color and cut out the baptism scene as one piece (do not cut along the dotted lines). Fold the top of the scene back along the top dotted line to show only the portion of John speaking to a group of people on the bank of the river. While retelling the story, fold the scene down along the bottom dotted line to show John baptizing Jesus (see the example). Use this activity to retell the story of John baptizing Jesus.

Satan Tempts Jesus

Matthew 4: Satan Tempts Jesus

Temptation Storybook

Supplies

- copy of the Temptation Storybook scenes for each child (continued on p. 154)
- construction paper (1 sheet per child, any color)
- crayons or markers
- scissors
- glue
- stapler

Directions

Color and cut out each of the six scenes. Cut a sheet of construction paper in half widthwise. Fold the two pieces of construction paper in half to make a book (see the example). Staple the book at the center. Write "Satan Tempts Jesus" on the front cover and decorate the cover. Then glue each scene to a page in the order they are numbered, starting on the inside of the front cover. Use the book to retell the story of Satan tempting Jesus. Describe what is shown in each picture and then look up the correlating Bible verse to tell how Jesus answered each temptation using words from Scripture.

1) Jesus was hungry after 40 days in the desert. Satan tried to convince Jesus to turn stones into bread.
2) Look up the verse to find out what Jesus said.
3) Satan tried to convince Jesus to jump off a very high place on top of the temple. He told Jesus that God would not let Him get hurt.
4) Look up the verse to find out what Jesus said.
5) Satan offered to give Jesus many things if Jesus would bow down and worship him.
6) Look up the verse to find out what Jesus said.

Matthew 4:4

2

3
Matthew 4:7
4
5
Matthew 4:10
6

Jesus' First Followers

John 1: Jesus' First Followers

Followers Puppets

Supplies

- copy of the Followers Puppets for each child
- crayons or markers
- scissors
- tape

Directions

Color and cut out each of the five finger puppets. Wrap the puppet bases and attach them using tape, so that each one can be worn as a finger puppet. Place the puppets on separate fingers in the following order: Jesus (thumb), Andrew (pointer finger), Peter (center finger), Philip (ring finger), Nathanael (little finger). Use the finger puppets to retell the story of Jesus' first followers:

1) Andrew decided to follow Jesus and brought his brother Peter to Jesus too (show the Jesus, Andrew, and Peter puppets).
2) Jesus called Philip to follow Him (add the Philip puppet).
3) Philip went and found Nathanael and told him about Jesus (add the Nathanael puppet), but Nathanael wasn't sure about who Jesus was.
4) Jesus told Nathanael that He had seen him under a tree before Philip called him. Then Nathanael believed that Jesus was God's Son.

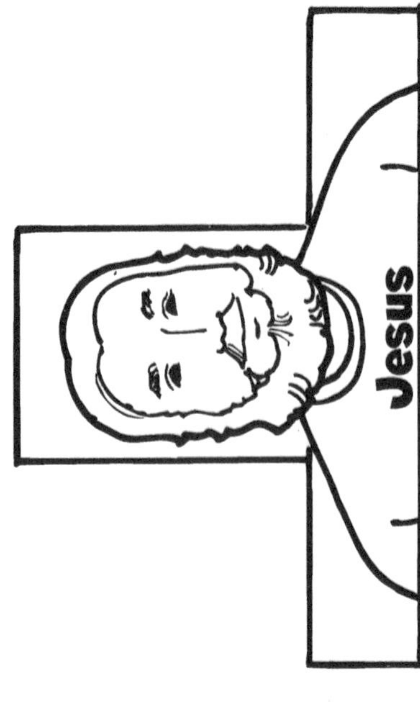

Jesus Teaches about God

John 3, 19: Jesus Teaches about God

Jesus Teaches Flip-Flap Book

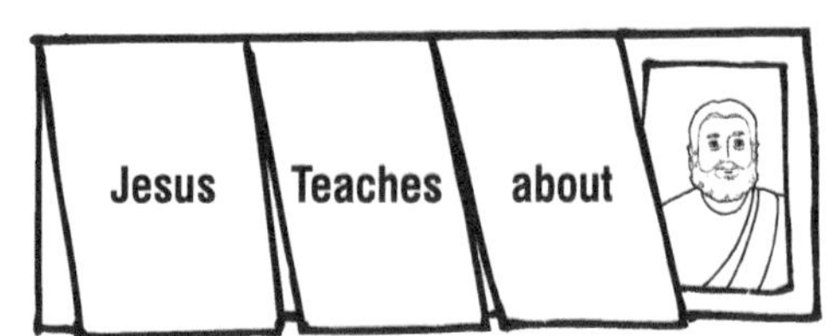

Supplies

- copy of the Jesus Teaches Flip-Flap Book for each child
- construction paper (1 sheet per child, any color)
- crayons or markers
- scissors
- glue

Directions

Color and cut out each of the four scenes. Fold a sheet of construction paper in half lengthwise. Lay the folded paper in front of you and cut the top half of the sheet into four equal sections, being careful to stop at the fold line. You should now have four flaps (each approximately 3" wide) that can be lifted up (see the example). Lift and attach one scene under each flap, attaching the scenes in order according to the numbers on the scenes. With the flaps folded closed, write "Jesus Teaches about God" (one word on each flap). Use the flip-flap book, lifting the flaps in order, to retell the story of Jesus teaching Nicodemus about God:

1) Nicodemus was an important Jewish leader.
2) Nicodemus came to Jesus at night to ask Him about His teaching.
3) Nicodemus was confused by what Jesus said.
4) Jesus told Nicodemus why God had sent Him into the world.

Jesus and a Woman from Samaria

John 4: Jesus and a Woman from Samaria

Story Well

Supplies

- copy of the Story Well and jar scenes for each child (continued on p. 161)
- brown paper lunch bags (1 per child)
- crayons or markers
- scissors
- glue

Directions

Color and cut out the jar scenes and the well. Cut off 3½" from the top of a brown paper lunch bag. Attach the well to the front of the bag. Place the jar scenes inside the bag. Use the Story Well to retell the story of what happened when Jesus met a woman from Samaria. Pull the jars out of the bag in order as you retell the story (refer to the numbers on the jars for help with the order of the story):

1) Jesus was resting by a well when a woman came to get water.
2) Jesus asked the woman for water, and the woman was surprised that Jesus spoke to her.
3) Jesus talked to the woman about her life. The woman believed that Jesus had been sent from God.
4) The woman went home and told others about Jesus.

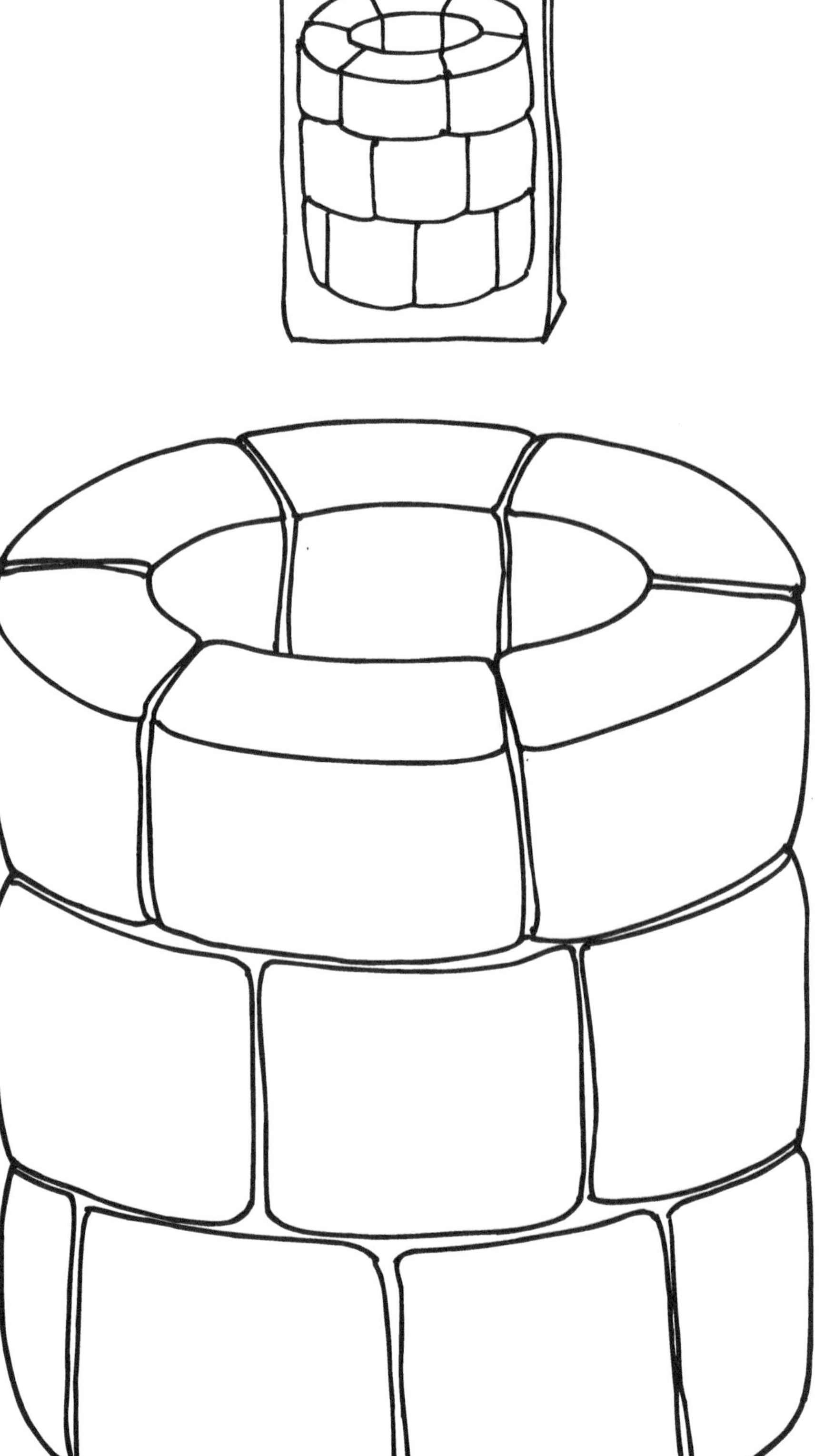

1
2
3
4

Jesus Heals an Official's Son

John 4: Jesus Heals an Official's Son

Healing Story Box

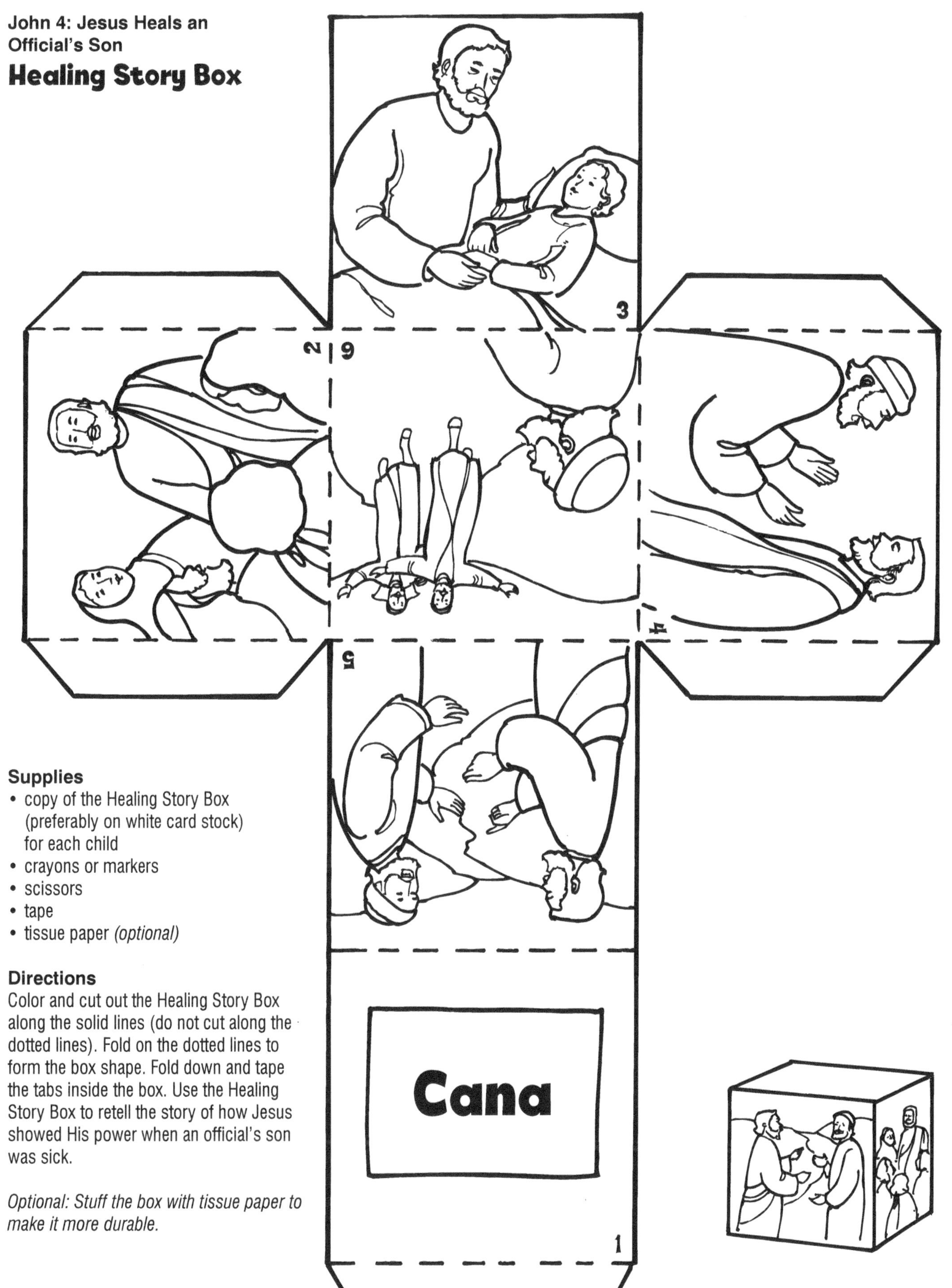

Supplies

- copy of the Healing Story Box (preferably on white card stock) for each child
- crayons or markers
- scissors
- tape
- tissue paper *(optional)*

Directions

Color and cut out the Healing Story Box along the solid lines (do not cut along the dotted lines). Fold on the dotted lines to form the box shape. Fold down and tape the tabs inside the box. Use the Healing Story Box to retell the story of how Jesus showed His power when an official's son was sick.

Optional: Stuff the box with tissue paper to make it more durable.

Jesus Chooses Four Followers

Mark 1; Luke 5: Jesus Chooses Four Followers

Four Followers Book

Supplies

- copy of the Four Followers Book for each child (continued on p. 166)
- construction paper (1 sheet per child)
- crayons or markers
- scissors
- glue
- stapler

Directions

Color and cut out the six scenes. Cut a sheet of construction paper in half widthwise. Fold the two pieces of construction paper together to make a book (see the example). Staple the book at the center. Write "Jesus Chooses Four Followers" on the front cover and decorate the cover as you like. Glue each scene to a separate page of the book in the order in which they are numbered, starting on the inside of the front cover. Use the book to retell the story of how Jesus called four fishermen to follow Him:

1) Jesus was teaching by a lake.
2) The crowd was so large that Jesus got into one of the fishing boats and asked the fisherman named Peter to take the boat out into the water. Jesus taught the people from the boat.
3) Jesus told the fishermen to go out into deeper water. He said they would catch fish. Peter did not believe they would catch anything, but he did as Jesus said.
4) Peter and Andrew let down their nets and caught so many fish that their nets began to break.
5) James and John, also fishermen, hurried to help from another boat. But both boats were so full they began to sink.
6) Peter, Andrew, James, and John realized how special Jesus was. When Jesus asked the four fishermen to follow Him, they did!

1

2

3
4
5
6

Jesus and a Man Who Is Paralyzed

Mark 2: Jesus and a Man Who Is Paralyzed

Paralyzed Man Rebus

Supplies

- copy of the Paralyzed Man Rebus for each child
- crayons or markers

Directions

Color the pictures in the rebus. Use the rebus to tell what happened when four men brought their friend to Jesus. See the picture descriptions for what each picture stands for.

Jesus

Crowds

Four Friends

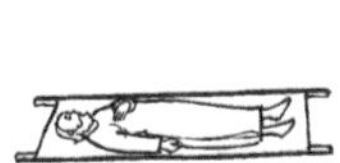
Paralyzed Man

House

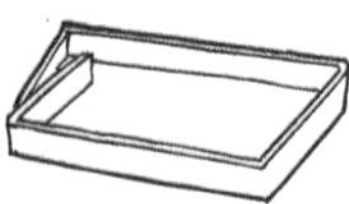
Roof

 **went to a town called Capernaum.**  **gathered at a**

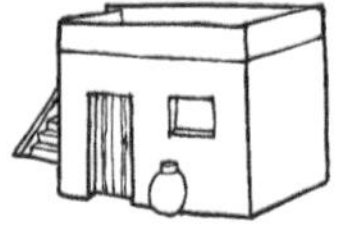 **to hear**  **teach.**  **carried a** 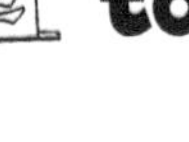 **to**

. They wanted  **to help the**  **walk. The** 

were so thick that the  **could not get into the** 

where  **was teaching. Then one friend had an idea. The**

 **climbed onto the** 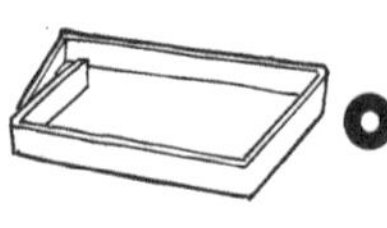 **of the** 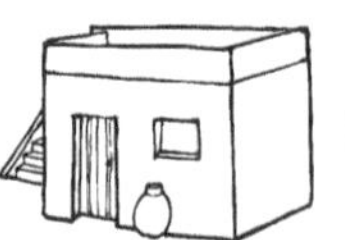 **and cut a**

hole in the 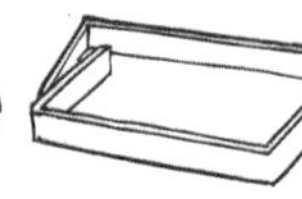 **. They lowered the**  **down into the**

 **through the hole in the** 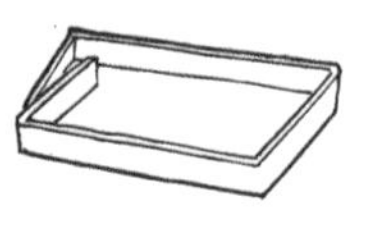 **.**  **said the**

was forgiven and told him to get up and walk. The

jumped up and carried his mat out the door of the 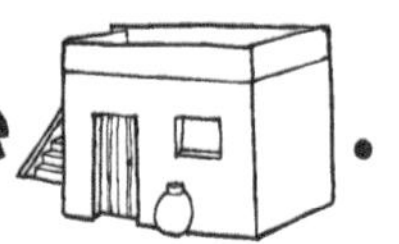 **.**

The  **were amazed and praised God.**

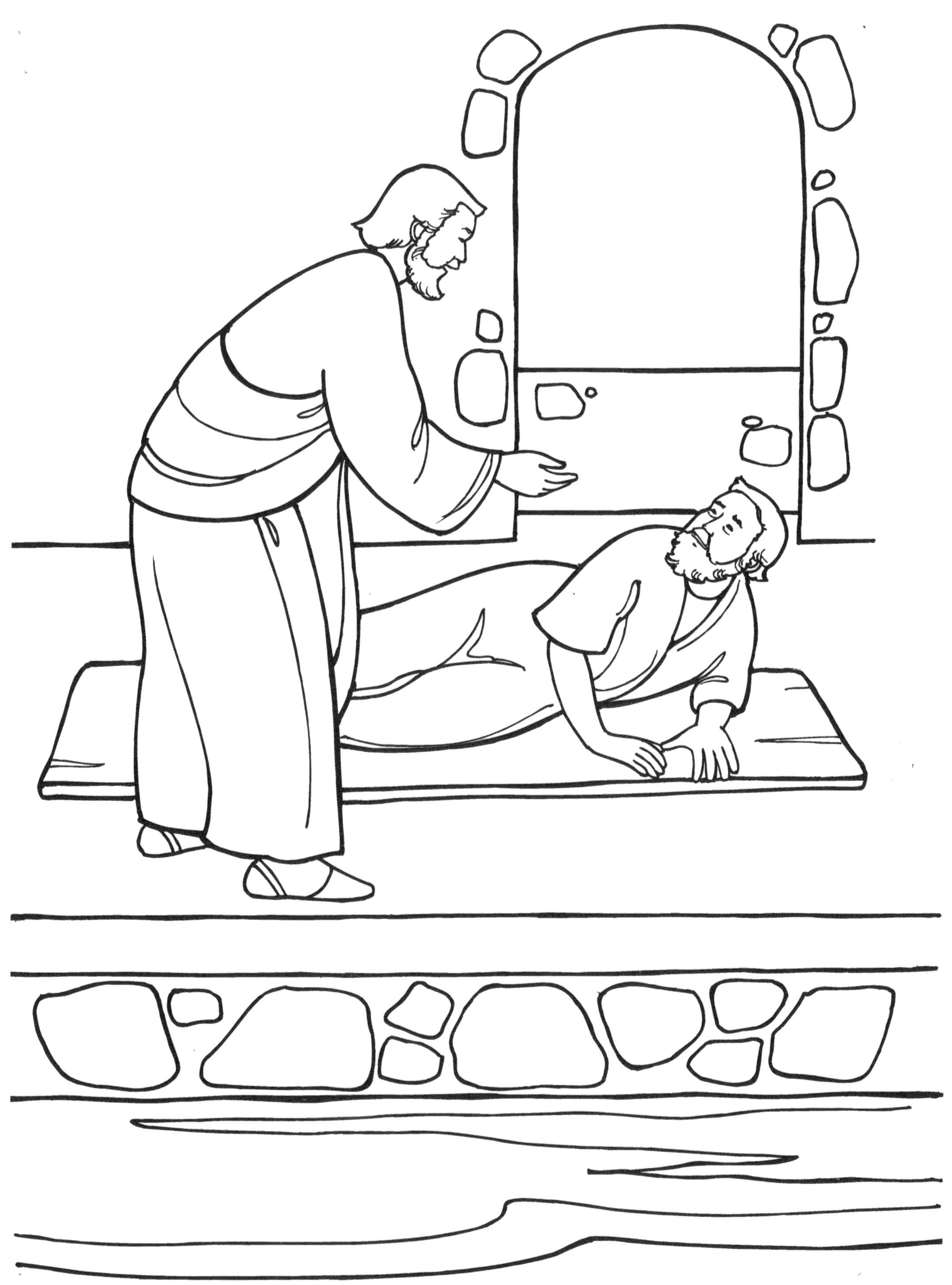

Jesus Heals a Man at a Pool

John 5: Jesus Heals a Man at a Pool

Healing Story Smush Book

See page 7 for supplies and directions for this activity.
Use the book to tell how Jesus helped a man in need.

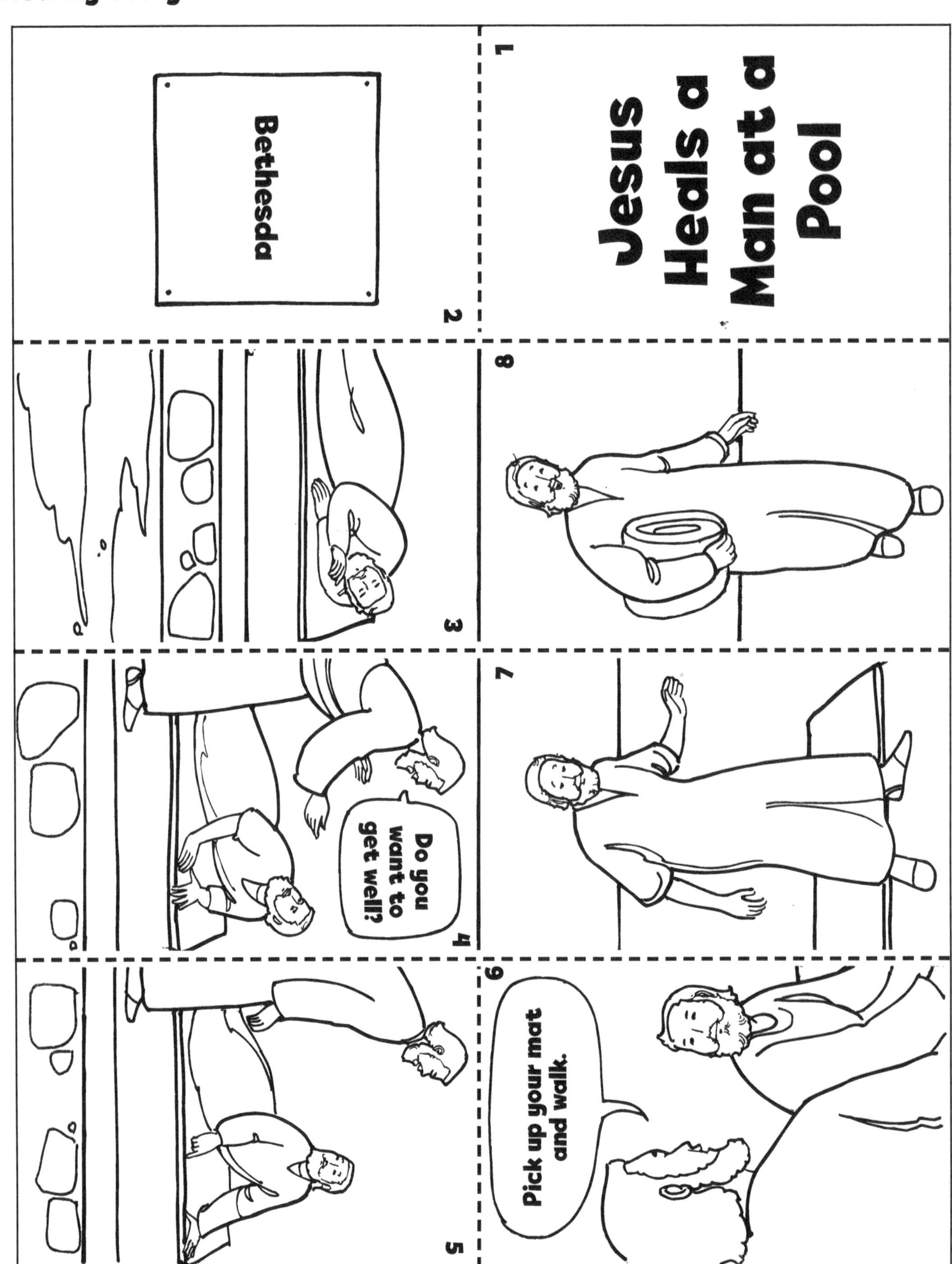

Jesus and a Woman Needing Forgiveness

Luke 7: Jesus and a Woman Needing Forgiveness

Perfume Jar Storybook

Supplies

- copy of the Perfume Jar Storybook for each child
- crayons or markers
- scissors

Directions

Color and cut out the Perfume Jar Storybook as one piece (do not cut along the dotted lines). Fold the jars in half along the dotted lines so that jars 1 and 4 are behind jars 2 and 3. Cut out the center space between the jars. Then fold the jars in half again so jars 2 and 3 are on the inside of the book. Use the Perfume Jar Storybook to retell the story of Jesus forgiving a woman who came to Him:

1) While Jesus was at Simon's house, a woman who did not have a good reputation came to Him crying.
2) The woman washed Jesus' feet with an expensive jar of perfume and then wiped His feet with her hair.
3) The guests were upset about the woman, and Jesus knew their thoughts.
4) Jesus told the guests that she was being kind to Him, and He forgave her sins.

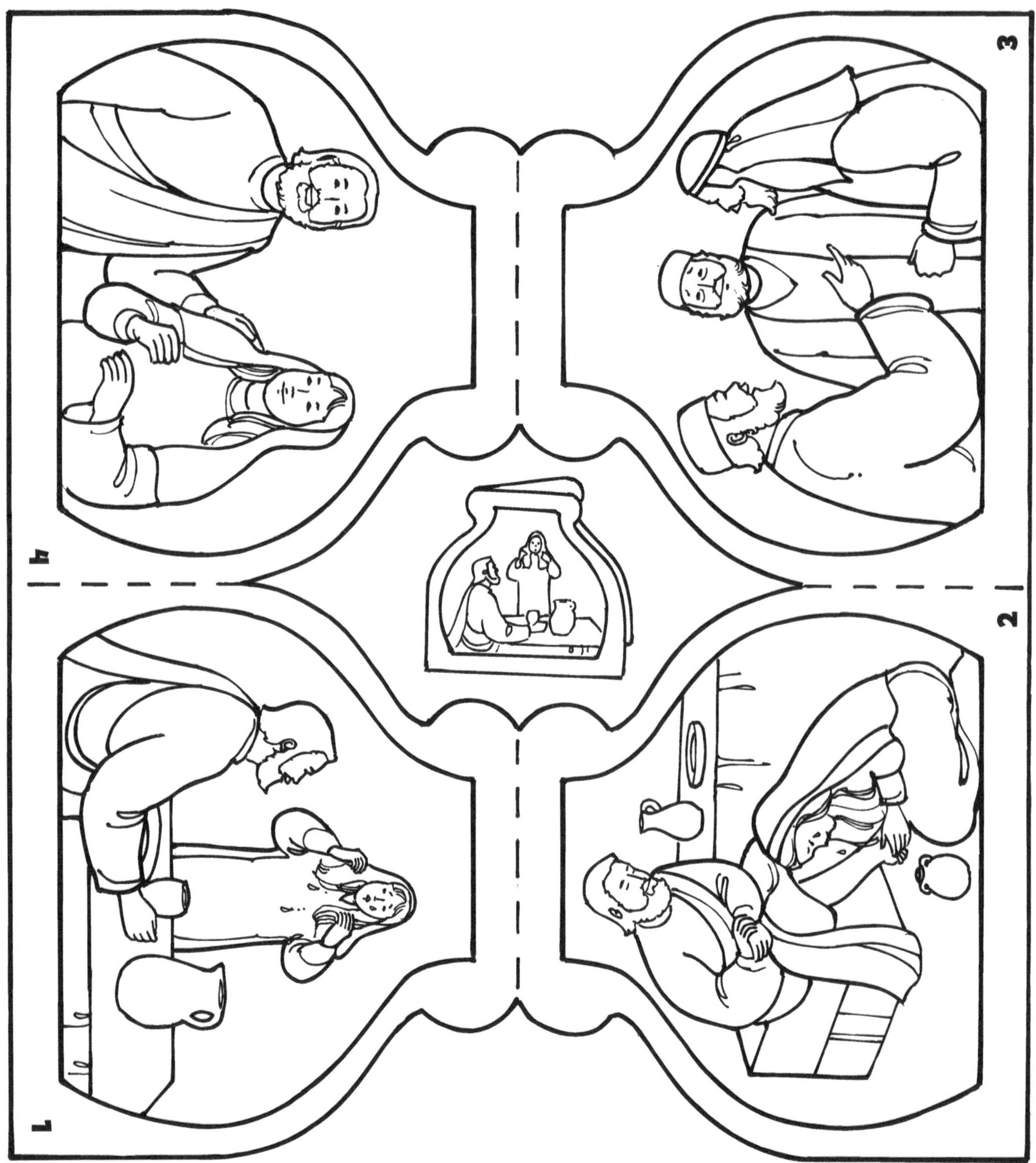

Jesus Stops a Storm

Mark 4: Jesus Stops a Storm

Storm Story Pamphlet

Supplies

- copy of the Storm Story Pamphlet for each child
- crayons or markers
- scissors

Directions

Color and cut out the six scenes as one piece. Fold the scenes in half along the dotted line so scenes 1, 3, and 6 are behind scenes 2, 4, and 5. Lay the pamphlet in front of you with scenes 2, 4, and 5 facing up. Fold scene 5 in along the dotted line to cover scene 4. Scenes 2 and 3 should now be facing out. Fold scene 2 in to cover scene 3; scene 1 now shows as the front cover. Unfold the scenes one at a time as you retell the story of how Jesus showed His power over nature.

1) Jesus was teaching crowds from a boat just off the shore (show scene 1).
2) After He finished teaching, Jesus and His disciples sailed across the lake (open the first panel to reveal scenes 2 and 3).
3) When a storm came up, Jesus spoke to the wind and told the storm to stop (open scene 3 so scenes 2, 4, and 5 are showing).
4) The sea calmed, and the disciples were amazed at what Jesus had done (fold scene 5 over scene 4 so scenes 2 and 3 are showing again).

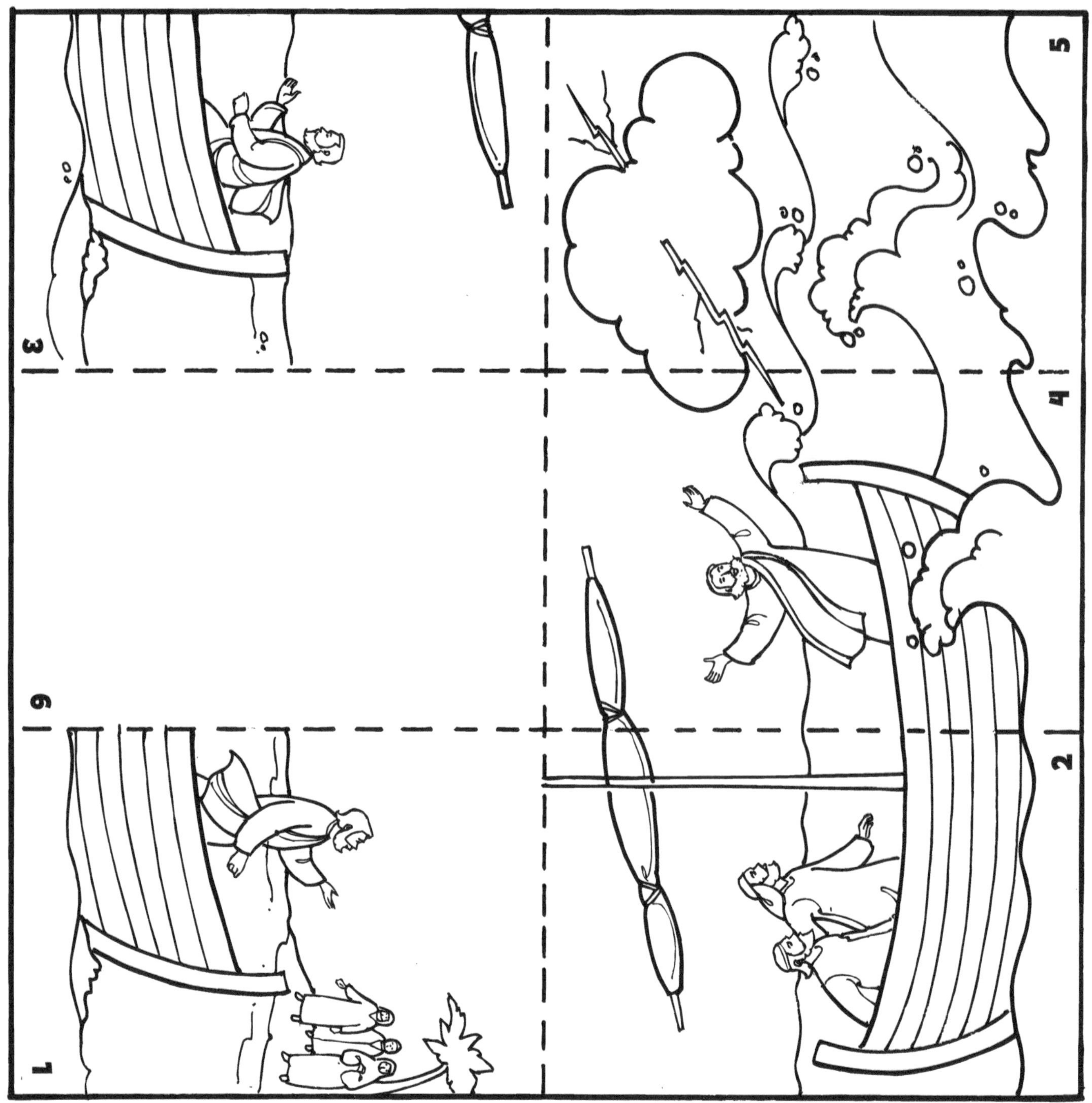

Jesus Heals a Woman and a Young Girl

Mark 5: Jesus Heals a Woman and a Young Girl

Jesus Heals Peel-a-Picture

Supplies

- copy of the Jesus Heals Peel-a-Picture sentence strips for each child (enlarged to 120%)
- scissors
- crayons
- copy of p. 175 for each child
- glue

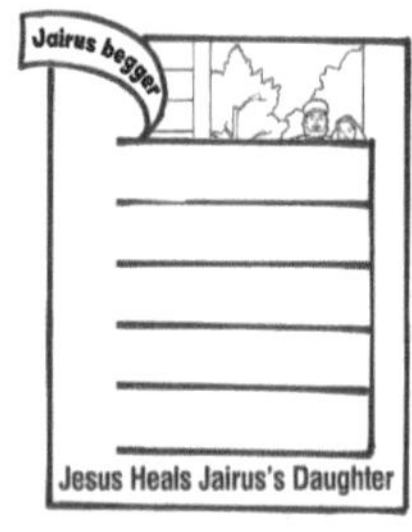

Directions

Cut around the outside edge of the sentence strips rectangle and along the dividing lines between each strip, being careful to stop at the dotted line. Color the Jesus Heals a Woman and a Young Girl coloring picture. Apply glue to the right side of the sentence strips rectangle between the dotted line and the edge only (do not apply any glue to the sentence strips themselves). Turn the rectangle over and attach the sentence strips over the coloring page (sentence side down) by pressing along the glued section. Peel back each strip in order to reveal the picture underneath and tell that part of the story.

Jairus begged Jesus to heal his daughter.

Jesus agreed to go to Jairus's house.

On the way, a woman who had been sick came to Jesus. Jesus healed her.

Some people came from Jairus's house to tell him his daughter had died.

Jesus told Jairus to not be afraid, but believe.

Jesus went into the girl's room. Jesus told the girl to stand up, and she did!

Glue here

Jesus Feeds 5,000

John 6: Jesus Feeds 5,000

Fish and Bread Mobile

Supplies

- copy of the Fish and Bread Mobile for each child (continued on p. 179)
- paper plates (1 per child)
- crayons or markers
- scissors
- hole punch
- yarn (any color)

Directions

Color and cut out the two fish and the five loaves of bread (the oval-shaped scenes). Punch holes in each of the seven pieces where indicated by the open circles and tie a length of yarn to each piece. Write "Jesus Can Give You What You Need" on the back of the paper plate. Punch seven holes, evenly spaced, around the rim of the plate, and then punch a hole in the center of the plate. Using varying lengths of yarn, tie the seven mobile pieces to the rim of the paper plate, alternating between loaves and fish (tie the five loaves in order per the numbers in the lower right corners—see the example). Tie a piece of yarn through the center of the plate to hang the mobile. Use the Fish and Bread Mobile to retell the story of what Jesus did for a large crowd of people.

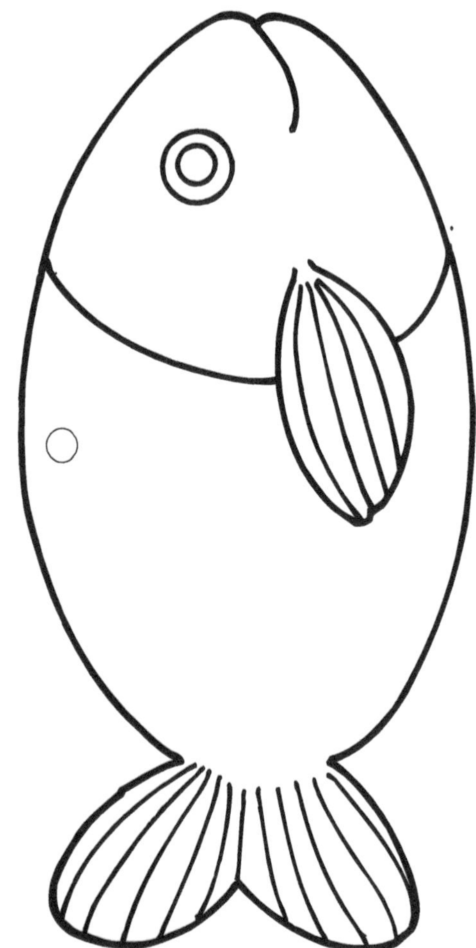

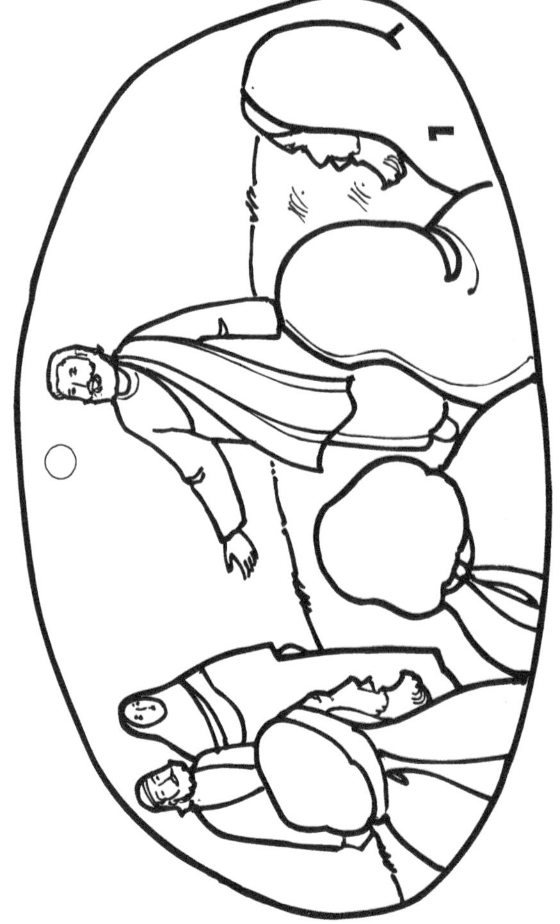

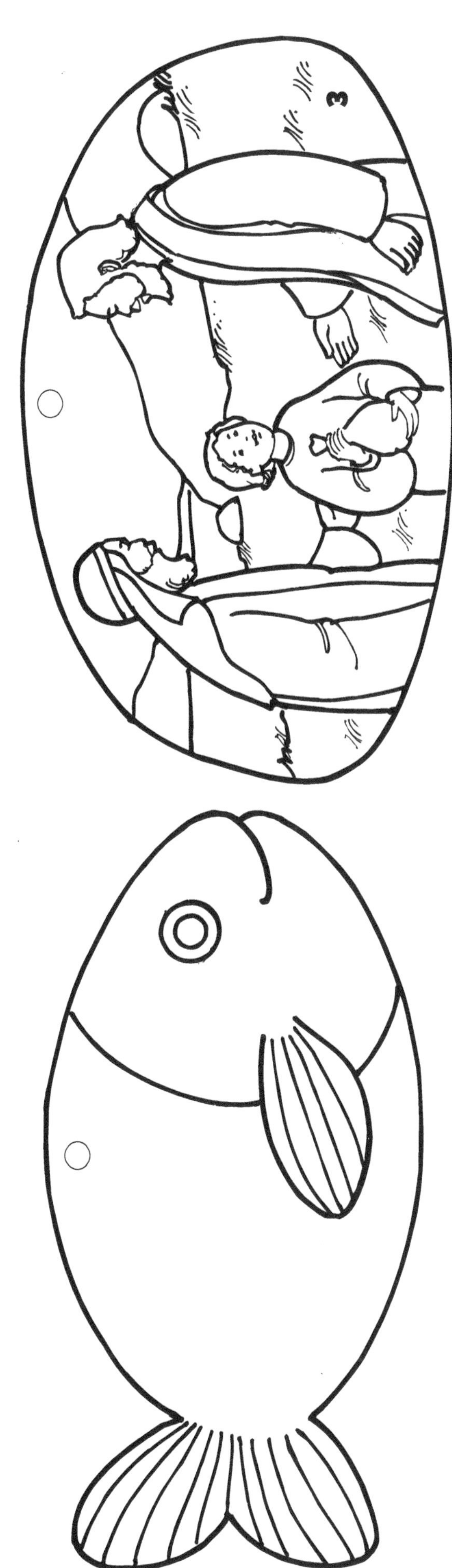

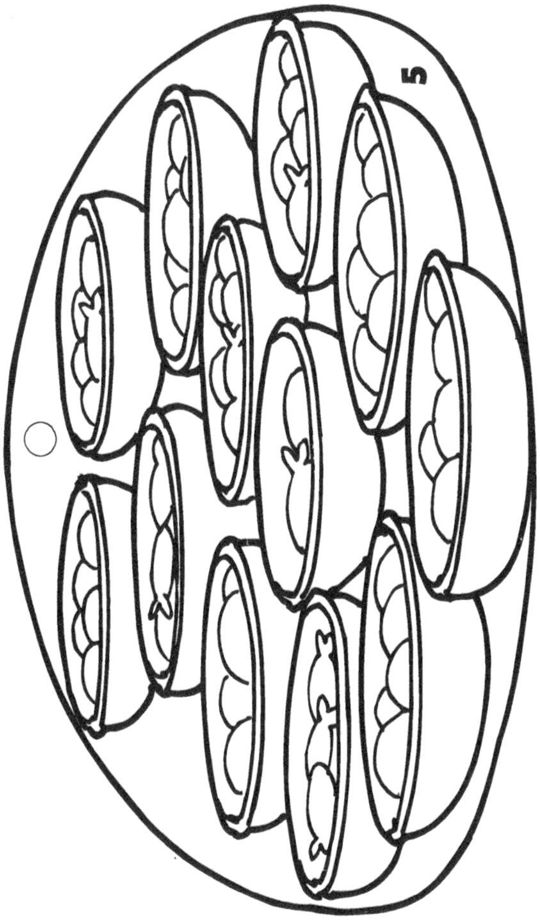

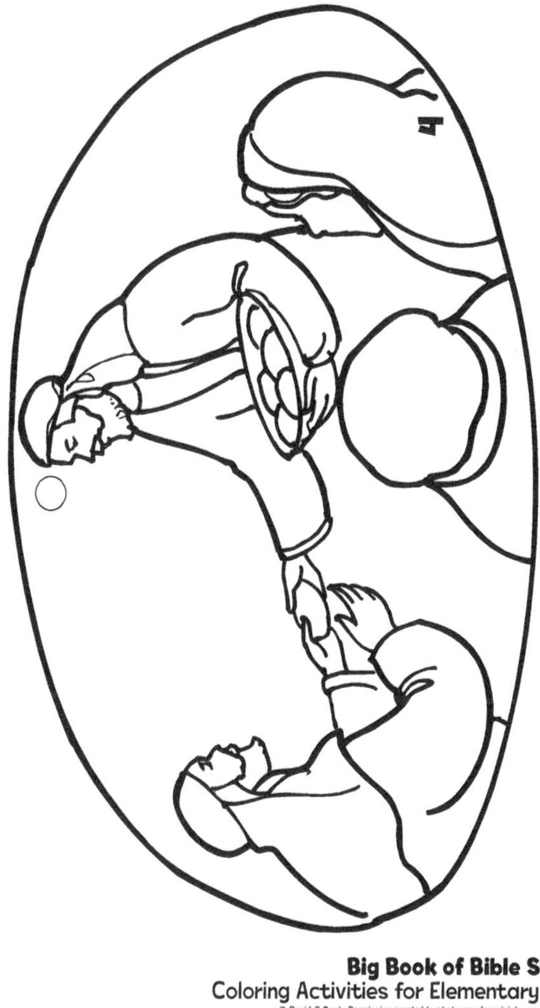

Jesus Walks on Water

Matthew 14: Jesus Walks on Water

Jesus and Peter Puppets

Supplies

- copy of the Jesus and Peter Puppets (preferably on card stock) for each child
- blue construction paper
- crayons or markers
- scissors
- hole punch *(optional)*
- craft sticks (1 per child)
- glue

Directions

Color and cut out the Jesus and Peter Puppets. Cut (or punch) out the circles for the legs on both puppets. Cut a piece of blue construction paper to look like water. Glue a craft stick to the back of the water piece (see example). Put two fingers through the leg holes in the Jesus and Peter Puppets. Use the water piece and the puppets as you retell the story of Jesus walking on water.

Jesus Heals a Man Who Can't Hear

Mark 7: Jesus Heals a Man Who Can't Hear

Healing Storybook

Supplies

- copy of the Healing Storybook for each child (continued on p. 184)
- construction paper (any color, 1 sheet per child)
- crayons or markers
- scissors
- glue
- hole punch
- yarn (any color)

Directions

Color and cut out each story scene and sentence strip. Cut a piece of construction paper in half widthwise. Fold the two pieces of construction paper in half and put them together to make a book (see the example). Write "Jesus Heals a Man Who Can't Hear" on the front cover of the book and decorate the cover as you like. Starting on the inside of the front cover, glue each scene and its correlating sentence strip to a separate page of the book in numbered order (glue the sentence strip below the picture). Punch two holes at the fold of the book and tie the book together using colorful yarn. Use the book to tell about Jesus healing a man who could not hear.

Some people brought a man who could not hear to Jesus for healing.	**Jesus put His fingers in the man's ears.**
Jesus spit and touched the man's tongue.	**Jesus looked up to heaven and said, "Be opened!"**

The man could hear and speak clearly!
The people were amazed. They said, "Jesus has done everything well!"
3
4
5
6

Jesus with Moses and Elijah

Matthew 17: Jesus with Moses and Elijah

Mountain Men

Supplies

- copy of the Mountain Men story triangle for each child
- crayons or markers
- scissors
- tape

Directions

Color and cut out the Mountain Men story triangle. Cut along the solid lines (do not cut along the dotted lines). Fold on the dotted lines and tape the tab to the back of the side with words. Use the story triangle to retell the story of Moses and Elijah appearing with Jesus on the mountain during His transfiguration:

1) Jesus took Peter, James, and John up on a high mountain.
2) Jesus' appearance changed, and His face and clothes were bright like the sun. Moses and Elijah appeared with Jesus and talked with Him.
3) A voice from heaven said, "This is my Son, whom I love.... Listen to him!"

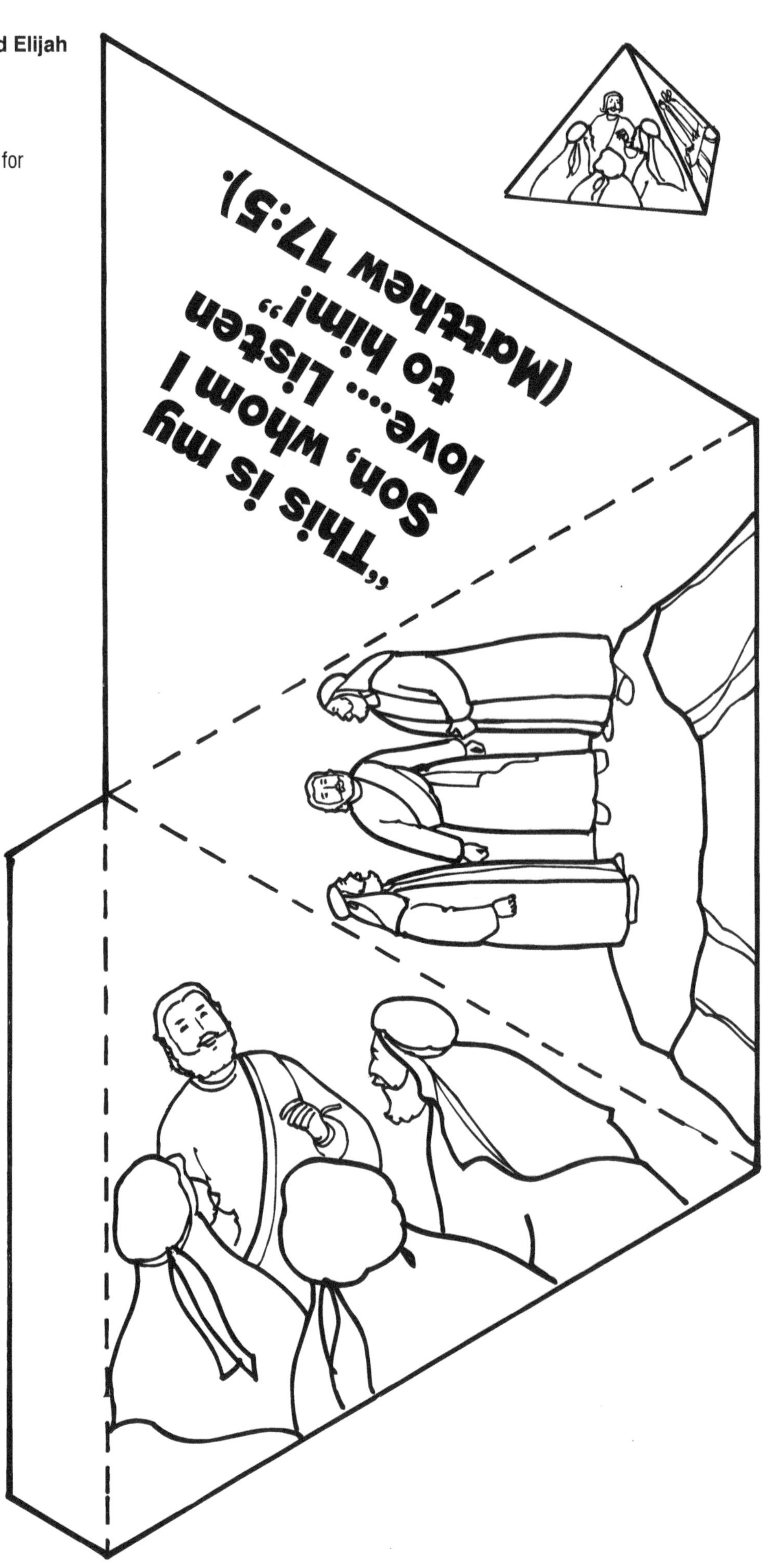

Jesus Heals a Man Who Can't See

John 9: Jesus Heals a Man Who Can't See

Healing Time Line

Supplies

- copy of the Healing Time Line scenes and blind man figure for each child (continued on p. 189)
- crayons or markers
- scissors
- craft sticks (1 per child)
- glue
- tape

Directions

Color and cut out each time line scene and the blind man figure (leaving the blind man figure as one piece). Fold the figure on the dotted line. Glue a craft stick between the two sides of the blind man figure, at the bottom. Tape the time line scenes together in order per the numbers in the lower right corners. Move the blind man through the time line, placing him in the empty spaces in each scene as you retell the story of how Jesus healed a man and showed God's power:

1) As Jesus was walking, He saw a man who could not see (show side of the man with eyes shut).
2) Jesus spit on the ground and made mud with the dirt.
3) Jesus put the mud on the man's eyes.
4) Jesus sent the man to wash in the Pool of Siloam.
5) When the man washed off the mud, he could see (turn the blind man over to show his eyes opened)! The man told others about what Jesus did, and the people were amazed.

1

2

3

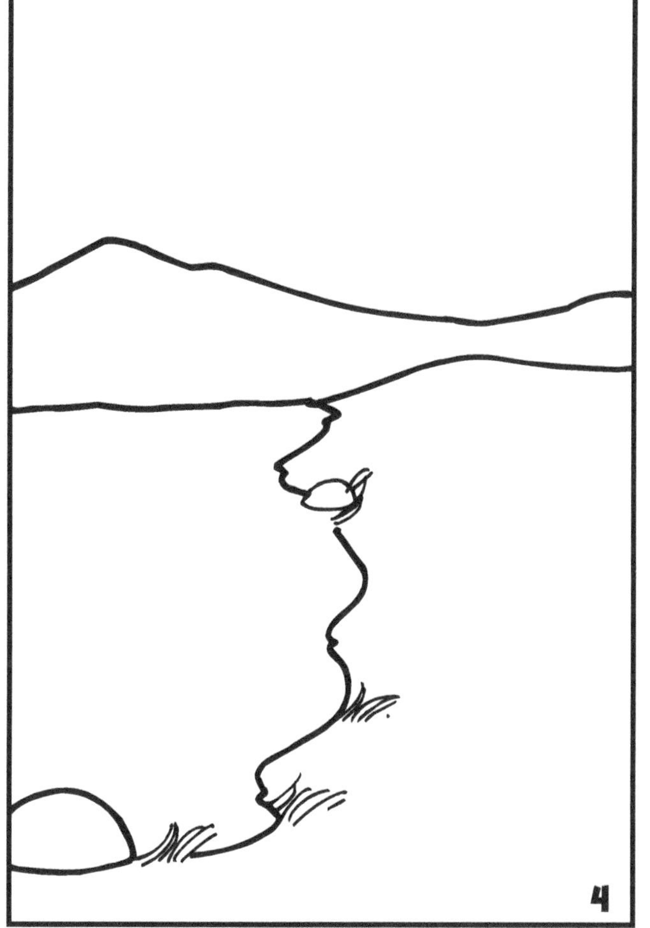
4

5

Jesus Teaches about Helping

Luke 10: Jesus Teaches about Helping

Injured Man Story Mask

Supplies

- copy of the Injured Man Story Mask (preferably on card stock) for each child
- crayons or markers
- scissors
- jumbo craft sticks (1 per child)
- tape

Directions

Color and cut out the story mask. Cut out the spaces for the eyes and the space inside the mouth. Attach the mask to a craft stick by taping the stick to the back center of the mask. Use the story mask to retell Jesus' story about helping others, from the perspective of the injured man.

Jesus Teaches about Prayer

Matthew 6; Luke 11: Jesus Teaches about Prayer

Prayer Pop-Up Card

Supplies

- copy of the Prayer Pop-Up Card for each child
- crayons or markers
- scissors

Directions

Color and cut out the pop-up card. Fold the card back along the horizontal dotted line so the scenes are back-to-back. Fold the center piece down along the dotted lines and then fold the card in half so the pop-up piece is folded inside. Use the Prayer Pop-Up Card to retell the story of Jesus teaching about prayer:

1) One day Jesus was teaching about prayer.
2) Jesus said not to pray in public in order to get attention and not to use a lot of unnecessary words.
3) Jesus said to pray in a room behind a closed door and to trust that God knows what you need before you ask Him.
4) Jesus taught a model prayer to His followers in Matthew 6:9–13.

Encourage students to find Matthew 6:9–13 in their Bibles and to memorize the prayer Jesus taught His disciples.

Jesus Teaches about Sharing

Luke 12: Jesus Teaches about Sharing

Story Barn

Supplies

- copy of the Story Barn (preferably on card stock) for each child
- crayons or markers
- scissors
- tape

Directions

Color and cut out the Story Barn along the solid lines (do not cut along any of the dotted lines). Fold each panel on the dotted lines and attach the roof panels together using tape. Tape the side panels together at the seam. Use the Story Barn to retell the story of Jesus teaching about sharing:

1) A rich man had a good crop and he was happy.
2) The man realized he did not have enough room for all his crops.
3) The man decided to build bigger barns to hold all his crops rather than share the extras with others.
4) The man was told he was going to die that night and that he had made a bad choice in storing up things for himself.

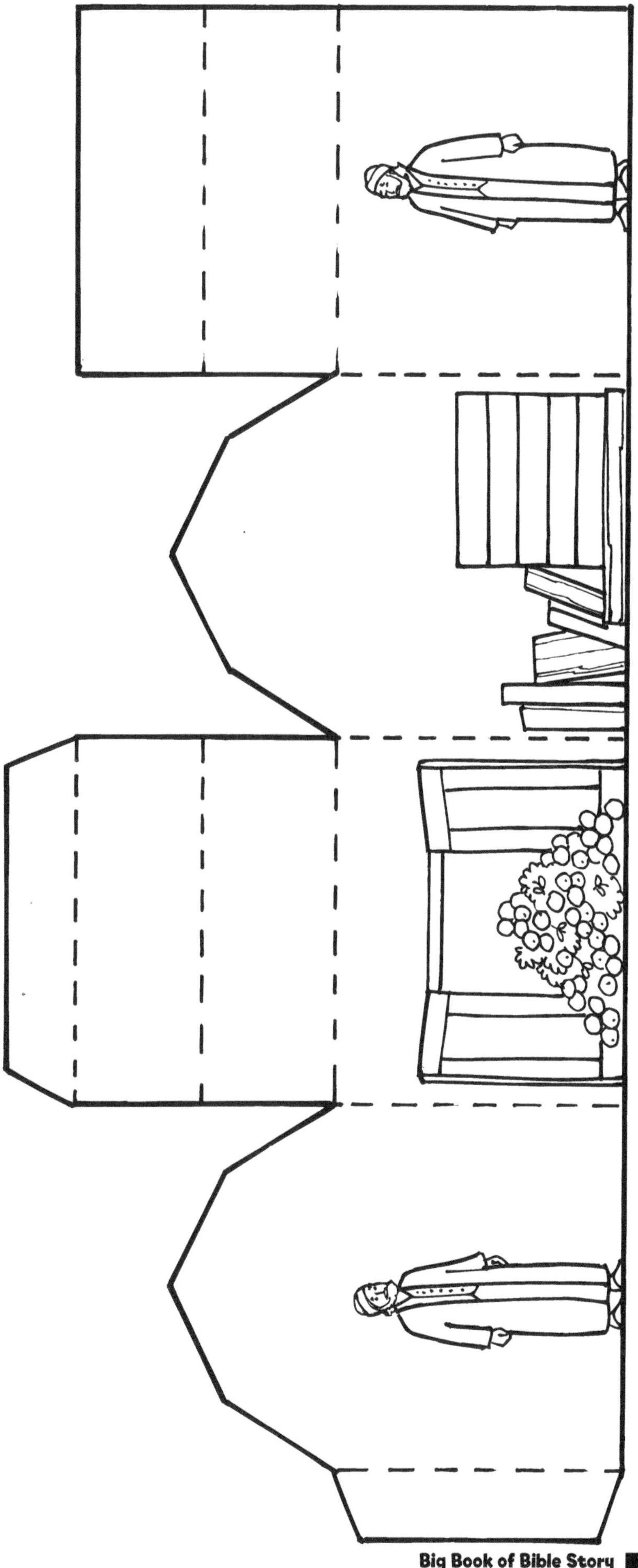

Jesus Brings Lazarus Back to Life

Luke 10; John 11: Jesus Brings Lazarus Back to Life

Lazarus Box

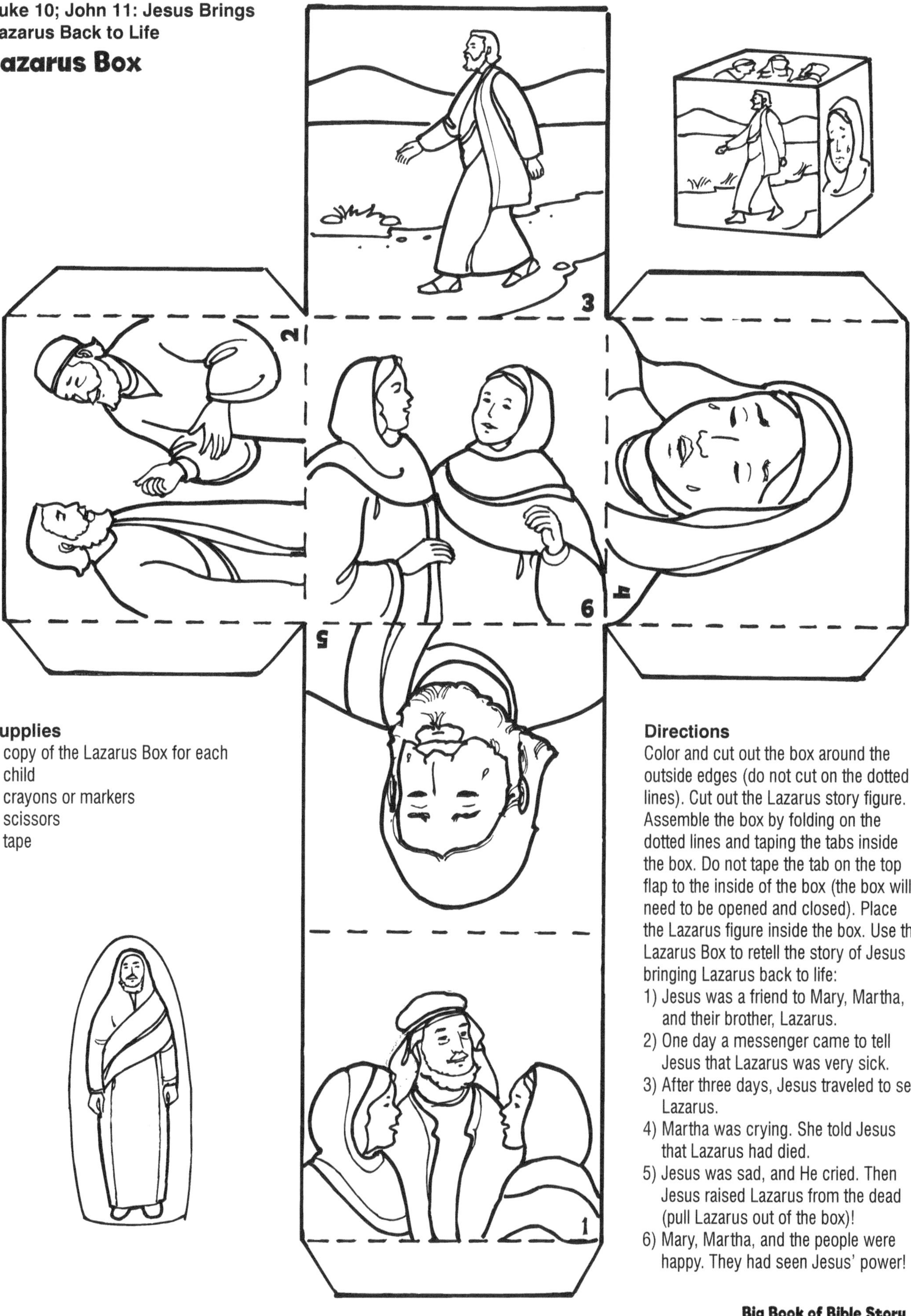

Supplies

- copy of the Lazarus Box for each child
- crayons or markers
- scissors
- tape

Directions

Color and cut out the box around the outside edges (do not cut on the dotted lines). Cut out the Lazarus story figure. Assemble the box by folding on the dotted lines and taping the tabs inside the box. Do not tape the tab on the top flap to the inside of the box (the box will need to be opened and closed). Place the Lazarus figure inside the box. Use the Lazarus Box to retell the story of Jesus bringing Lazarus back to life:

1) Jesus was a friend to Mary, Martha, and their brother, Lazarus.
2) One day a messenger came to tell Jesus that Lazarus was very sick.
3) After three days, Jesus traveled to see Lazarus.
4) Martha was crying. She told Jesus that Lazarus had died.
5) Jesus was sad, and He cried. Then Jesus raised Lazarus from the dead (pull Lazarus out of the box)!
6) Mary, Martha, and the people were happy. They had seen Jesus' power!

Jesus and Ten Men with Leprosy

Luke 17: Jesus and Ten Men with Leprosy

Ten Men Maze

Supplies

- copy of the Ten Men Maze for each child (continued on p. 200)
- crayons or markers (including the colors red, green, and blue for each child)
- tape

Directions

Connect the two sections of the maze by taping them together at the seam. Color the towns and the people in the maze. Use the maze to retell the story of Jesus and ten men with leprosy:

1) Jesus was traveling to Jerusalem. As He was entering a village, ten men with leprosy called out asking for help. (Trace a red path from Jesus to the ten men outside the village.)
2) Jesus told the ten men to go and show themselves to a priest, and as they went they were healed. (Trace a green path leading the ten men from the village toward the priest.)
3) Jesus continued on His path, but one of the men came back to Jesus and thanked Him. (Trace a red path from Jesus at the village to the place where one man is thanking Him. Trace a blue path leading one man from the group with the priest to the place where he is thanking Jesus.)
4) Jesus asked the man where the rest were. Jesus told the man who came back that it was his faith that had healed him. Jesus continued on His way. (Trace a red path from Jesus with the one man to the city of Jerusalem.)

Jesus and the Children

Mark 10: Jesus and the Children

Jesus and the Children Flip-Flap Book

Supplies

- copy of the Jesus and the Children Flip-Flap Book for each child
- crayons or markers
- construction paper (1 sheet per child, any color)
- scissors
- glue

Directions

Color and cut out each of the four scenes. Fold a piece of construction paper in half lengthwise. Lay the folded paper in front of you horizontally and cut the top half into four equal sections, stopping at the fold line (see the example). Each flap should be about 3" wide. Attach the four scenes in order under each of the four flaps so a scene appears when each flap is lifted (see the example). Write the words "Jesus and the Children" on the front of the flaps, one word per flap. Use the flip-flap book to retell the story of how Jesus showed love to the children:

1) People were bringing their children to Jesus.
2) Jesus' followers told the people to leave Jesus alone.
3) Jesus corrected His followers and said they should let the children to come to Him.
4) Jesus took the children in His arms and He blessed them. Jesus said people who wanted to be part of God's kingdom should be like a child.

Jesus and Zacchaeus

Luke 19: Jesus and Zacchaeus

Jesus and Zacchaeus Puppets

Supplies

- copy of the Jesus and Zacchaeus Puppet faces for each child
- brown paper lunch bags (2 per child)
- crayons or markers
- scissors
- glue

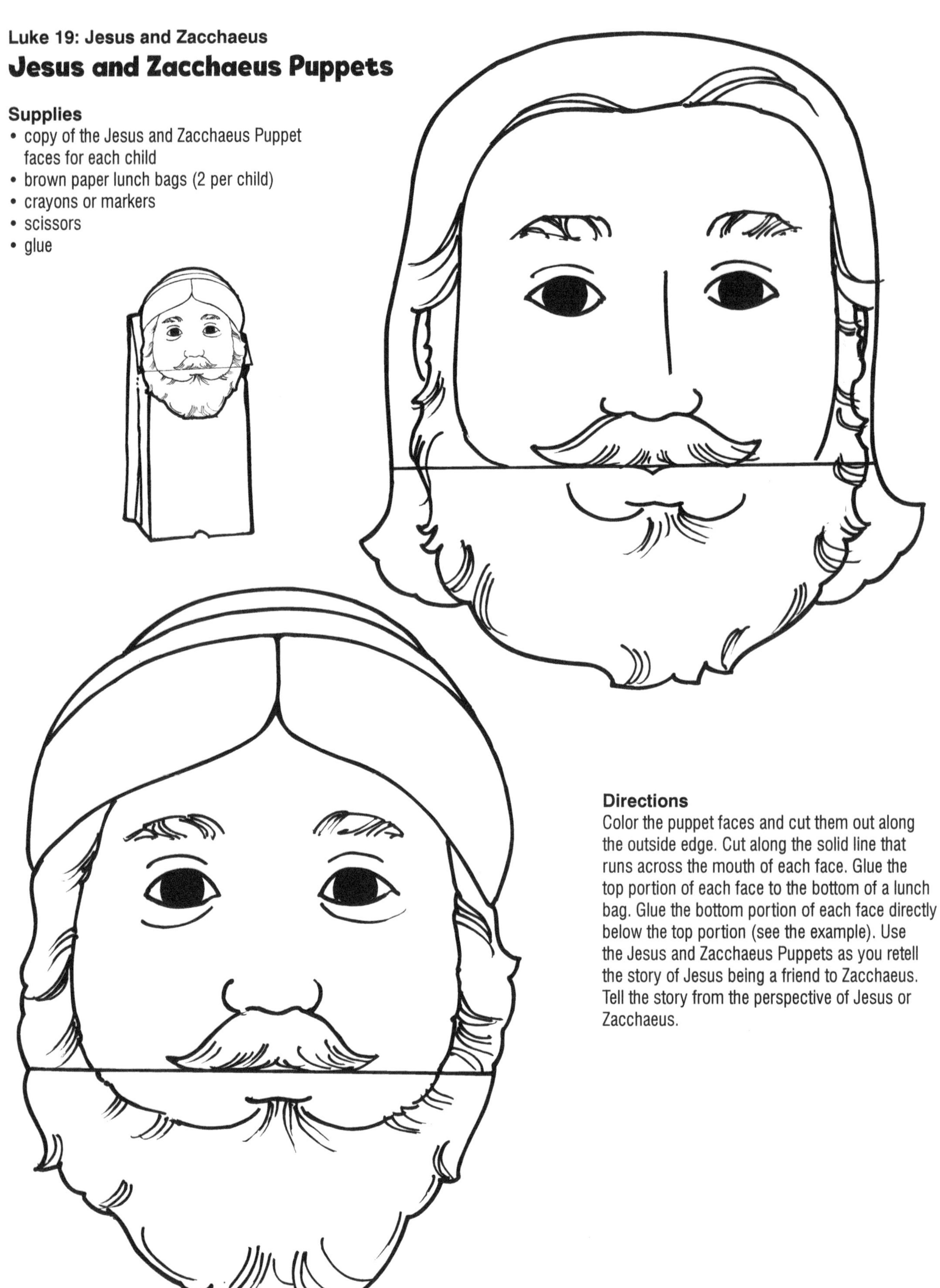

Directions

Color the puppet faces and cut them out along the outside edge. Cut along the solid line that runs across the mouth of each face. Glue the top portion of each face to the bottom of a lunch bag. Glue the bottom portion of each face directly below the top portion (see the example). Use the Jesus and Zacchaeus Puppets as you retell the story of Jesus being a friend to Zacchaeus. Tell the story from the perspective of Jesus or Zacchaeus.

People Praise Jesus

Matthew 21; John 12: People Praise Jesus

Praise Pamphlet

Supplies

- copy of the Praise Pamphlet for each child
- crayons or markers
- scissors

Directions

Color and cut out the Praise Pamphlet as one piece (do not cut along the dotted lines). Fold the pamphlet in half so the scenes are back-to-back with three scenes on each side. Lay the pamphlet down so scenes 1, 2, and 3 are facing up. Fold the right side of the pamphlet in so scene 4 covers scene 2. Fold the left side of the pamphlet in so only the cover is showing. Use the Praise Pamphlet to retell the story of people praising Jesus as He rode into Jerusalem:

1) Jesus and His followers were going to Jerusalem. A young donkey was found for Jesus to ride as He entered Jerusalem (open the cover and show scenes 1 and 4 together).
2) Jesus rode into Jerusalem on the colt while people praised Him and cheered (open scene 4 to show scenes 1, 2, and 3).

People Praise Jesus

4

1

2

3

The Last Week

Matthew 21, 27; Luke 19–22:
The Last Week

Last Supper Slide Show

Supplies

- copy of the Last Supper Slide Show (preferably on card stock) for each child
- crayons or markers
- scissors
- glue

Directions

Color the house and four story scenes. Cut out the story scenes along the outside border (do not cut apart each individual scene). Cut out the house around the outside edge. Cut two slits in the window of the house where indicated by the bold, vertical lines on either side of the window. Slide the scenes through the slits in the window (as shown in the example) as you retell the story of one of the main events that took place during the week before Jesus' death:

1) Jesus told two of His disciples to follow a man carrying water to a house and ask the owner of that house for a room where they could eat the Passover meal.
2) Jesus' disciples prepared the meal.
3) During the meal, Jesus took some bread and broke it into pieces. Jesus said the bread represented His body that was going to be given for them. He told them to remember Him as they ate the bread.
4) At the meal, Jesus took a cup and told His followers they should drink from it. The drink represented Jesus' blood and the forgiveness He gives to all who follow and obey Him.

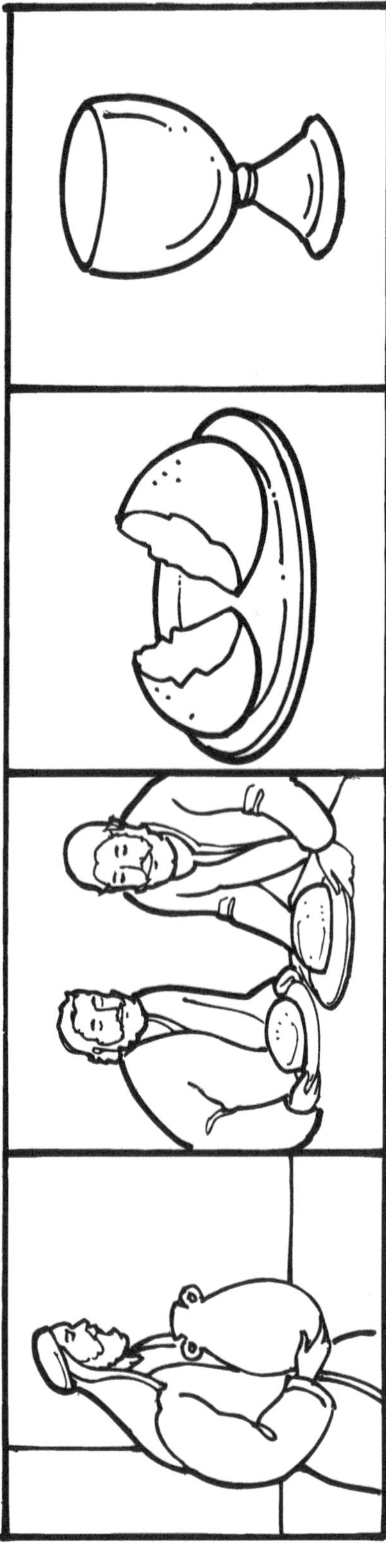

Jesus Dies and Lives Again

John 18–20: Jesus Dies and Lives Again

Jesus Lives Story Wheel

Supplies

- copy of the Jesus Lives Story Wheel for each child
- copy of the Story Wheel Cover (p. 243) for each child
- crayons or markers
- scissors
- hole punch
- paper fasteners (1 per child)

Directions

Color the scenes on the story wheel. Cut out the wheel around the outside edge. On the Story Wheel Cover, write: "Jesus Dies and Lives Again." Then color the rest of the cover gray to look like a stone. Place the wheel cover on top of the story wheel and punch a hole through the center of both the cover and the wheel. Use a paper fastener to loosely attach the cover to the wheel. Rotate the cover to reveal each section as you retell the story of Jesus' death and resurrection:

1) Jesus died on a cross.
2) Jesus' body was placed in a tomb, and a stone was rolled over the entrance.
3) Mary Magdalene came to the tomb. When she saw that it was open, she ran to tell the disciples.
4) Peter and John ran to the tomb to see if what Mary said was true. They saw the tomb was empty.
5) Jesus appeared to Mary Magdalene at the empty tomb and told her not to cry. He was going to return to His Father.

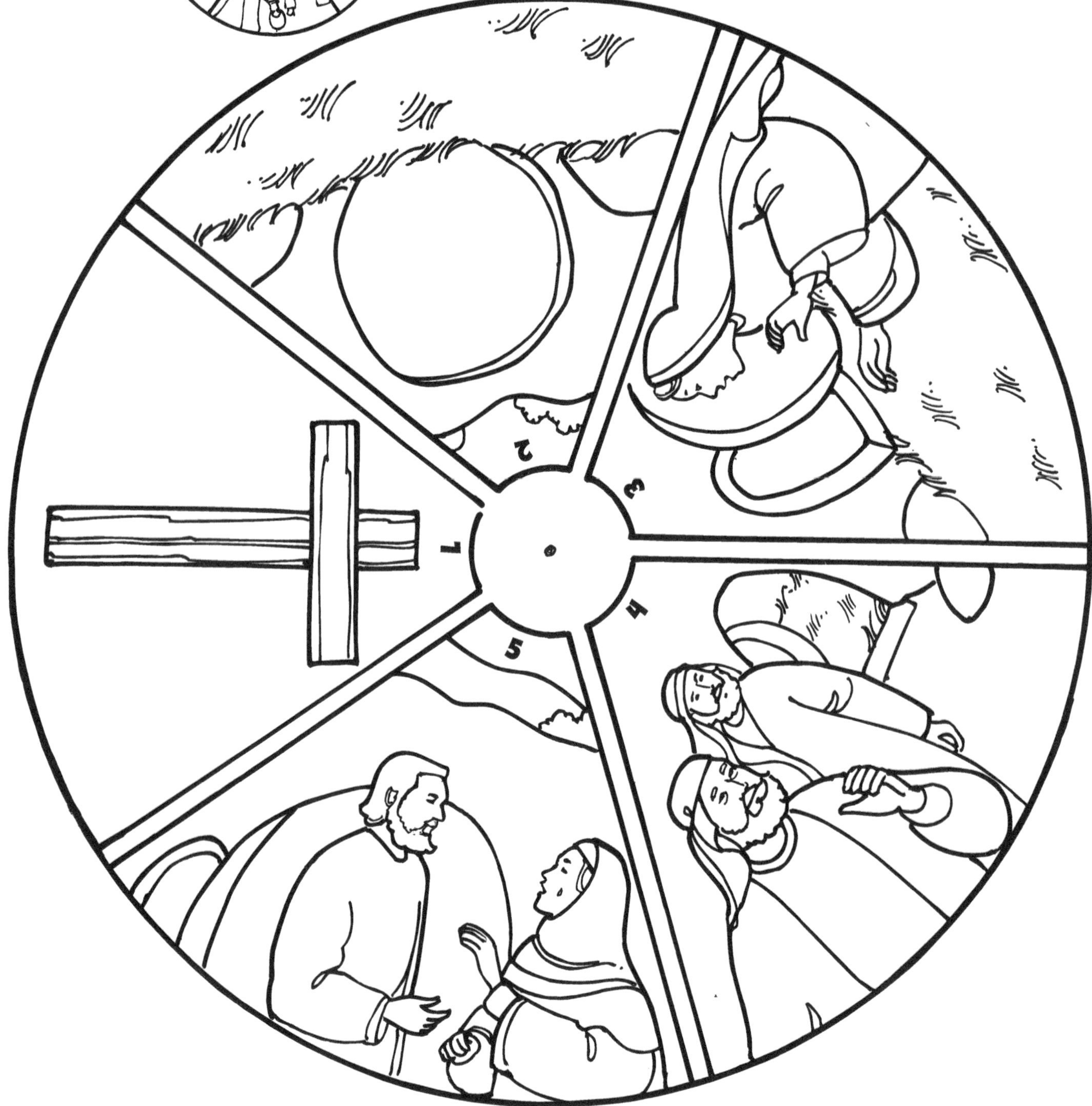

Jesus Is Alive

Matthew 26–28: Jesus Is Alive

Jesus Is Alive Smush Book

See page 7 for supplies and directions for this activity.
Use the book to tell how Jesus showed His power over death.

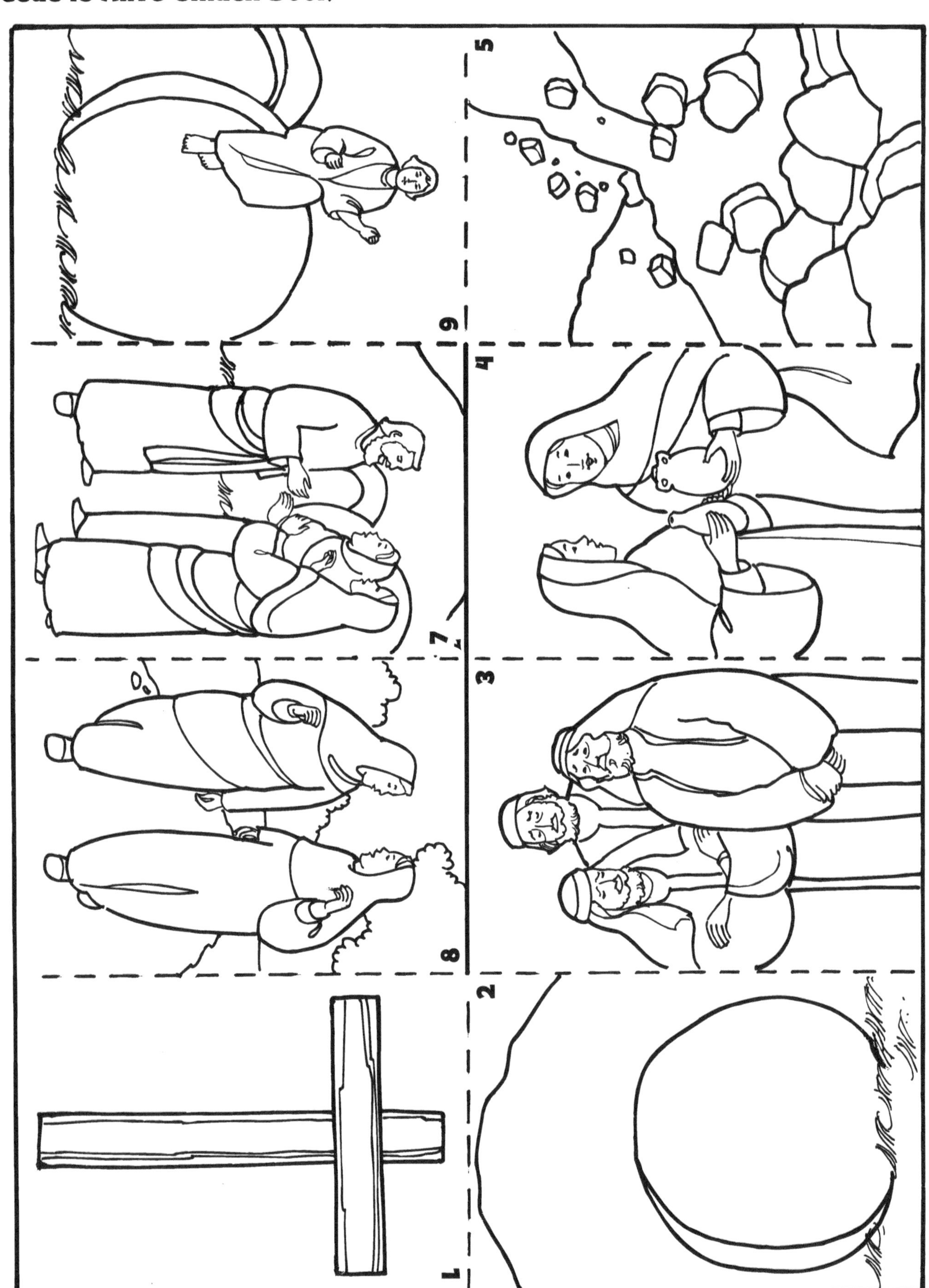

Jesus Appears and Returns to Heaven

Mark 16; Luke 24; John 20–21: Jesus Appears and Returns to Heaven

Ascension Pop-Up Card

Supplies

- copy of the Ascension Pop-Up Card for each child
- crayons or markers
- scissors

Directions

Color and cut out the pop-up card. Fold the card in half along the horizontal dotted line so the scenes are back-to-back. Fold the center piece down along the dotted line and fold the card in half so the pop-up piece is folded inside. Use the Ascension Pop-Up Card to retell the story of what happened after Jesus came back to life:

1) The day Jesus came back to life, He appeared to two men who were walking from Jerusalem to Emmaus.
2) Jesus appeared more times to many of His followers.
3) One day Jesus walked with His followers outside a village. He talked to His disciples. Then Jesus was taken up to heaven. The disciples knew Jesus is the Son of God.

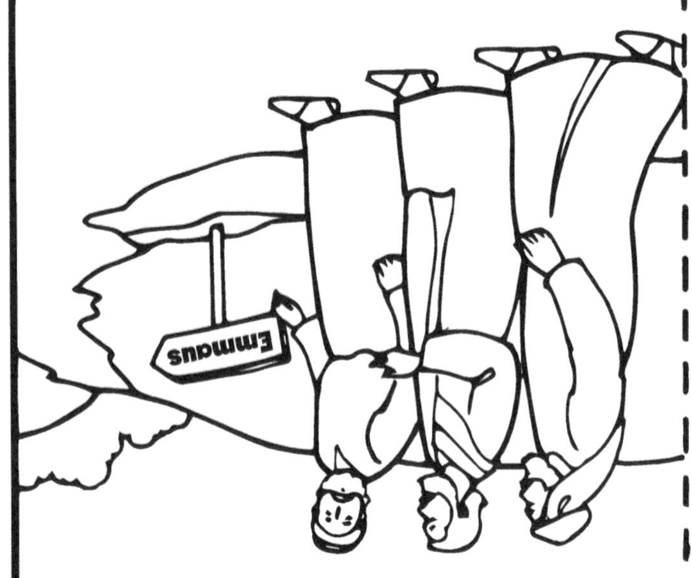

We can tell others that Jesus is alive!

Peter Preaches about Jesus

Acts 1–2: Peter Preaches about Jesus

Peter Tells about Jesus Book

Supplies

- copy of the Peter Tells about Jesus Book for each child
- crayons or markers
- scissors

Directions

Color and cut out the Peter Tells about Jesus Book and fold along the dotted line so scenes 1 and 4 are behind scenes 2 and 3. Fold the book in half again so scene 1 shows on the front and scene 4 is on the back. Use the Peter Tells about Jesus Book to retell the story of what happened when Peter told a large crowd about Jesus:

1) The disciples were gathered on the Day of Pentecost. A sound like a blowing wind filled the house where they were, and what looked like tongues of fire came to rest on each of them.
2) A crowd gathered because people from all different nations heard the disciples speaking in their own languages.
3) Peter stood up and spoke to the crowd. They asked what they should do to be saved.
4) Peter told the crowd, "Repent and be baptized … in the name of Jesus Christ for the forgiveness of your sins. And you will receive the gift of the Holy Spirit" (Acts 2:38).

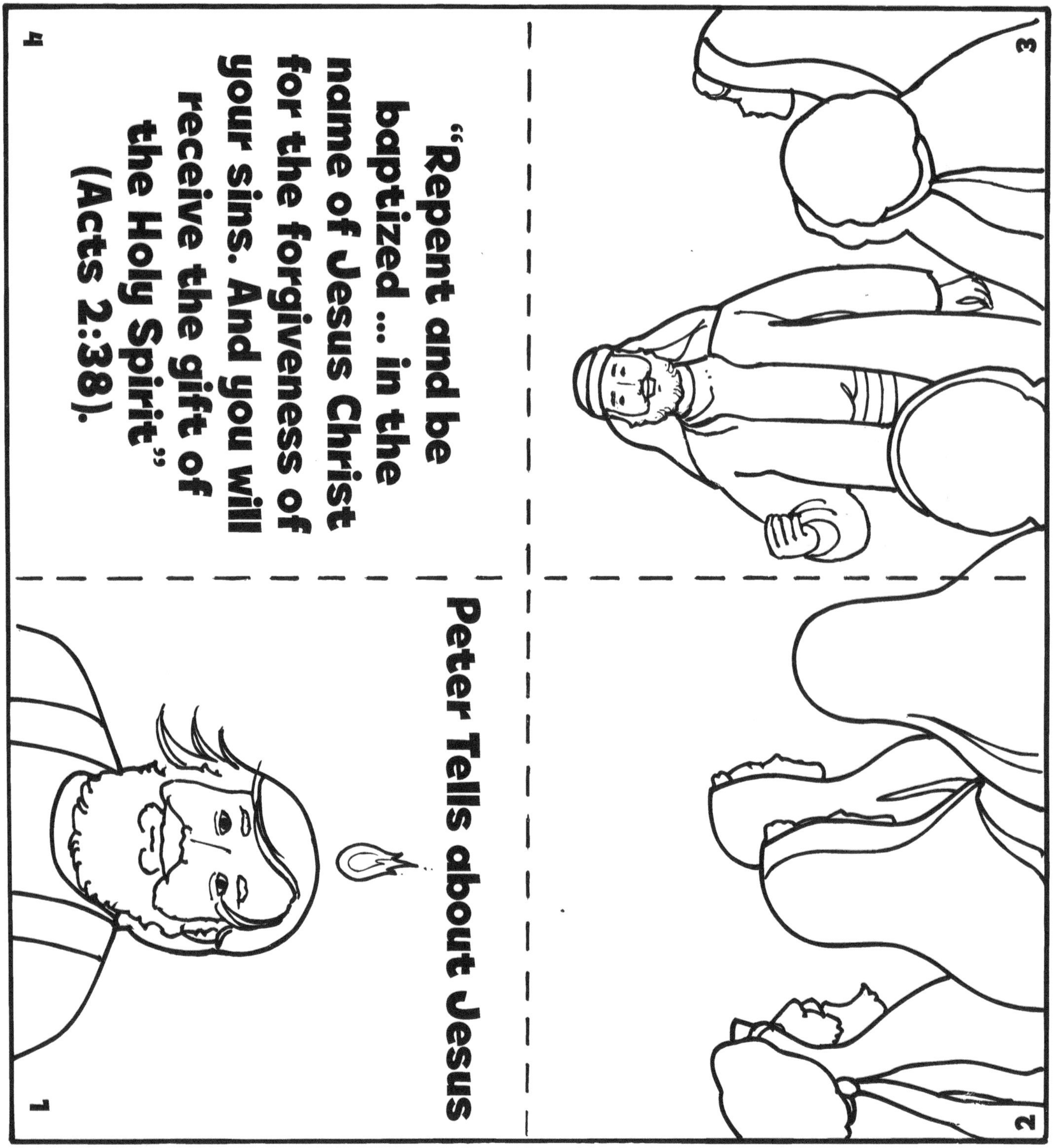

4

"Repent and be baptized … in the name of Jesus Christ for the forgiveness of your sins. And you will receive the gift of the Holy Spirit" (Acts 2:38).

3

1

Peter Tells about Jesus

2

Peter and John at the Temple

Acts 3–4: Peter and John at the Temple

Temple Gate Puzzle

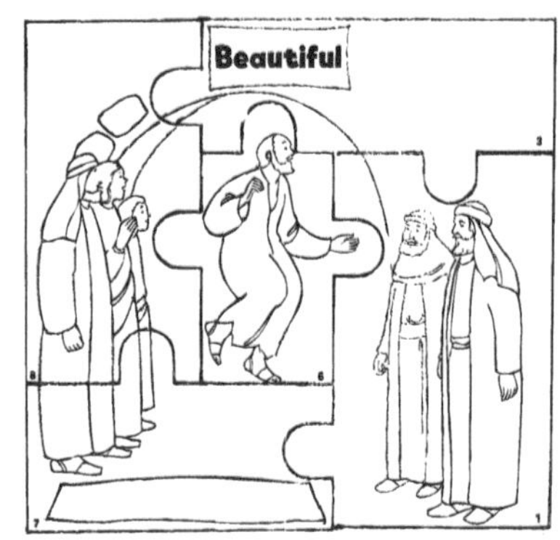

Supplies

- copy of the Temple Gate Puzzle (preferably on white card stock) for each child (continued on p. 219)
- crayons or markers
- scissors

Directions

Color and cut out the Temple Gate Puzzle pieces. Assemble pieces 1 through 5 as you retell the first half of the story of Peter and John at the temple:

1) Peter and John were going to the temple (piece 1).
2) On their way, they saw a man who could not walk being brought to the temple gate called Beautiful (add pieces 2 and 3).
3) The man asked Peter and John for money (add piece 4).
4) Peter said he did not have money to give the man but instead told him to get up and walk in the name of Jesus (add piece 5).

Remove pieces 2, 4, and 5 and replace them with pieces 6, 7, and 8 as you finish the story.

5) The man jumped to his feet (replace pieces 4 and 5 with pieces 6 and 7).
6) The people were amazed at what had happened (replace piece 2 with piece 8).

(See the examples of the two finished puzzles for reference.)

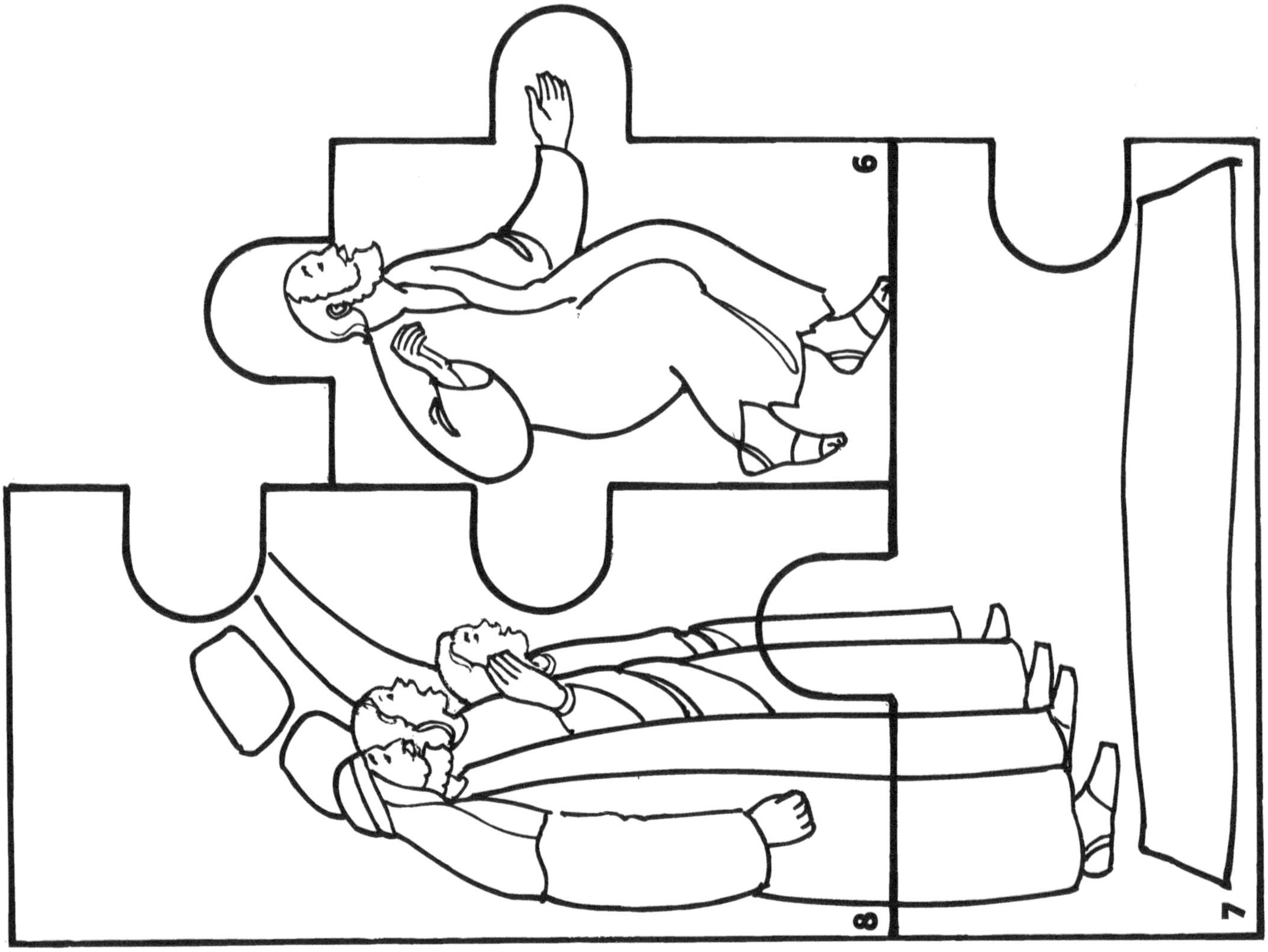

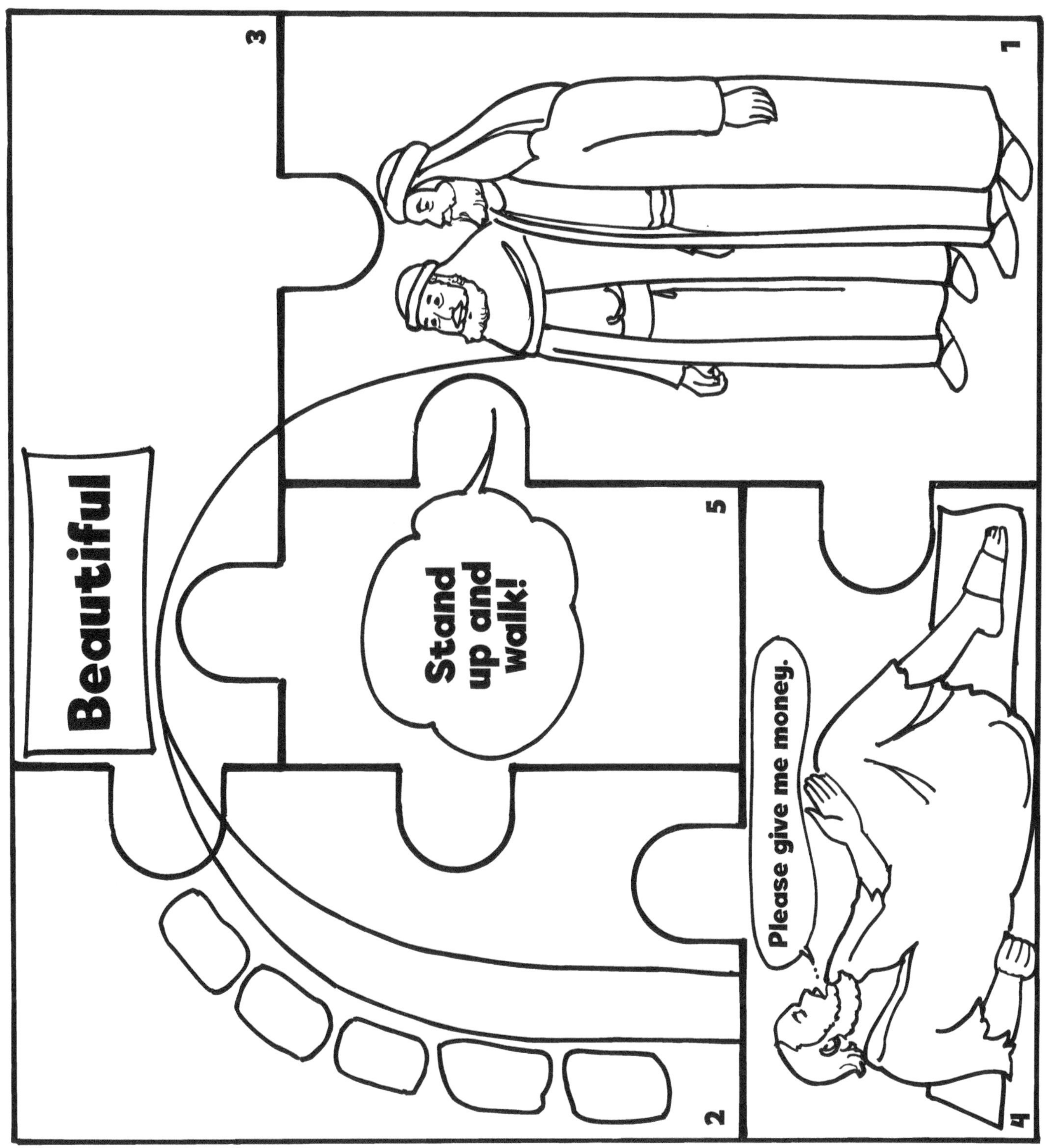
Beautiful
3
1
5
Stand up and walk!
Please give me money.
2
4

Peter and John Speak Boldly

Acts 4: Peter and John Speak Boldly

Speak Boldly Stand-Up Figures

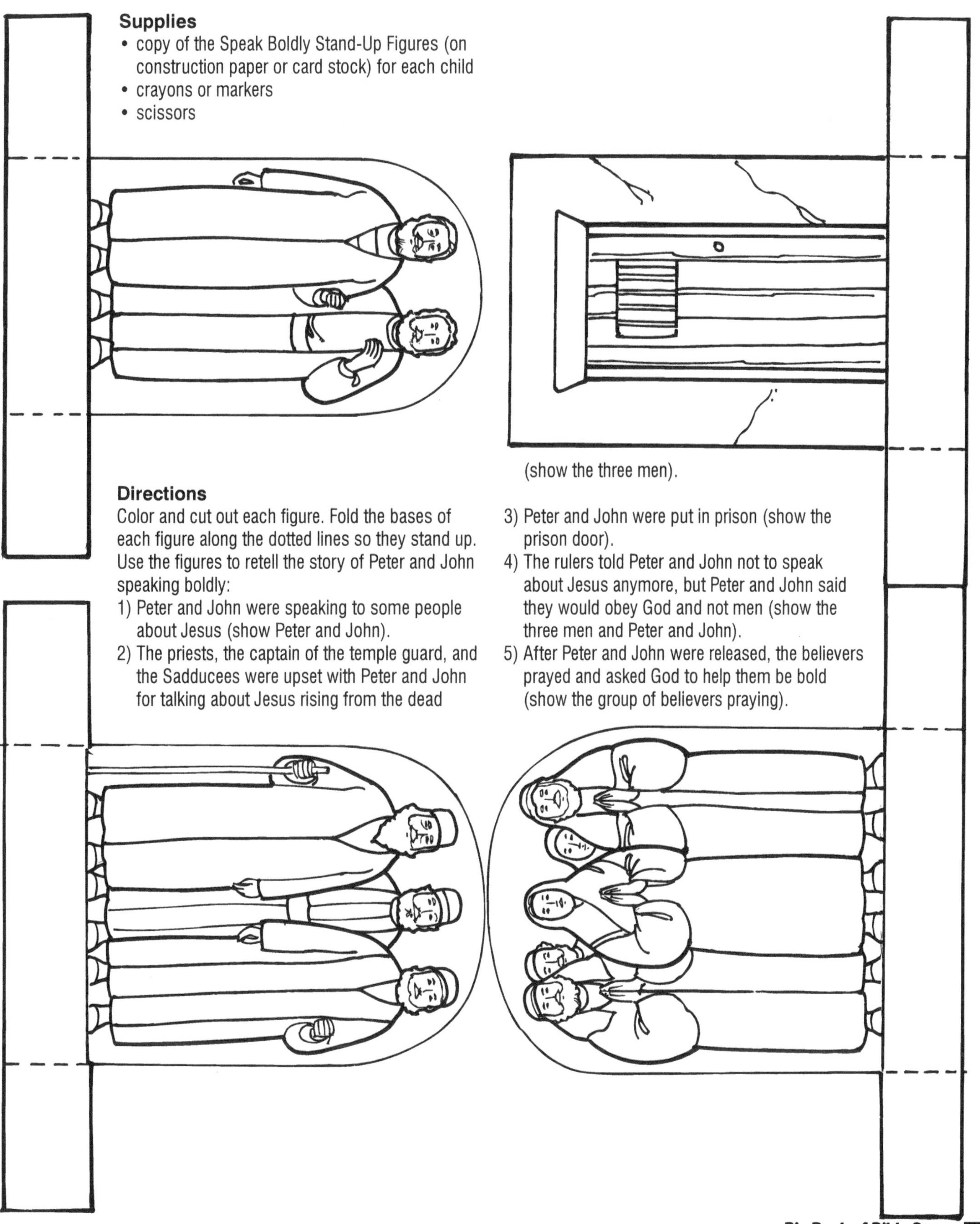

Supplies

- copy of the Speak Boldly Stand-Up Figures (on construction paper or card stock) for each child
- crayons or markers
- scissors

Directions

Color and cut out each figure. Fold the bases of each figure along the dotted lines so they stand up. Use the figures to retell the story of Peter and John speaking boldly:

1) Peter and John were speaking to some people about Jesus (show Peter and John).
2) The priests, the captain of the temple guard, and the Sadducees were upset with Peter and John for talking about Jesus rising from the dead (show the three men).
3) Peter and John were put in prison (show the prison door).
4) The rulers told Peter and John not to speak about Jesus anymore, but Peter and John said they would obey God and not men (show the three men and Peter and John).
5) After Peter and John were released, the believers prayed and asked God to help them be bold (show the group of believers praying).

Philip Teaches a Man from Ethiopia

Acts 8: Philip Teaches a Man from Ethiopia

Story Scroll

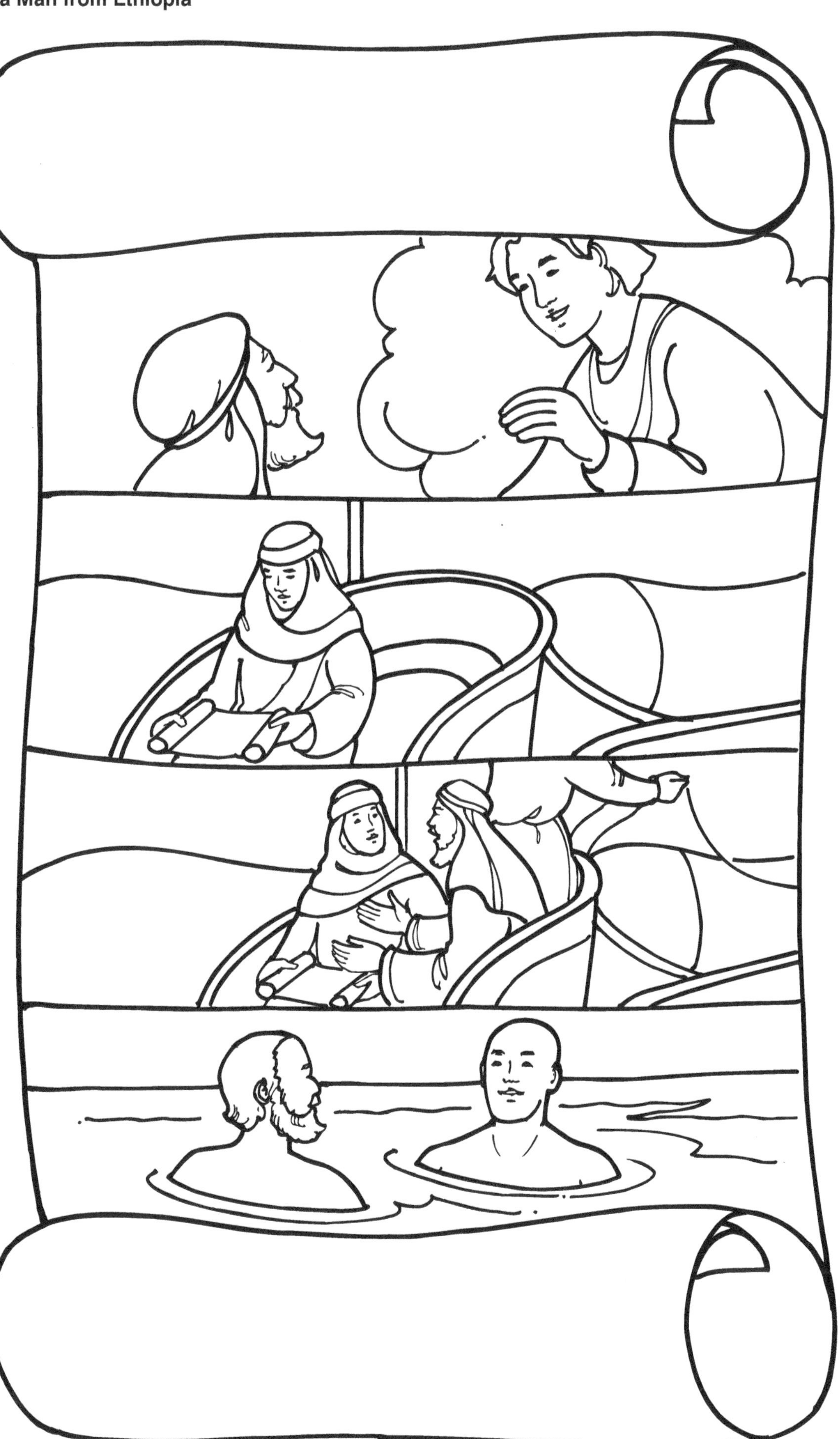

Supplies

- copy of the Story Scroll for each child
- crayons or markers
- scissors
- decorative ribbon

Directions

Color and cut out the scroll as one piece. Roll up the scroll and tie it with ribbon at the center. Unroll the scroll and use it to retell the story of Philip teaching a man from Ethiopia:

1) An angel told Philip to go to the desert road that went from Jerusalem to Gaza.
2) On his way, Philip saw an Ethiopian who was sitting in a chariot and reading from the book of Isaiah. The man did not understand what he was reading.
3) Philip explained the Scripture to the man and told him about Jesus.
4) The Ethiopian wanted to be baptized, so Philip baptized him in some water that was nearby.

Peter and Tabitha

Acts 9: Peter and Tabitha

Peter and Tabitha 3-D Scene

Supplies

- copy of the Peter and Tabitha 3-D Scene pieces (preferably on card stock) for each child
- crayons or markers
- scissors
- glue
- construction paper (any color)

Directions

Color and cut out the 3-D pieces. Fold a sheet of construction paper in half widthwise. Color the top half of the construction paper to look like a bedroom (see the example). Fold the bases of each figure back on the dotted line. Glue the bases to the bottom half of the construction paper (see the example). Lay the pieces down and fold them up one at a time as you retell the story of Peter and Tabitha:

1) Peter was called to come to Joppa because a disciple named Tabitha had died.
2) Peter was taken to an upstairs room. The widows were crying (show Peter, the crying widows, and Tabitha lying on the bed).
3) Peter sent everyone out of the room and prayed. He told Tabitha to get up. She opened her eyes and Peter helped her up (show Peter with Tabitha now standing).
4) Peter showed Tabitha to the widows, and they were very happy (show Peter, Tabitha, and the happy widows).

Paul Begins to Follow Jesus

Acts 9, 22: Paul Begins to Follow Jesus

Paul and Friends Finger Puppets

Supplies

- copy of the Paul and Friends Finger Puppets for each child
- crayons or markers
- scissors
- tape

Directions

Color and cut out each of the four finger puppets. Wrap the puppet bases and attach them using tape so each one can be worn as a finger puppet. Place the puppets on separate fingers in the following order: Angry Paul (pointer finger, right hand), High Priest (center finger, right hand), Ananias (pointer finger, left hand), Joyful Paul (center finger, left hand). Use the finger puppets to retell the story of Paul learning about Jesus:

1) Paul did not like Christians (show Angry Paul).
2) Paul asked the high priest for permission to go to Damascus to arrest Christians (add the High Priest).
3) Jesus blinded Paul by a bright light on the way, and Paul waited in Damascus until Ananias came to see him. Ananias came to tell Paul about Jesus (remove High Priest; add Ananias).
4) Paul believed in Jesus and was able to see again. He joyfully told others about Jesus (remove Angry Paul; add Joyful Paul).

Paul and Barnabas Help Others Learn about Jesus

Acts 11, 13: Paul and Barnabas Help Others Learn about Jesus

Go-and-Tell Sandals

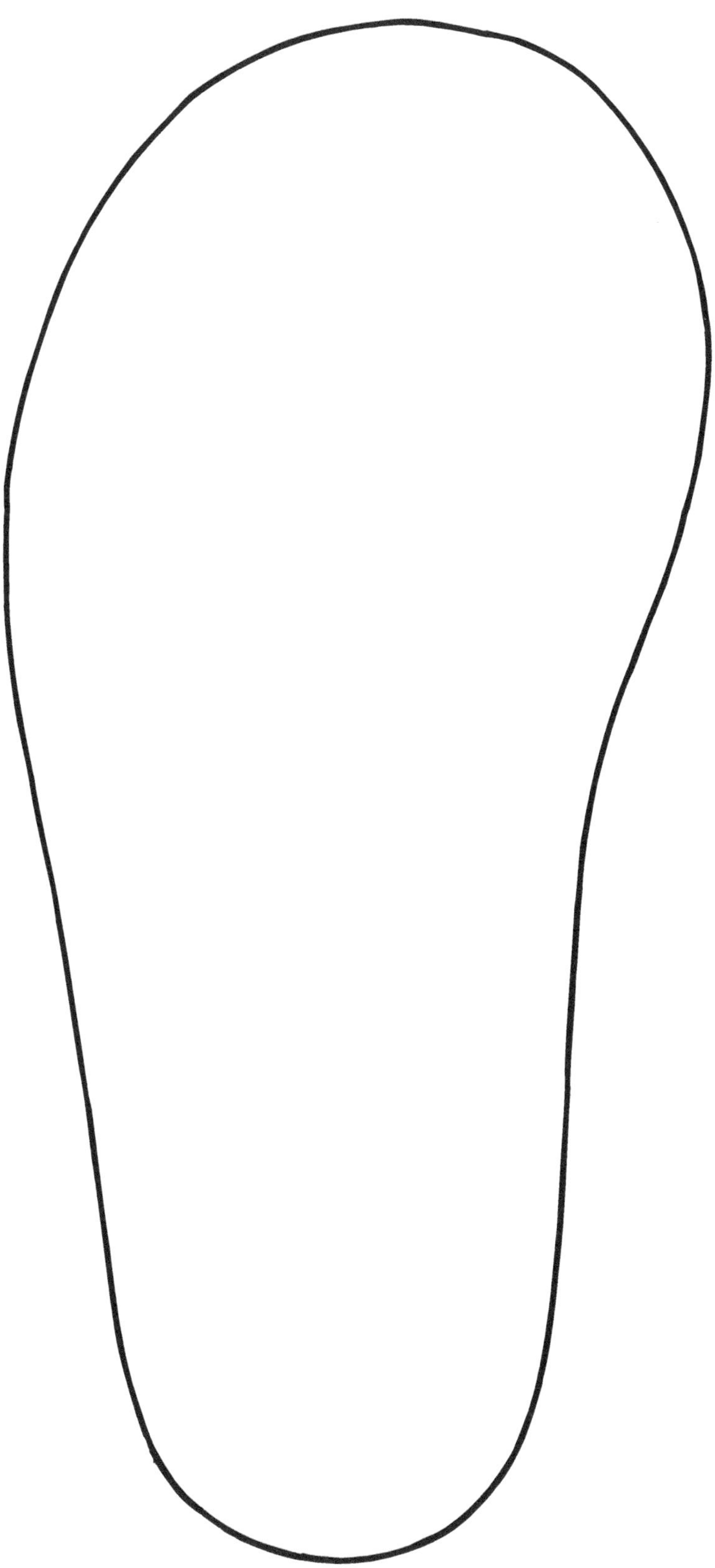

Supplies

- copy of the Go-and-Tell Sandal pattern for each child
- white card stock (3 sheets per child)
- crayons or markers
- scissors
- stapler
- tape
- construction paper
- glitter and glue

Directions

Cut out the sandal pattern. Trace the pattern twice on one sheet of card stock. Turn the pattern over, and trace it twice more on another sheet of card stock. Now you have two right sandals and two left sandals. Cut them out. Cut four strips of card stock for the straps—each approximately 8" long and $1^1/_2$" wide. Color the soles and straps. One pair of sandals should be plain (for Paul or Barnabas), and the other should have nicely decorated straps (for Sergius Paulus or his friend Elymas, to show they were important men). Wrap the straps of the sandals around the top of the soles, leaving enough room to place your feet under the straps. Staple the straps to the bottom of the soles (smooth side of the staple against your foot). Cover the ends of the staples with tape (on the bottom of the soles). Write the words "Antioch" and "Cyprus" on separate pieces of construction paper. Wear the sandals as you travel from Antioch to Cyprus to share the good news about Jesus. You can pretend to be Paul and Barnabas (wearing the plain sandals) telling others about Jesus, or pretend to be Sergius Paulus or his friend Elymas as you hear about Jesus. Encourage kids to participate as they act out the story. Remind them that Elymas tried to convince Sergius not to listen to Paul and Barnabas.

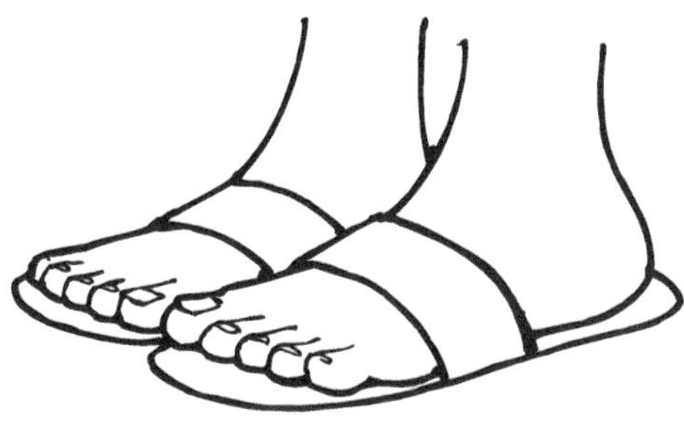

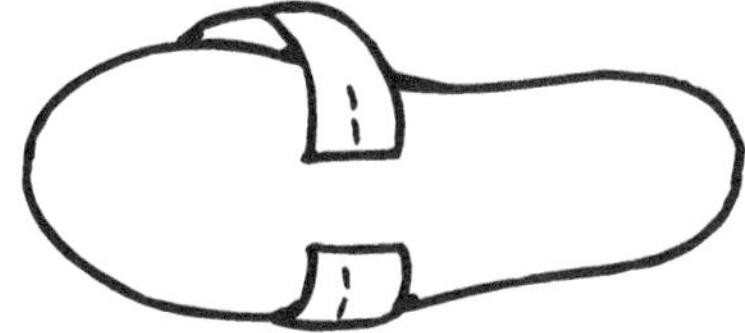

Paul and Barnabas Tell about the Living God

Acts 14: Paul and Barnabas Tell about the Living God

Paul and Barnabas Stand-Up Figures

Supplies

- copy of the Paul and Barnabas Stand-Up Figures (preferably on card stock) for each child
- crayons or markers
- scissors

Directions

Color and cut out each figure. Fold the base of each figure along the dotted lines so they stand up. Use the figures to retell the story of Paul and Barnabas helping people know about the living God:

1) Paul and Barnabas told people in Lystra about Jesus (show Paul and Barnabas).
2) A man who couldn't walk was listening (show the man sitting on the ground).
3) Paul knew the man believed in Jesus. Paul told him to stand up. The man jumped up and began to walk (show the man walking).
4) The people in the crowd were amazed and thought Paul and Barnabas were gods (show the amazed crowd).
5) Paul and Barnabas said they were humans, not gods. Then they told the crowd about the true and living God (show Paul and Barnabas speaking to the amazed crowd).

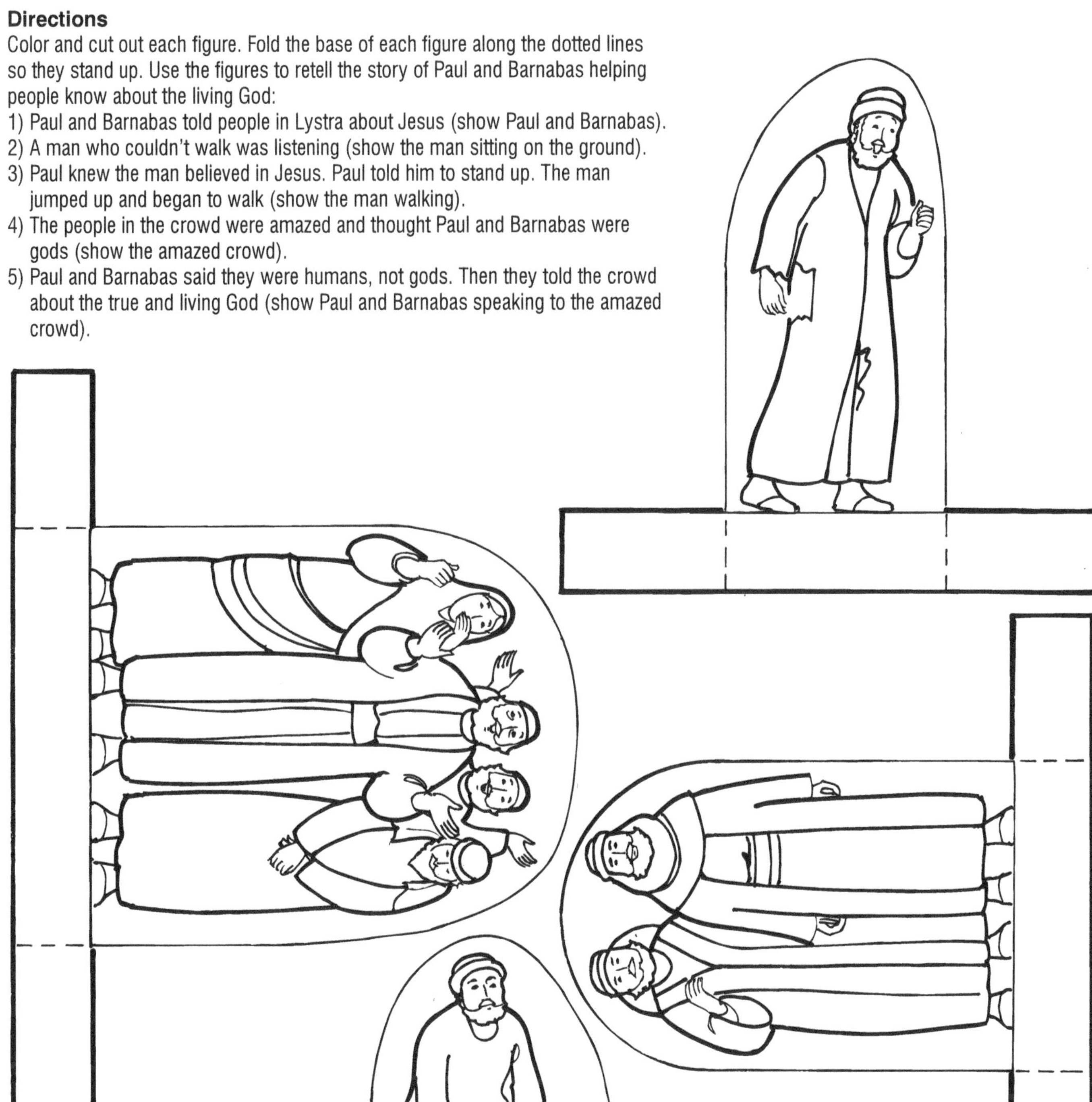

Lydia Learns to Follow Jesus

Acts 16: Lydia Learns to Follow Jesus

Lydia Matching Game

Supplies

- copy of the memory cards and game spinner (preferably on card stock) for each child (continued on p. 234)
- paper fasteners (1 per child)
- crayons or markers
- scissors
- hole punch

Directions

Color and cut out the ten memory cards and game spinner. Assemble the spinner by punching a hole in the square and in the arrow where indicated by the open circles. Using a paper fastener, attach the arrow to the spinner square. (Attach it loosely so it will easily spin.) In teams of two, play a game of memory using the cards and spinner. Turn the cards upside down (20 cards total; ten for each player). Spin the arrow to see how many cards you may turn over. To win, you must collect one of each card in order per the numbers on the cards. (Example: If the spinner stops on the number 2, turn over any two cards. If neither card is number 1, you must turn both cards back over and the other player spins. On your next turn, try again to find card number 1. Once you've found the first card, you may move on to trying to find the second card on your next turn.) The game is over when one player has collected a full set of all ten cards in order.

Using the cards collected (and in the correct order), the winner should retell the story of Lydia learning to follow Jesus:

1) Paul and
2) Silas were in
3) Philippi.
4) They went to the river to pray.
5) They found a group women who were praying.
6) Lydia was one of the women.
7) Lydia sold purple cloth.
8) Lydia and her family believed what Paul said about Jesus.
9) Lydia and her family were baptized.
10) Lydia invited Paul and Silas to stay at her house in Philippi while they taught others about Jesus.

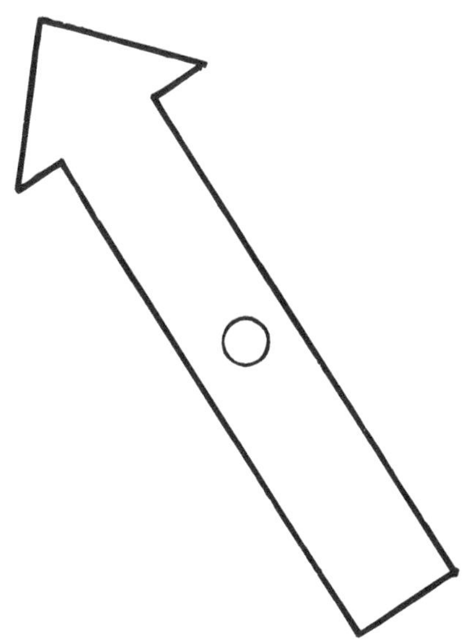

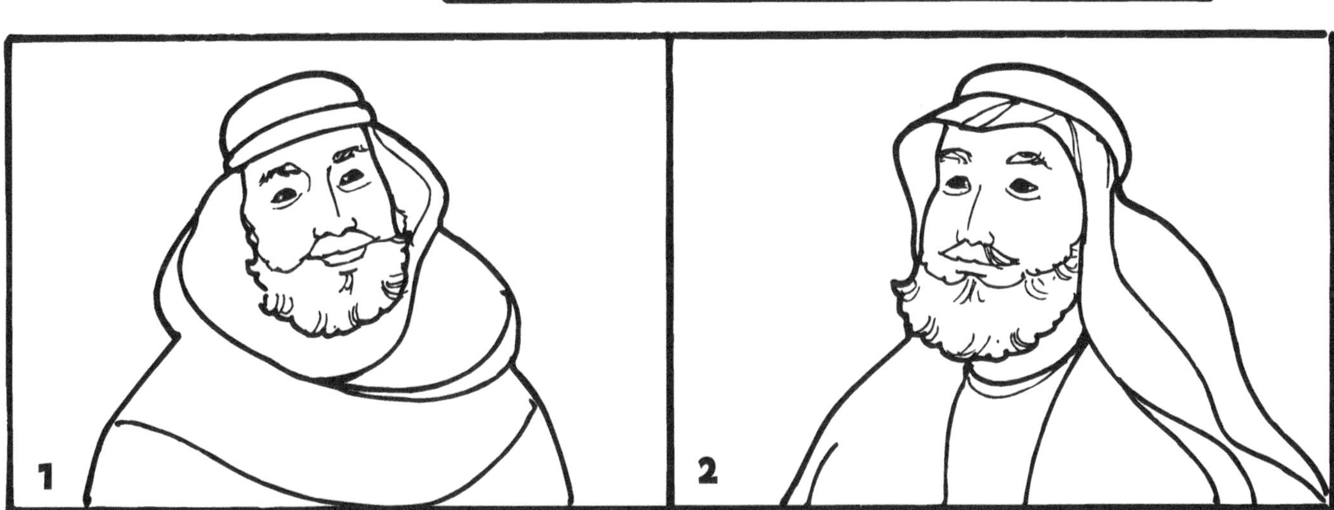

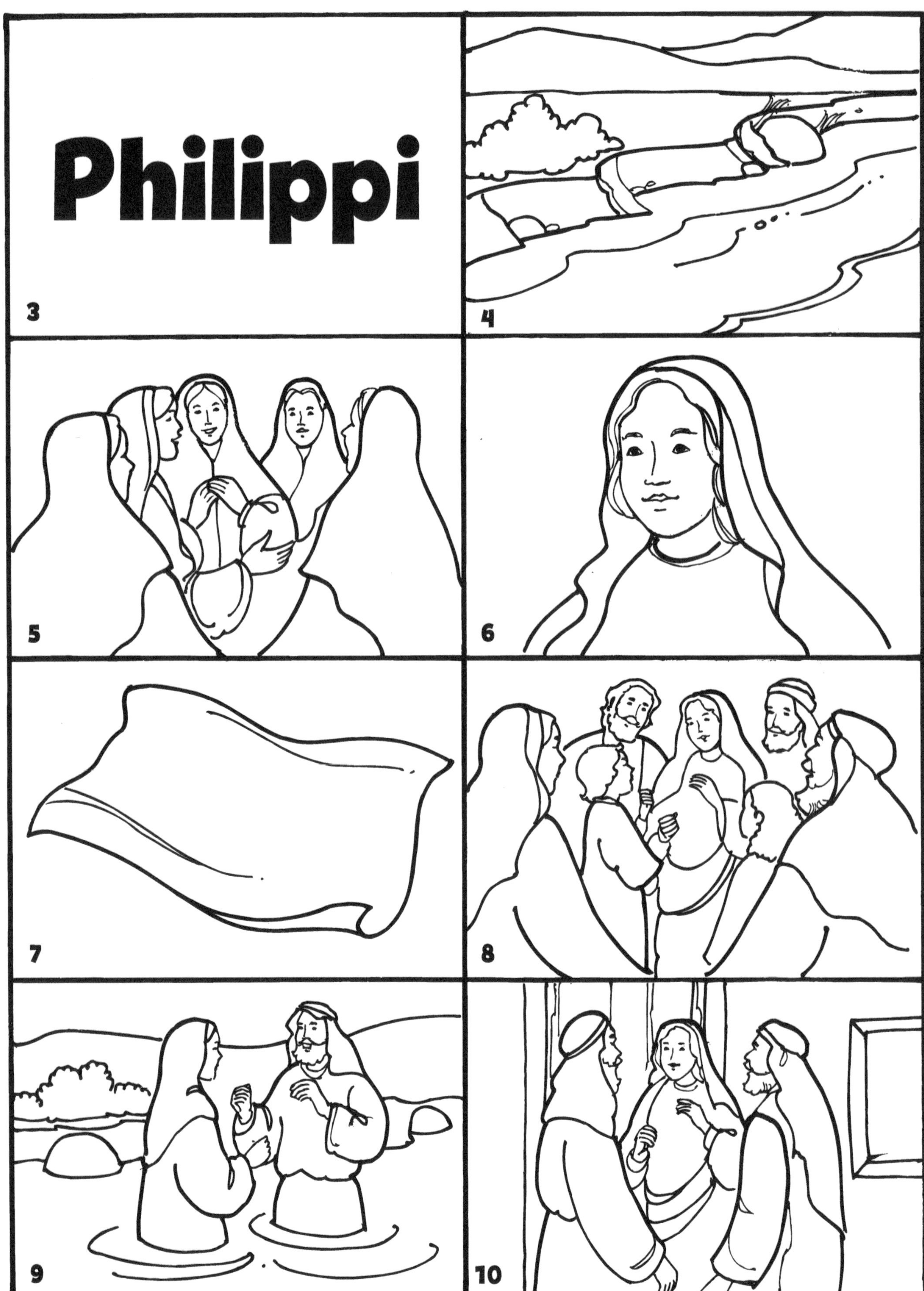
Philippi
3
4
5
6
7
8
9
10

Paul and Silas Sing in Prison

Acts 16: Paul and Silas Sing in Prison

Prison Puzzle

Supplies

- copy of the Prison Puzzle (on card stock) for each child
- crayons or markers
- scissors

Directions

Color and cut out the puzzle pieces. Use the Prison Puzzle to retell the story of Paul and Silas in prison:

1) Paul and Silas healed a young slave girl, but her owners were very angry. They said things about Paul and Silas that made others angry too.
2) Paul and Silas were thrown into prison.
3) Paul and Silas sang songs to God in prison. God sent an earthquake that opened the door and broke their chains.
4) The jailer was frightened because the earthquake freed the prisoners. He was afraid he would get into trouble.
5) Paul explained that the jailer should not be afraid, because the prisoners were all there. The jailer asked Paul about Jesus.
6) The jailer believed what Paul said about Jesus. He and his family were baptized that night.

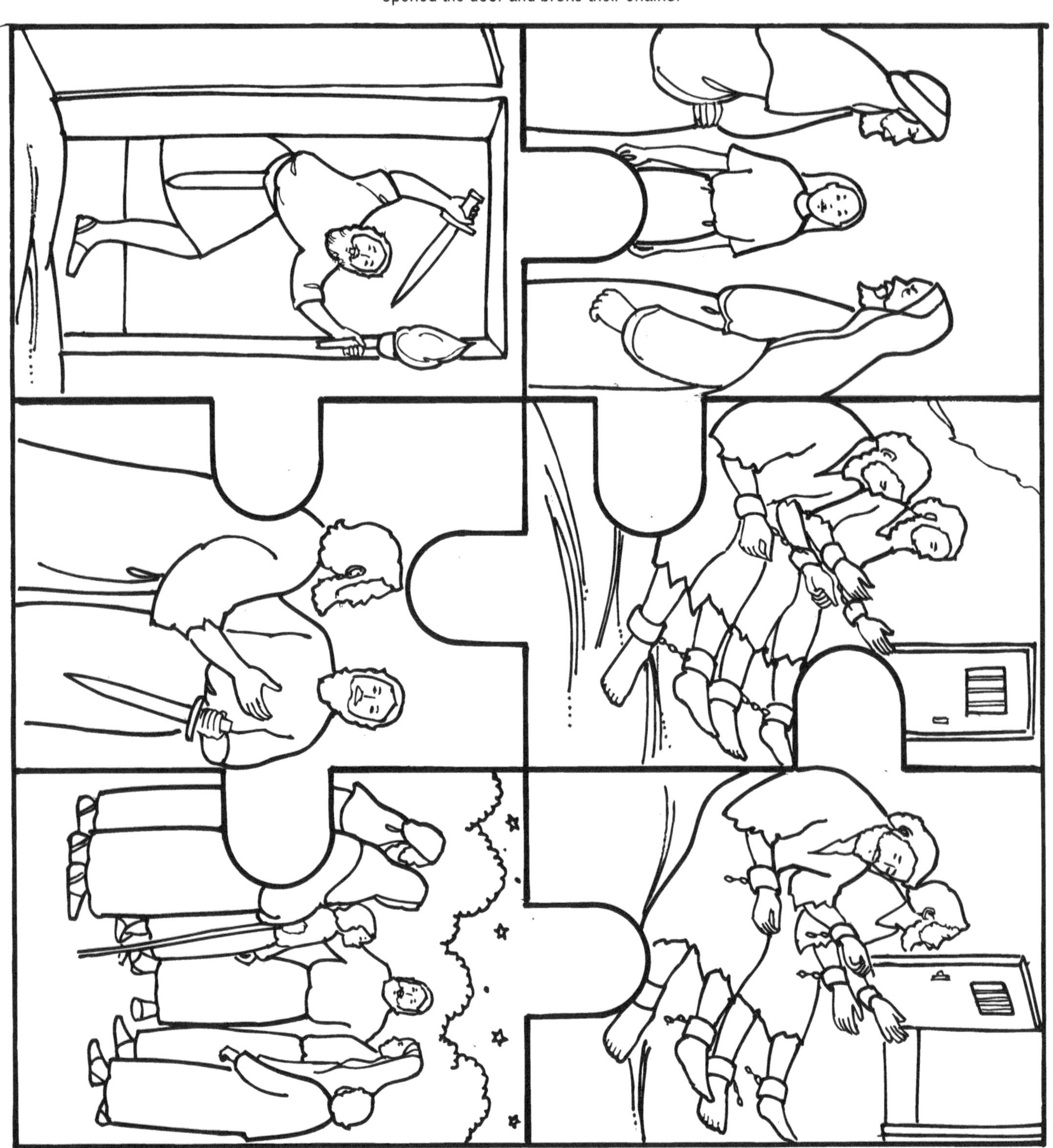

Paul Tells a Crowd about Jesus

Acts 21–22: Paul Tells a Crowd about Jesus

Paul Tells 3-D Scene

Supplies

- copy of the 3-D scene for each child (preferably on card stock)
- construction paper (1 sheet per child, preferably gray or tan)
- crayons or markers
- scissors
- glue

Directions

Color and cut out the scene pieces. Fold a sheet of construction paper in half widthwise. On the top half of the paper, draw what the front of the army building and steps might have looked like (see the example). Fold each figure along the dotted lines to form bases. Glue each base to the bottom half of the background scene. Lay the figures down and pop them up as you retell the story of Paul telling a crowd about Jesus:

1) Paul was in the temple one day when some men grabbed him and stirred up a crowd against him (show Paul and the angry crowd).
2) The commander of the Roman army and his soldiers came and arrested Paul (put on Paul's prison outfit and show the two soldiers and army commander).
3) On the steps of the army building, Paul asked the commander if he could speak to the crowd (leave all figures standing).
4) Paul spoke to the crowd and bravely told them how Jesus had helped him (leave all figures standing).

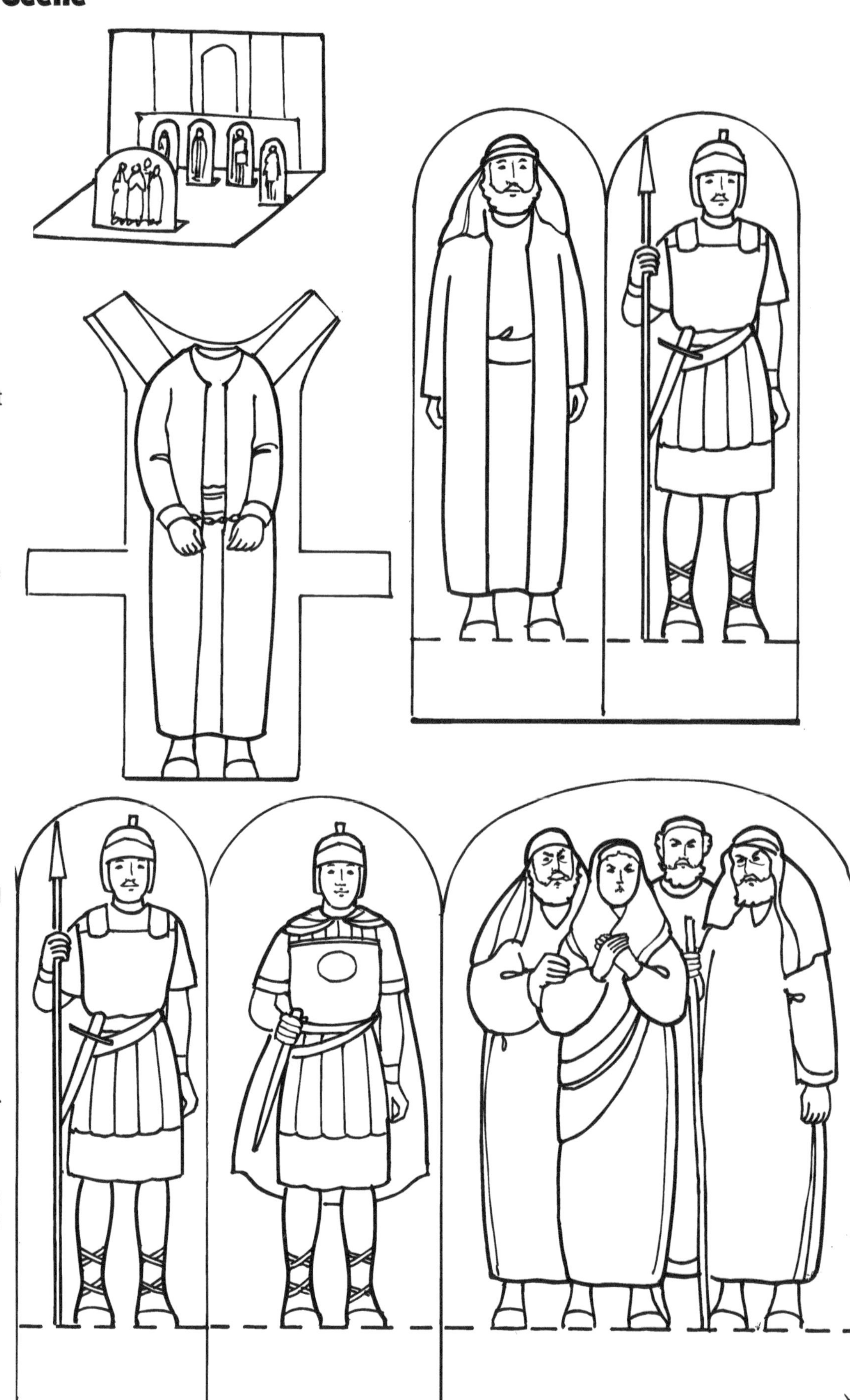

Paul Is Shipwrecked

Acts 27–28: Paul Is Shipwrecked

Shipwreck Mobile

Supplies

- copy of the Shipwreck Mobile for each child
- scissors
- crayons or markers
- white construction paper or card stock (1 sheet per child)
- hole punch
- yarn or twine

Directions

Color and cut out the four shipwreck pieces. Punch holes where indicated by the open circles. Make a sail from white construction paper or card stock (see the example). Place the longest edge of the sail at the bottom. Punch four holes along the bottom of the sail and one hole in the top. Tie a piece of yarn to each shipwreck piece and tie each piece to the bottom of the sail with the scenes hanging in story order. Tie another piece of yarn to the top of the sail to hang the mobile.

Use the Shipwreck Mobile to retell the story of Paul's shipwreck:

1) Paul was chained as a prisoner on a ship headed for Rome when a storm came.
2) Paul told the others on the ship not to be afraid because an angel had told him that no one would die in the storm.
3) The ship broke into pieces along the shore of an island, and everyone made it safely to shore.
4) The leader of the island allowed passengers of the ship to stay in his home, and Paul healed the leader's father. Paul spent the rest of the time on the island healing many who were sick.

Paul Tells about Jesus in Rome

Acts 28; Philippians 1: Paul Tells about Jesus in Rome

Paul Preaches Doorknob Hanger

Supplies

- copy of the Paul Preaches Doorknob Hanger (on card stock) for each child
- crayons or markers
- scissors
- glue

Directions

Color and cut out the two-sided doorknob hanger as one piece. Fold along the dotted line so the words are on the back of the scene. Glue the two sides together. Cut out the holes. Use the doorknob hanger to retell the story of Paul telling about Jesus in Rome. Place the hanger on a doorknob as a reminder that you can tell your family and those in your home about Jesus.

Story Wheel Cover

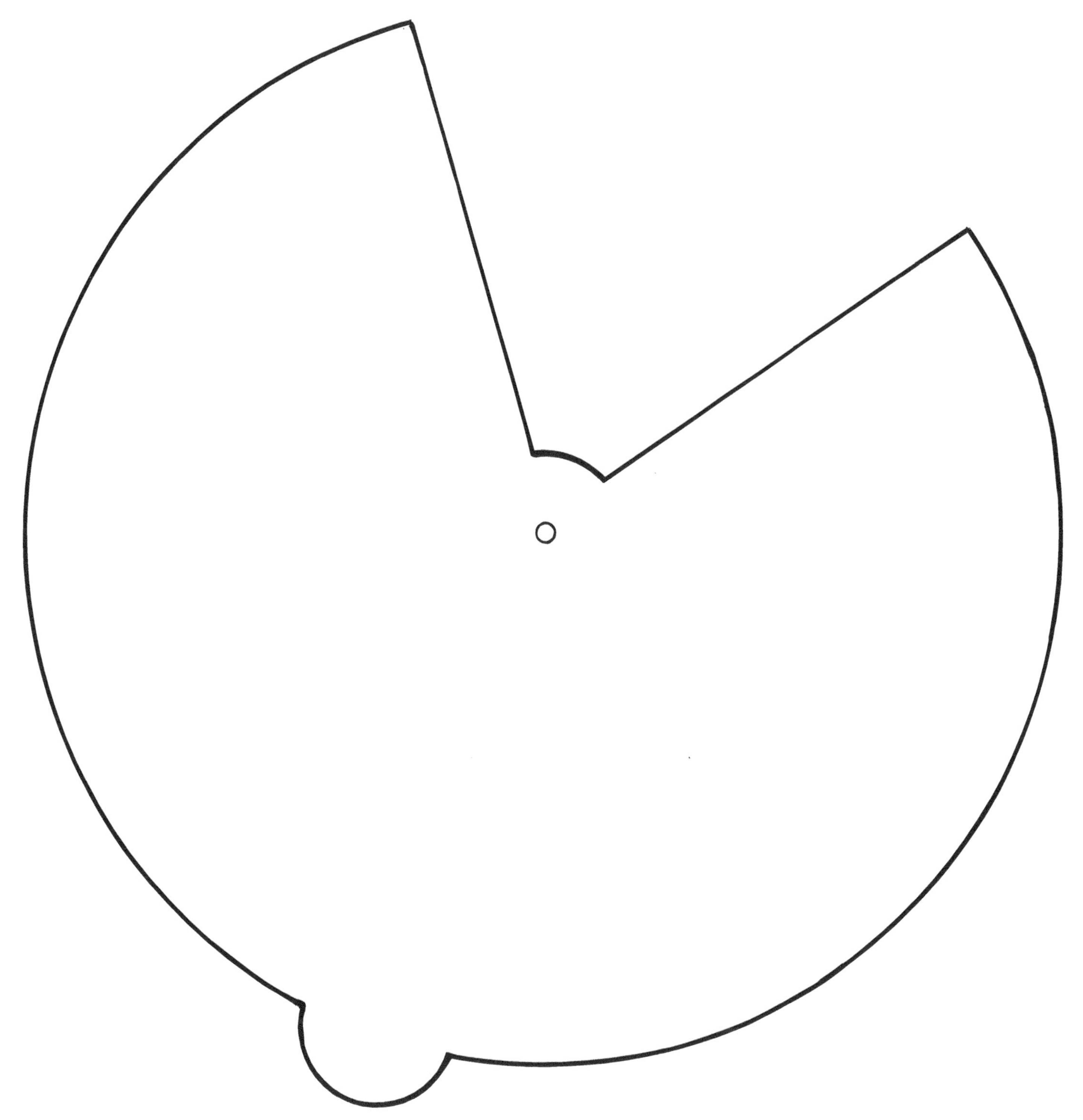

Early Elementary Scope & Sequence

Fall Year 1
- God Makes the World (pp. 10–12)
- God Makes the Animals (pp. 13–14)
- God Makes People (pp. 15–16)
- Noah Trusts and Obeys God (pp. 17–18)
- God Keeps His Promise to Noah (pp. 19–20)
- Abraham's New Home (pp. 21–22)
- The Birth of Isaac (pp. 26–27)
- God Cares for Jacob (pp. 33–34)
- God Cares for Moses (pp. 39–40)
- God Cares for His People (pp. 41–42)
- God's People Cross the Red Sea (pp. 43–44)
- God Gives Food and Water (pp. 45–47)
- God Gives Ten Rules (pp. 48–49)

Winter Year 1
- An Angel Visits Mary (pp. 129–130)
- Jesus Is Born (pp. 133–134)
- Shepherds Tell Others (pp. 138–139)
- Wise Men Worship Jesus (pp. 144–146)
- Jesus Grows Up (pp. 147–149)
- Jesus Chooses Four Followers (pp. 164–166)
- Jesus and the Children (pp. 201–202)
- Jesus Brings Lazarus Back to Life (pp. 196–197)
- Jesus and Ten Men with Leprosy (pp. 198–200)
- Jesus and a Woman from Samaria (pp. 159–161)
- Jesus and Zacchaeus (pp. 203–204)
- Jesus and a Woman Needing Forgiveness (pp. 171–172)
- Jesus and a Man Who Is Paralyzed (pp. 167–168)

Spring Year 1
- The Last Week (pp. 207–208)
- Jesus Is Alive (pp. 211–212)
- Jesus Stops a Storm (pp. 173–174)
- Jesus Heals a Man Who Can't Hear (pp. 182–184)
- Jesus Heals a Man Who Can't See (pp. 187–189)
- Paul Begins to Follow Jesus (pp. 226–227)
- Paul and Barnabas Help Others Learn about Jesus (pp. 228–229)
- Paul and Barnabas Tell about the Living God (pp. 230–231)
- Lydia Learns to Follow Jesus (pp. 232–234)
- Paul and Silas Sing in Prison (pp. 235–236)
- Paul Tells a Crowd about Jesus (pp. 237–238)
- Paul Is Shipwrecked (pp. 239–240)
- Paul Tells about Jesus in Rome (pp. 241–242)

Summer Year 1
- 12 Spies Explore Canaan (pp. 50–52)
- God Is with Moses and Joshua (pp. 53–54)
- Joshua Obeys God at Jericho (pp. 55–56)
- God's People Choose to Serve Him (pp. 57–58)
- Deborah and Barak (pp. 59–60)
- Gideon (pp. 61–62)
- Naomi and Ruth (pp. 63–64)
- Jonah (pp. 123–125)
- Hannah (pp. 65–66)
- God Talks to Samuel (pp. 67–68)
- Samuel Talks to God (pp. 69–70)
- Saul Chooses Not to Listen (pp. 71–72)
- Samuel Anoints David as King (pp. 73–74)

Fall Year 2

- God Helps David Do His Jobs (pp. 75–77)
- God Helps David Be Brave (pp. 78–80)
- Jonathan Is a Good Friend to David (pp. 81–82)
- David Chooses God's Way (pp. 83–84)
- Elijah Trusts and Obeys God (pp. 87–88)
- God Provides for Elijah and a Woman in Zarephath (pp. 89–91)
- God Shows His Power (pp. 92–93)
- God Helps Elisha and a Family in Shunem (pp. 94–95)
- Naaman Learns to Obey God (pp. 96–97)
- Solomon Asks God for Wisdom (pp. 85–86)
- Hezekiah Asks for God's Help (pp. 98–99)
- Jehoshaphat and God's People Pray and Worship God (pp. 102–103)
- Manasseh Asks God for Forgiveness (pp. 104–105)

Winter Year 2

- Zechariah Praises God (pp. 127–128)
- Mary Rejoices (pp. 131–132)
- Shepherds Tell about Jesus (pp. 135–137)
- Simeon and Anna Thank God (pp. 140–141)
- Wise Men Worship Jesus (pp. 142–143)
- John Baptizes Jesus (pp. 150–151)
- Satan Tempts Jesus (pp. 152–154)
- Jesus' First Followers (pp. 155–156)
- Jesus with Moses and Elijah (pp. 185–186)
- Jesus Teaches about Prayer (pp. 192–193)
- Jesus Teaches about Sharing (pp. 194–195)
- Jesus Teaches about Helping (pp. 190–191)
- Jesus Teaches about God (pp. 157–158)

Spring Year 2

- People Praise Jesus (pp. 205–206)
- Jesus Dies and Lives Again (pp. 209–210)
- Jesus Appears and Returns to Heaven (pp. 213–214)
- Jesus Heals an Official's Son (pp. 162–163)
- Jesus Heals a Man at a Pool (pp. 169–170)
- Jesus Heals a Woman and a Young Girl (pp. 175–176)
- Jesus Feeds 5,000 (pp. 177–179)
- Jesus Walks on Water (pp. 180–181)
- Peter Preaches about Jesus (pp. 215–216)
- Peter and John at the Temple (pp. 217–219)
- Peter and John Speak Boldly (pp. 220–221)
- Philip Teaches a Man from Ethiopia (pp. 222–223)
- Peter and Tabitha (pp. 224–225)

Summer Year 2

- Abraham Follows God (pp. 23–25)
- Abraham's Servant Asks for God's Help (pp. 28–30)
- Isaac Listens to God (pp. 31–32)
- Joseph Moves from Canaan to Egypt (pp. 35–36)
- Joseph Forgives and Helps His Family (pp. 37–38)
- King Josiah Hears God's Word (pp. 100–101)
- God's People Pray for Queen Esther (pp. 110–111)
- Nehemiah and God's People Rebuild the Wall (pp. 108–109)
- Ezra Teaches God's Law (pp. 106–107)
- Job Trusts God (pp. 112–114)
- Daniel and His Friends Choose God's Way (pp. 115–117)
- Daniel's Friends Face a Fiery Furnace (pp. 118–120)
- Daniel and the Lions' Den (pp. 121–122)

BIG BOOK

BIG BIBLE Learning Fun for Kids of All Ages!

Big Books will provide hours of creative Bible learning and fun for any children's ministry program! You'll find games, art activities, coloring pages, creative storytelling, object lessons, Bible talks, crafts, puzzles, science experiments, and more! **Plus each Big Book is reproducible** and comes with perforated pages and a Scripture index.

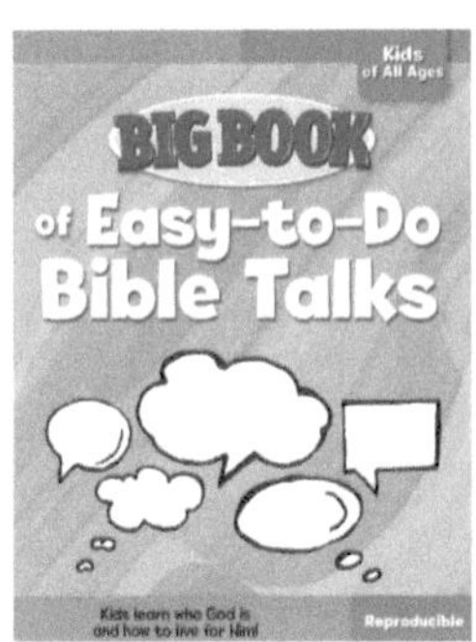

Kids of All Ages

Big Book of Easy-to-Do Bible Talks
ISBN 978-0-8307-7243-8

Big Book of Bible Crafts
ISBN 978-0-8307-7239-1

Big Book of Coloring Pages with Bible Stories
ISBN 978-0-8307-7236-0

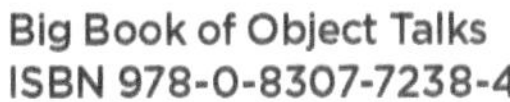

Big Book of Object Talks
ISBN 978-0-8307-7238-4

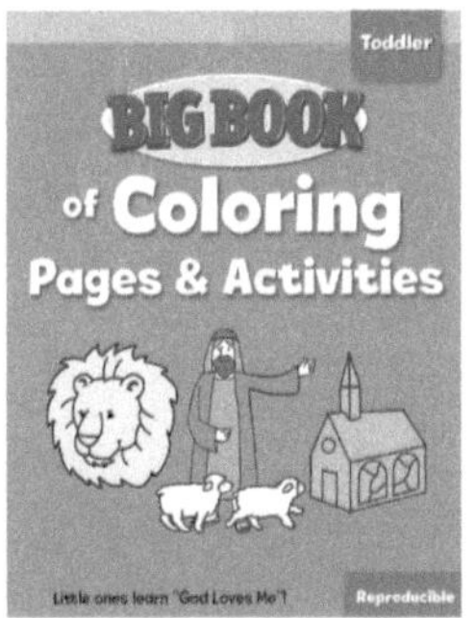

Toddler

Big Book of Coloring Pages and Activities
ISBN 978-0-8307-7237-7

Early Childhood

Big Book of Bible Story Coloring Pages
ISBN 978-0-8307-7232-2

Big Book of Bible Story Coloring Activities
ISBN 978-0-8307-7234-6

Big Book of Bible Activities, Songs, and Rhymes
ISBN 978-0-8307-7241-4

Big Book of Bible Puzzles
ISBN 978-0-8307-7235-3

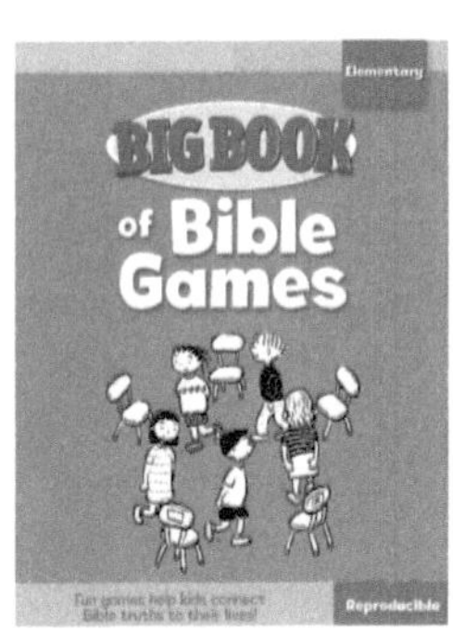

Elementary

Big Book of Bible Story Coloring Activities
ISBN 978-0-8307-7230-8

Big Book of Bible Story Coloring Pages
ISBN 978-0-8307-7233-9

Big Book of Bible Facts and Fun
ISBN 978-0-8307-7247-6

Big Book of Bible Games
ISBN 978-0-8307-7231-5

Big Book of Science Fun
ISBN 978-0-8307-7244-5

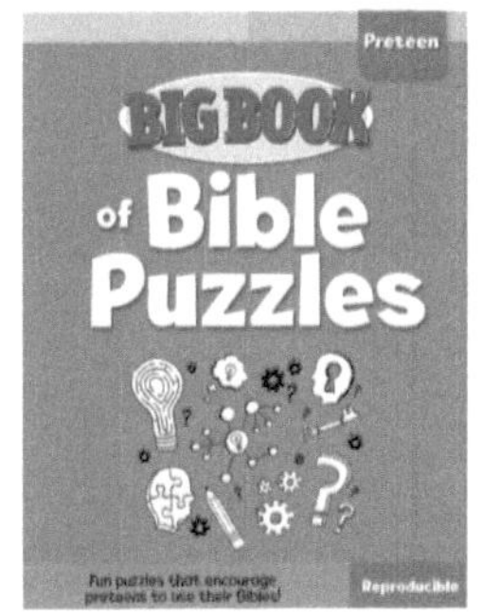

Preteen

Big Book of Bible Puzzles
ISBN 978-0-8307-7242-1

Ministry Activities for 5 DIFFERENT AGE LEVELS!

Available from David C Cook
and everywhere books are sold